Managing Culture and Interspace in Cross-border Investments

This book focuses on the dialectics between spatio-organisational gaps and local contexts that characterise cross-border investments. "Interspatial" investments—be it mergers & acquisitions or greenfield investments—are usually characterised by what is referred to as "otherness", that is organisational and cultural distances of the firms involved in relation to their regional contexts.

At the same time, economic, political and sociocultural linkages are decisive for attracting cross-border investments to regions and for providing firms with conditions supportive of their market success. As a consequence of being locked into complex structures of proximities, cross-border investments are situated in contested terrain. This terrain triggers learning processes in both regional actors and investors, which can result in the convergence of mindsets and organisational issues.

This book is unique in that it combines interspace (defined as the distance between the new owner and the cross-border venture), place (the target region), interpretation (perception and understanding of the investment by the actors involved) and context (institutions, actor networks and interaction), thus offering better understanding of recent processes of globalisation. Crossing disciplinary boundaries by integrating economic geography and management studies, the volume adopts an innovative and spatially informed perspective on foreign direct investments.

This perspective will be of great value to scholars, students and practitioners. The volume is inventive in its approach in that it offers fresh readings from interdisciplinary theoretical approaches and combines these with valuable empirical insights from developed as well as emerging economies.

Martina Fuchs holds the chair of Economic and Social Geography at the Faculty of Management, Economics and Social Sciences at the University of Cologne.

Sebastian Henn holds the chair of Economic Geography at the Institute of Geography at Friedrich Schiller University of Jena.

Martin Franz holds the chair of Human Geography at the Institute of Geography at the University of Osnabrück.

Ram Mudambi is a professor and Perelman Senior Research Fellow in Strategic Management at the Fox School of Business and Management at Temple University.

Routledge Studies in International Business and the World Economy

For a full list of titles in this series, please visit www.routledge.com

60 **Born Globals, Networks and the Large Multinational Enterprise**
Insights from Bangalore and Beyond
Shameen Prashantham

61 **Big Business and Brazil's Economic Reforms**
Luiz F. Kormann

62 **The Nature of the Firm in the Oil Industry**
International Oil Companies in Global Business
Basak Beyazay-Odemis

63 **Sustainable Management Development in Africa**
Building Capabilities to Serve African Organizations
Edited by Hamid H. Kazeroony, Yvonne du Plessis, and Bill Buenar Puplampu

64 **Global Mindsets**
Exploration and Perspectives
Edited by John Kuada

65 **Management and Organizations in Transitional China**
Yanlong Zhang and Lisa A. Keister

66 **Global Advertising Practice in a Borderless World**
Edited by Linda Brennan and Robert Crawford

67 **Social and Solidarity Economy**
The World's Economy with a Social Face
Sara Calvo, Andres Morales, Video Edited by Yanni Zikidis

68 **Managing Culture and Interspace in Cross-border Investments**
Building a Global Company
Edited by Martina Fuchs, Sebastian Henn, Martin Franz and Ram Mudambi

Managing Culture and Interspace in Cross-border Investments

Building a Global Company

**Edited by Martina Fuchs,
Sebastian Henn, Martin Franz
and Ram Mudambi**

Routledge
Taylor & Francis Group
LONDON AND NEW YORK

First published 2017 by Routledge

2 Park Square, Milton Park, Abingdon, Oxfordshire OX14 4RN
52 Vanderbilt Avenue, New York, NY 10017

Routledge is an imprint of the Taylor & Francis Group, an informa business

First issued in paperback 2019

Library of Congress Cataloging-in-Publication Data
A catalog record for this book has been requested

ISBN: 978-1-138-92946-3 (hbk)
ISBN: 978-0-367-24307-4 (pbk)

Typeset in Sabon
by Apex CoVantage, LLC

Contents

Figures and Tables

Figures

Tables

Contributors

Claes G. Alvstam is Professor emeritus for Economic Geography at the University of Gothenburg, School of Business, Economics and Law, Sweden.

Florian Bauer is Professor for Strategic Management at Innsbruck University, Department of Strategic Management, Marketing and Tourism, and Senior Lecturer at MCI Management Center Innsbruck, Austria.

Christian Baumeister is a former teaching and research associate at the Catholic University of Eichstätt-Ingolstadt, Economic Geography working group, Eichstätt, Germany.

Luigi De Bernardis is an expert of the Commissione Nazionale per le Società e la Borsa and teacher of Organization at LUISS Guido Carli University in Rome, Department of Business and Management, Italy.

Kai Bollhorn works as a consultant in Hamburg, Germany.

Mai Anh Dao is a research and teaching assistant at the MCI Management Center Innsbruck, Department of Business and Management, Austria.

Daniel Degischer is a research and teaching assistant at the MCI Management Center Innsbruck, Department of Management and Law, Austria.

Muriel Durand is Professor for International Human Resources and Talent Management and Head of Organisation and Management Department at Group ESC Troyes, France.

Manuel Erlacher is a graduate of the MCI Management Center Innsbruck, Department of Management and Law, Austria.

Martin Franz is Professor for Human Geography at the University of Osnabrück, Department of Geography, Germany.

Martina Fuchs is Professor for Economic and Social Geography at the University of Cologne, Faculty of Management, Economics and Social Sciences, Germany.

Luca Giustiniano is Associate Professor for Business Organisation at the LUISS Guido Carli University in Rome, Department of Business and Management, Italy.

Sophie Golinski is a project coordinator at the Ministry of Regional Development and Transport of Saxony-Anhalt, Magdeburg, Germany.

Sebastian Henn is Professor for Economic Geography at the Institute of Geography at Jena University, Germany.

Lucas Huter is a research assistant at the MCI Management Center Innsbruck, Department of Business and Management, Austria.

Inge Ivarsson is Professor for Economic Geography at the Gothenburg University, Centre for International Business Studies, School of Business, Economics and Law, Sweden.

Erja Kettunen is Docent of Economic Geography at University of Turku, Turku School of Economics, Finland.

Elmar Kulke is Professor for Geography at the Humboldt-University Berlin, Department of Economic Geography, Germany.

Ingo Liefner is Professor for Economic Geography at Leibniz Universität Hannover, Institute of Economic and Cultural Geography, Germany.

Ram Mudambi is Frank M. Speakman Professor of Strategy at Fox School of Business, Temple University, Philadelphia, Pennsylvania, U.S.

Michael D. Nolan is a partner at Milbank, Tweed, Hadley & McCloy LLP, Washington, DC, U.S.

Christina Öberg is Professor for Marketing at the Örebro University, Sweden, and is associated with the Ratio Institute, Sweden, and Leeds University and University of Exeter in the United Kingdom.

Päivi Oinas is Professor for Economic Geography at University of Turku, Turku School of Economics, Finland.

Javier Revilla Diez is Professor for Economic Geography at the University of Cologne, Department of Human Geography, Germany.

Reinhard Röhrig is Project Secretary in the project Work 2020 in North Rhine-Westphalia of IG Metall North Rhine-Westphalia, Düsseldorf, Germany.

Karl P. S. Sauvant is Resident Senior Fellow at the Columbia University, Columbia Center on Sustainable Investment, Columbia Law School, The Earth Institute, New York, New York, U.S.

Martin Schalljo is a research assistant at the University of Cologne, Faculty of Management, Economics and Social Sciences, Germany.

Christoph Scheuplein is a Research Fellow at the Institute for Work and Technology of the Westfälische Hochschule in Gelsenkirchen, Germany.

Daniel Schiller is Professor for Economic and Social Geography at the Ernst Moritz Arndt University Greifswald, Germany.

Yvonne Stockhammer is a graduate of the MCI Management Center Innsbruck, Department of Management and Law, Austria.

Lech Suwala is a postdoctoral fellow at the Humboldt University Berlin, Department of Geography, Germany, and Visiting Associate Professor for Innovation Management at Ritsumeikan University, College of Business Administration, Kyoto, Japan.

Susan M. Walcott is Professor for Geography at the University of North Carolina, Department of Geography, Greensboro, North Carolina, U.S.

Hans-Martin Zademach is Professor for Economic Geography at the Catholic University of Eichstätt-Ingolstadt, Germany.

Daria Zvirgzde holds a doctoral degree in Economic Geography, Bonn, Germany.

Abbreviations

CEO	chief executive officer
CFIUS	Committee on Foreign Investment in the United States
COFDI	Chinese outward foreign direct investment
CSR	corporate social responsibility
EU	European Union
FDI	foreign direct investment
FIDC	Fundo de Investimentos em Direitos Creditórios
GPN	global production network
IT	information technology
M&A	merger and acquisition
MNE	multinational enterprise
OECD	Organisation for Economic Co-operation and Development
OEM	original equipment manufacturer
OFDI	outward foreign direct investments
OI	organisational identity
OLI	ownership–location–internationalisation
PE	private equity
PE-FDI	private equity foreign direct investment
R&D	research and development
SCF	supply chain finance
UK	United Kingdom
UN	United Nations
UNCTAD	United Nations Conference on Trade and Development
U.S.	United States

1 Introduction

Managing Culture and Interspace in Cross-border Investments: Building a Global Company

Martina Fuchs, Sebastian Henn, Martin Franz and Ram Mudambi

Introduction

Cross-border investments connect people from different countries. When a cross-border acquisition is still fresh, managers and employees from the acquired firm come into contact with new colleagues from the investing firm. Often, these colleagues act on the basis of fairly different practices and habits, and they may be guided by experiences and expectations significantly different to their own. Particular sentiments are in the air, with the situation perhaps characterised by great enthusiasm or paralyzing scepticism. In critical cases, the parties involved might distance themselves from their international counterparts even where close collaboration is needed. There are many cases in which a cross-border acquisition does not really result in the formation of a "global" unit as may be intended by top management as the agents involved do not share similar views and values. Rather, there may be gaps in understanding each other, frictions in interaction or simply a perceived lack of need for approaching each other—a situation that eventually creates what we refer to as "interspaces" within the emerging international company. Such diverse interspaces challenge executives in the pre- and post-investment stage of mergers and acquisitions (M&As), as well as managers of young greenfield foreign direct investments (FDI) who must balance relations between the foreign headquarters and the subsidiary to keep the company on a long-term path of growth (Teerikangas 2012). As a result, the respective managers face two main challenges: on one hand, they are themselves involved in cross-border encounters and thus subjects who need to adapt to the new situation; on the other hand, they are executives that need to guide employees' attitudes towards, and their interactions with, their international counterparts. At the same time, it is not only the managers of the respective firms who are confronted with issues of interspace. By connecting different locations, cross-border acquisitions involve a multitude of actors, such as employees, politicians, chambers, trade unions and the media (e.g. Bollhorn and Franz 2016; Golinski and Henn 2015). This new arena is a complex and multiscalar setting composed of markets, institutional arrangements, actors' networks and sociocultural rules, all of which may differ considerably from country to country (Geppert et al. 2016).

This volume deals with the question of whether and in what manner interspatial differences, frictions and gaps challenge cross-border acquisitions and the regions involved. It proposes a range of conceptual approaches for better understanding cross-border acquisitions, and offers empirical evidence for different types of industrial sectors, involving cross-border acquisitions located in the established core economies as well as in the dynamically rising emerging economies. By combining recent interdisciplinary perspectives on interspace, in particular from international business studies and economic geography, this book aims to inspire researchers dealing with cross-border acquisitions and regional development, as well as practitioners working in management, trade unions, policy-makers and organisations responsible for economic and regional development.

Culture and Interspace

Actors involved in cross-border acquisitions often perceive frictions and gaps in interspace; they commonly refer to them as "cultural differences". Some of the earliest work on this was done by Hofstede (1984) who responded to the differences evolving in the globalising world by introducing categories to measure culture, such as masculinity, power distance, uncertainty avoidance, individualism and long-term orientation. Even though his approach was well received by practitioners and academics, it seems problematic to speak of "typical" cultural characteristics of an entire country when considering the regional variety of cities and rural areas or when picturing globally integrated versus more isolated regions. Furthermore, an essentialist view of culture ignores the diversity of cultural flows and networks (Appadurai 1986) that are never confined by national borders. The same holds true for corporate "cultures": when accepting the fact that multinational companies link subsidiaries and diverse organisational units on an international scale, it seems rather problematic to speak of *the* culture of the company.

Here we refer to culture as the

> norms, rules, convictions, moral codes, and philosophies of life (. . .) [which] have developed through a history of social relations and are shaped, produced, and reproduced in everyday practices of human action and interaction (and) help create meaning and a cultural identity (. . .)
>
> (Depner and Bathelt 2005, 58)

Culture hence comprises commonly shared symbolic systems, values and beliefs (Cartwright and Magni 2009, 45) as well as collective assumptions, expectations and traditions (Weber and Drori 2008, 121). It includes patterns of interpretation that guide economic and social life, and it influences individual activities as people cannot leave behind what they have learnt and experienced during their socialisation and habitualisation. In general, such rules are often hidden and taken-for-granted patterns that implicitly guide human behaviour (Fuchs 2014; Fuchs and Schalljo 2016). When managers or employees work abroad, for example in the context of cross-border investments, their perceptions and activities are clearly influenced by such sociocultural backstage rules. Of course, there is no deterministic relation between particular cultural backstage rules and individual activities, all the more so as people might be exposed to varying normative contexts.

Cultural identity is based on the similarity of shared norms and the dissimilarity to observed differences (Ibert and Müller 2015). In the business world, this means that the "Western" management perspective would see its own position as "we" and the behaviour of foreign counterparts as "other" (the practice of othering; Reuter 2002), a contrast that is reinforced by certain stereotypes and prejudices. Recent studies on investors from emerging economies illustrate that such othering is not restricted to individuals but also happens amongst firms (see *Sophie Golinski* and *Sebastian Henn* as well as *Martina Fuchs* and *Martin Schalljo* in this volume).

The term *interspace*, as we understand it, addresses the rather complex matter of perceived differences in the context of cross-border acquisitions. As such, it explicitly includes the sociocultural patterns that underlie human agency, as well as the power of rules that influence an individual's sense of identity and otherness. More so than "space", the notion of "interspace" thus emphasises the multifaceted sphere of rapprochement and distancing and ties and fissures within international encounters.

With regard to cross-border acquisitions, interspace implies that executives manage interspatial socio-economic relations within their enterprises—as well as relations with the respective external regional settings (Beugelsdijk et al. 2010). Executives of global enterprises, in other words, face "multiple embeddedness" across heterogeneous global contexts. They organise their interspatial networks and, at best, are able to utilise the different settings of their multiple host locations for reaching corporate goals (Henn 2012; Meyer et al. 2011, 235). During the post-investment process, those involved learn to combine the diverse international experiences, expectations, routines and practices gained by gradually tapping into the different international arrangements of both home and host country (Cagliano et al. 2011, 299; Pudelko and Harzing 2007). We refer to this as the double adaptation process of cross-border acquisitions: adaptation by the international parties involved in the acquisition and adaptation by the newly established organisations and their environmental settings.

With regard to the latter, the acquisition is of course shaped by *national* settings. Although foreign investors are usually capable of quickly adapting to formal rules and procedures that are, in the first instance, prescribed by the national state, they typically need more time to adapt to their *local and regional* environments and build social networks there (Liu and Dicken 2006). This book argues that the need to handle local differences in interspace has even grown in importance in times of globalisation (see Meyer et al. 2011). Moreover, cross-border investments must succeed in *internationally contested* environments, in particular, in worldwide customer and factor markets which are shaped by politics and institutional arrangements. Diverse international customer requirements, different resource availability at the international level, and patterns of global governance should therefore also be considered part of the environment of cross-border investments.

This means that the "borders" referred to in the term *cross-border investment* are first and foremost national borders. As Beugelsdijk and Mudambi (2013) have emphasised, national borders often represent qualitative discontinuities in interspace and places where spatial heterogeneity comes to the fore. This is because national borders demarcate not only different legal systems but also different institutional and sociocultural settings. At the same time, spatial heterogeneity is not only demarcated by national borders—the international and subnational levels also play a role. This opens a seminal research area for international business studies and economic geography, as this volume illustrates.

Interspace is thus crucial for explaining cross-border investments and their spatial embeddedness (Alvstam et al. 2016, 47). The contributions of this book clearly illustrate this, for example by focusing on how managers and regional actors react to and manage interspace within the cross-border investment and between a firm and its local or regional surroundings. Figure 1.1 gives an outline overview of the idea of the book.

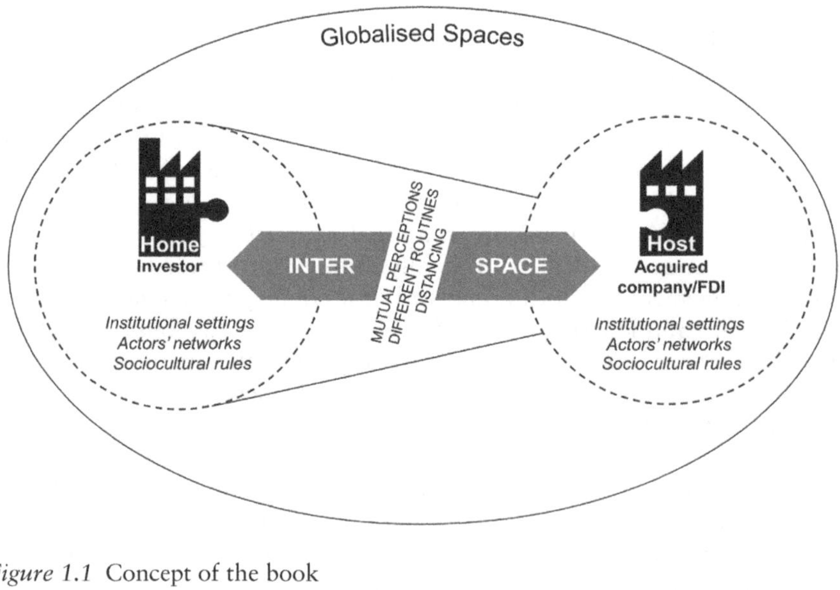

Figure 1.1 Concept of the book

Source: The authors; illustration: Theresa Pies and Jonathan Mauersberger.

Structure of the Book

Given the diversity of spaces where cross-border investments bridge locations on a worldwide scale, this volume focuses on players in the core economies as well as in emerging economies. The latter, sometimes also referred to as "Southern Engines", have recently attracted great attention in international business studies and economic geography (e.g. Aleksynska and Havrylchyk 2013; Alvstam et al. 2014; Awate et al. 2012; Bollhorn 2015). This volume seeks to close the research gap that remains with respect to culture and interspace in this context.

Following on from the Introduction, the book considers how actors involved in cross-border acquisitions perceive and handle sociocultural interspace. *Sophie Golinski* and *Sebastian Henn* highlight that despite the many economic benefits resulting to industrialised countries through FDI from the global South, investors often see themselves confronted with various patterns of resistance by the workforce of the acquired firms, as well as with diffuse concerns within the target country's population. Their discourse analysis shows that othering is strongly influenced by media reporting in that the latter structures the public discourse. By employing a methodology of structural hermeneutics and with a particular focus on top managers, *Martina Fuchs* and *Martin Schalljo* demonstrate that top managers in the early stage of an acquisition emphatically extended a warm welcome to the new owners but distanced themselves from the new owners in the post-acquisition process. *Martin Franz, Kai Bollhorn* and *Reinhard Röhrig* shift the perspective towards labour, examining industrial relations and FDI from China and India in Germany. In Germany, the engagement of FDI from emerging markets often results in felt insecurities on the part of the employees in the target firm. Common fears are that the new foreign owner will not accept pre-existing standards of industrial relations and social standards but try to undermine them in order to align them with the situation in the home country. *Muriel Durand* further explains distancing by adopting the cultural friction perspective when investigating the contacts between middle managers in post-merger integration processes in cross-border acquisitions. She provides an example for saving face in "Western" M&A with Asian counterparts.

Whereas the first contributions focus on "Western" and "Asian" views, *Luca Giustiniano* and *Luigi De Bernardis* shift the perspective towards organisational identities, in general. They consider a plurality of identities as a tolerable state rather than a source of problems to be solved. Although othering usually produces frictions and gaps between the cross-border parties involved, dealing with dissimilarities in a reasonable way can be economically successful and organisationally sustainable at the same time. This view is further exemplified by *Claes G. Alvstam* and *Inge Ivarsson* who report on the acquisition of Volvo Car Corporation by Zhejiang Geely, illustrating a grey zone between "foreign" and "domestic". They propose that this recent event has given rise to a new "hybrid" identity of the company. *Lucas Huter, Mai Anh Dao, Daniel Degischer, Florian Bauer, Yvonne Stockhammer* and *Manuel Erlacher* relate distancing to the direction of the cross-border acquisition (incoming versus outgoing). By comparing inbound and outbound cross-border transactions, they provide evidence on the asymmetric effects of cultural distance. Such effects are further explained by *Christoph Scheuplein*, who focuses on inbound cross-border brownfield investments by comparing strategic investors to private equity investors in the German automotive parts industry. He shows that the latter work as a door opener for investors from emerging economies.

With a particular emphasis on jurisdictional aspects, *Karl P. S. Sauvant* and *Michael D. Nolan* show that the rapid rise of China's investments and related fears of their "Western" trade partners make China react to such developments, not only in its national policies but also in the country's international investment agreements. Furthermore, they show that politics is closely connected to sociocultural settings—a connection which has often been ignored in the research context of cross-border acquisitions (Mudambi and Navarra 2003, Mudambi 2011).

Still, further crucial spatial settings exist beyond national states and related international politics. Thus, the subsequent chapters take a regional view. *Susan M. Walcott* and *Ingo Liefner* illustrate that Chinese outward FDI tends to cluster in established German and U.S. industry locations either known for certain industrial traditions and infrastructures or for a history of previous investment inflow. "Laggards" benefit from established networks that early investors cannot rely on (see Cantwell and Mudambi 2011). *Daria Zvirgzde, Daniel Schiller* and *Javier Revilla Diez* analyse how multinationals perceive local institutional quality in different regions of Ukraine. By comparing the capital region (Kyiv) to border regions, they show that institutional change is perceived to be faster in the capital region than in other regions—a fact that is explained by the different degrees of Soviet legacy in the regions. *Päivi Oinas* and *Erja Kettunen* present a systematic framework for identifying different negotiation contexts between multinational enterprises and their host regions, assuming the *local* government to be the predominant negotiation partner.

Additionally, local customer markets play a significant role. *Lech Suwala* and *Elmar Kulke* discuss the internationalisation of grocery retailers in emerging markets. The chapter argues that business activities abroad generate additional costs for foreign firms when compared to their domestic counterparts. In order to overcome these, foreign firms can choose between two ends of a continuum: embeddedness or otherness. *Christina Öberg* also focuses on the markets, in particular, the local customers of the acquired parties. She shows how local customers become a crucial part of the cross-border strategy, and how they are involved in the sensemaking process of a cross-border acquisition. Shifting the perspective towards the financial sphere as a relevant element of a company's environment, *Christian Baumeister* and *Hans-Martin*

Zademach discuss inter-firm financing in the automotive sector in Germany and Brazil. The chapter addresses the flows of financial means in the complex production systems resulting from such transactions. Financial management, blurring the boundaries of the single firm, is shown to be able to increase competitiveness, especially in a regional environment which affects the overall financing situation of all suppliers independent of their specific characteristics. A final *synopsis* takes a comprehensive view and highlights lessons learnt, research gaps and managerial implications.

Acknowledgements

This book emerged in the particular context of two independent research projects. One concerned managers' patterns of interpretation in international takeovers and was supported by the German Scientific Foundation (FU 424/15–1), carried out by Martina Fuchs and Martin Schalljo. The other project, BRICINVEST, was supported by the Hans Boeckler Foundation. It focused on work and labour relations in investments from Brazil, Russia, India and China in Germany and was conducted by Kai Bollhorn, Martin Franz, Sophie Golinski, Sebastian Henn, Reinhard Röhrig and Jörg Weingarten. We would like to thank the foundations for supporting the research projects whose different foci offered complementary insights on management styles and actual labour in cross-border acquisitions embedded within their respective sociocultural rules and institutional settings.

Ram Mudambi of our editorial team helped to include the management perspective in this volume, also by resorting to the International Business, Economic Geography and Innovation (iBEGIN) research network that he coordinates. This stimulating research environment inspired us to seek out other colleagues working in this subject area who were willing to contribute to this volume.

We would like to thank Kira Gee for linguistic editing and Catherine Rocktäschel, Theresa Pies, Judith Rötgers and Jonathan Mauersberger for support in further editorial work.

References

Aleksynska, M., and O. Havrylchyk. 2013. "FDI from the South: The Role of Institutional Distance and Natural Resources." *European Journal of Political Economy* 29: 38–53.

Alvstam, C. G., Dolles, H., and P. Strom. 2014. *Asian Inward and Outward FDI: New Challenges in the Global Economy*. Basingstoke: Palgrave Macmillan.

Alvstam, C. G., Ström, P., and R. Wentrup. 2016. "Heterogeneous Economic Space in a Global Archipelago: An Economic-Geography Perspective of Emerging Markets." In *Handbook of Contemporary Research on Emerging Markets*, edited by H. Merchant, 38–61. Cheltenham and Northampton: Edward Elgar.

Appadurai, A. 1986. "Introduction: Commodities and the Politics of Value." In *The Social Life of Things*, edited by A. Appadurai, 3–63. Cambridge: Cambridge University Press.

Awate, S., Larsen, M. M., and R. Mudambi. 2012. "EMNE Catch-Up Strategies in the Wind Turbine Industry: Is There a Trade-Off between Output and Innovation Capabilities?" *Global Strategy Journal* 2(3): 205–232.

Beugelsdijk, S., McCann, P., and R. Mudambi. 2010. "Introduction: Place, Space and Organization: Economic Geography and the Multinational Enterprise." *Journal of Economic Geography* 10(4): 485–493.

Beugelsdijk, S., and R. Mudambi. 2013. "MNEs as Border-Crossing Multi-Location Enterprises: The Role of Discontinuities in Geographic Space." *Journal of International Business Studies* 44(5): 413–426.

Bollhorn, K. 2015. "Acquisitions of German Companies by Chinese and Indian Corporations: A Threat to Employment and Knowledge Retention?" *Die Erde* 146(1): 16–20.

Bollhorn, K., and M. Franz. 2016. "Production Network Knowledge as a Foundation for Resistance: Workers Influence on a Chinese Acquisition in Germany." *Tijdschrift voor economische en sociale geografie* 107(4): 407–420.

Cagliano, R., Caniato, F., Golini, R., Longoni, A., and E. Micelotta. 2011. "The Impact of Country Culture on the Adoption of New Forms of Work Organization." *International Journal of Operations and Production Management* 31(3): 297–323.

Cantwell, J., and R. Mudambi. 2011. "Physical Attraction and the Geography of Knowledge Sourcing in Multinational Enterprises." *Global Strategy Journal* 1(3/4): 206–232.

Cartwright, S., and L. Magni. 2009. "The Value of Stories in Understanding the Past and Shaping the Future in Merged Organisations." *Advances in Mergers and Acquisitions* 8: 43–60.

Depner, H., and H. Bathelt. 2005. "Exporting the German Model: The Establishment of a New Automobile Industry Cluster in Shanghai." *Economic Geography* 81(1): 53–81.

Fuchs, M. 2014. Worldwide Knowledge? Global Firms, Local Labour and the Region. Farnham: Ashgate.

Fuchs, M., and M. Schalljo 2016. "'Western' Professional Ethics Challenged by Foreign Acquisitions: German Managers' Patterns of Interpretation Surrounding Chinese and Indian Investors." *Geoforum* 75(10): 20–28.

Geppert, M., Becker-Ritterspach, F., and R. Mudambi. 2016. "Politics and Power in Multinational Companies: Integrating the International Business and Organization Studies Perspectives." *Organization Studies* 37(9): 1209–1225.

Golinski, S., and S. Henn. 2015. "Imperialisten, Spione oder Retter? Zur Charakterisierung von Direktinvestitionen aus Russland, Indien und China in deutschen Tageszeitungen." *Zeitschrift für Wirtschaftsgeographie* 59(1): 1–19.

Henn, S. 2012. "Transnational Entrepreneurs, Global Pipelines and Shifting Production Patterns: The Example of the Palanpuris in the Diamond Sector." *Geoforum* 43(3): 497–506.

Hofstede, G. 1984. Culture's Consequences: Comparing Values, Behaviors, Institutions, and Organizations across Nations. Sage: Thousand Oaks.

Ibert, O., and F. C. Müller. 2015. "Network Dynamics in Constellations of Cultural Differences: Relational Distance in Innovation Processes in Legal Services and Biotechnology." *Research Policy* 44(1): 181–194.

Liu, W., and P. Dicken. 2006. "Transnational Corporations and 'Obligated Embeddedness': Foreign Direct Investment in China's Automobile Industry." *Environment and Planning A* 38(7): 1229–1247.

Meyer, K. E., Mudambi, R., and R. Narula. 2011. "Multinational Enterprises and Local Contexts: The Opportunities and Challenges of Multiple-Embeddedness." *Journal of Management Studies* 48(2): 235–252.

Mudambi, R. 2011. "Hierarchy, Coordination and Innovation in the Multinational Enterprise." *Global Strategy Journal* 1(3/4): 317–323.

Mudambi, R., and P. Navarra. 2003. "Political Culture and Foreign Direct Investment: The Case of Italy." *Economics of Governance* 4: 37–56.

Pudelko, M., and A. W. Harzing. 2007. "Country-of-Origin, Localization, or Dominance Effect: An Empirical Investigation of HRM Practices in Foreign Subsidiaries." *Human Resources Management* 46(4): 535–559.

Reuter, J. 2002. Ordnungen des Anderen: Zum Problem des Eigenen in der Soziologie des Fremden. Bielefeld: Transcript.

Teerikangas, S. 2012. "Dynamics of Acquired Firm Pre-Acquisition Employee Reactions." *Journal of Management* 38(2): 599–639.

Weber, Y., and I. Drori. 2008. "The Linkages between Cultural Differences, Psychological States, and Performance in International Mergers and Acquisitions." *Advances in Mergers and Acquisitions* 7: 119–142.

2 Othering FDI in the Media

How Chinese Investors Are Constructed as Deviating Others in German Dailies

Sophie Golinski and Sebastian Henn

Introduction

In the last 20 years, the world has faced an unprecedented rise of outward FDI from emerging economies, especially from China (Collins 2013, 2). In addition to a mere shift in scale, this development has been marked by an increasing number of investments directed towards Western economies (e.g. Meunier et al. 2014, 114). Given the many beneficial aspects of FDI for economic development (e.g. Collins 2013, 6–8), it comes as a surprise that Chinese firms often face strong resentments in their target countries. Studies carried out in the U.S. (Rosen and Hanemann 2011), in Sweden (Barlach and Puerto Elizalde 2010) and in Australia (Makin 2008) suggest that the rapid expansion of Chinese multinational companies often causes anxiety and opposition amongst decision makers in politics and the economy, as well as the general public. In Western economies, Chinese investors ("they") are usually perceived and presented as being significantly different from the domestic ("our") firms. Such differentiation, also known as "othering" (e.g. Lohnson et al. 2004; Van Houtum and Naerssen 2002), may result in patterns of "economic nationalism" (D'Costa 2012, 2) in the sense of ongoing production and reproduction of positions of economic domination (of the incumbents) and subordination (of the foreign investors; Jacobsen and Jacobsen 2011). In extreme cases, political measures may be taken that intentionally keep (potential) investors away (e.g. restrictive investment reviews; see *Karl P. S. Sauvant* and *Michael D. Nolan* in this volume) whereas in other situations the investors themselves may become deterred from investing in a particular country. In either case, the economy of the host country will (ceteris paribus) face economic disadvantages in the global competition for capital and jobs in the long run (Jacobsen and Jacobsen 2011).

Up to now, the question of how resentments towards foreign investors gain a foothold in a society has not been well researched. There is, however, ample reason to believe that the media play a decisive role in this context. Newspaper articles (e.g. "China Buys up the World" in The Economist 2010) and TV reports (e.g. "The Chinese Are Coming! Europe's Salvation or Decline?"[1] by Magali Serre 2012) often view foreign investors as homogenous groups of actors who share certain cultural values and beliefs considered to be typical for their home countries and significantly different from the domestic culture (Hanemann and Huotari 2015, 38–40; Mawdsley 2008, 511–512). In other words, "the bigger the cultural distance between the host and home country, the more difficult it is for multinational enterprises to gain normative legitimacy in the host country" (e.g. Kang and Jiang 2012, 48).

So far, only a very limited number of studies have dealt with the question of how foreign investors are portrayed in the media. These have focused on representations of single acquisitions in host country media (e.g. Barlach and Puerto Elizalde 2010; Tienari et al. 2003), the impact of media reporting on international politics (e.g. Zhang 2010), or the relationship between media coverage and location choice (e.g. Kulchina 2014). However, only little is known on how the media actually contribute to the othering of investors. Better understanding of such processes would increase our knowledge on international investment decisions and the institutional settings the investors are embedded in, as well as the daily challenges managers face when engaging in localities abroad. This chapter seeks to close this research gap by focusing on how Chinese investments in Germany are portrayed in German daily newspapers, with the aim of understanding the difficulties Chinese firms face when entering the German market. In particular, we analyse how (local) interest groups as well as the general public other Chinese investors.

We start by reviewing the literature on public perception of FDI and specifying the role of the media as an information and dissemination platform that influences how meanings are attributed to economic phenomena, such as FDI. Subsequently, we describe our research design and methodology. In the third section, we consider the portrayal of FDI from China in German daily newspapers and discuss how othering contributes to the construction of distinct images of the investors. Finally, we sum up the most important findings and shed light on future research issues.

Public Perception of Cross-border Investment Activities

FDI, in most cases, turns out to be beneficial for the economy of the host countries (e.g. Caves 1971). According to the literature on international businesses, they foster growth in production and the exchange of goods, create additional employment opportunities and generate knowledge spill-overs to domestic firms (e.g. Lipsey 2004, 344–346). Despite these positive impacts, national and local governments, as well as actors on the ground, often adopt an attitude towards foreign investors that can be described as critical or even hostile (Bandelj 2008, 675). In most cases, their interpretations are shaped by national interests that are related to the wish to sustain national ownerships, cultural traditions and the strength of the national economy. In fact, unfamiliarity of the host country's population (insiders) with foreign investors (outsiders) fosters black-and-white stereotypical patterns of interpretation that often imply an unfavourable perception of and resistance towards foreign takeovers (Meunier 2014, 145). Hence, as Zhang (2014, 410) mentioned, agents "tend to fixate on the potential losses brought about by foreign acquisitions [. . .], and their aversion to loss could therefore distort perception of the benefits of foreign takeovers". Such perceptions are all but new. Studies on hostile receptions of American investments in the European Economic Community in the 1960s and 1970s (Servan-Schreiber 1967) or German investments in Eastern Europe in the 1990s (Sinn and Weichenrieder 1997, 184) suggest that resentments towards foreign investors can be regarded as a universal phenomenon. At least two factors have been identified that systematically influence the way how inward FDI are perceived.

First, the type of investments matters: whereas foundations of new firms (greenfield investments) are expected to contribute to the national industrial base and create employment opportunities, investments in existing firms (brownfield investments) are often accused of leading to potential closures of factories, losses of sovereignty and increased unemployment rates (Meunier et al. 2014, 110; Zhang 2014, 410). Furthermore, in many situations, the purchase of domestic firms by foreign investors is feared to gain them a position that would allow them to exert control over critical infrastructures or strategic industries (Makin 2008, 11), thus putting national security at stake.

Second, different studies suggest that the perception of FDI differs with the investor's country of origin (Bandelj 2003, 385). In industrialised countries, international operations of firms from developed countries, such as the U.S. or the UK, are typically regarded as low risk, mainly because of a felt similarity with the domestic cultural backgrounds and institutional environments (Wong 2013, 51). By contrast, firms from emerging markets investing in industrialised nations for the purpose of acquiring brands, technological assets and/or knowledge are perceived with significant scepticism (Hanemann 2014, 140).

FDI in the Media—Between Information Industry and "Cultural Battlefield"

Following Gamson and Modigliani (1989, 2), we understand the media discourse and public opinion as parallel albeit interacting systems, with media coverage contributing to the social construction of meaning. At the same time, public opinion can be viewed as part of the processes by which journalists and extra-medial actors (e.g. politicians, firm representatives, experts) influence and develop meaning in public discourses. The latter aspect points to the crucial role of various (groups of) actors who use the mass media as a social platform for raising and spreading their subjective positions, perspectives or interpretations. This can be done by giving more weight to some aspects while marginalising or even neglecting others (Bandelj 2008,

678; Vaara and Tienari 2002, 281). Selected information and subjective positions stimulate the production of certain images and interpretations, thereby contributing to collective sensemaking among the public which, in turn, directly or indirectly affects common emotions and behaviour towards the subjects dealt with (Kepplinger and Glaab 2007, 338). Furthermore, the media tend to pay more attention to negative rather than positive information in order to attract greater attention (Kepplinger and Glaab 2007, 337). According to Zhang (2014, 417), such asymmetric negative reporting may lead to long-lasting emotional and social consequences on the side of the recipients, fuelling public fears and people's perception of risks. Finally, patterns of intolerance and social exclusion are raised when the mediated subjects are viewed as different or threatening the "normal way of life" (Greer and Jewkes 2005, 21).

Foreign firms usually attract high media attention (Friebel and Heinz 2014, 97), in particular, M&A because of their potential to provoke conflicting and contradictory interpretations (Vaara and Tienari 2002, 280). In these discourses, opinions on foreign investments are largely framed by the global (foreign)—local (national) dichotomy, meaning that global investment activities are contrasted with national interests to either welcome or reject them (Bandelj 2008, 673). Within this framework, the rational discourse in the media is accompanied by certain cognitive and emotional interpretations that are significantly linked to the investors' home countries and their economic, political or sociocultural repertoires (Tienari et al. 2003, 379–380). Immediately after the acquisition of the Swedish car manufacturer Volvo by Chinese Geely, for instance, Swedish newspapers described the strategic takeover as conflicting with national and historical Swedish values and contributing to a significant loss of economic and social capital (Barlach and Puerto Elizalde 2010, 2). Barlach and Puerto Elizalde (2010, 15 & 44–45) show in this context that newspaper reports were enriched with critical positions towards China as an unstable market economy or as an authoritarian and manipulative society and therefore conclude that the media in this particular case functioned as a "channel to look into the attitudes of Swedish people towards China" (Barlach and Puerto Elizalde (2010, 15). In general, journalists, as well as extra-medial actors given a voice in newspaper texts, do not simply express their opinions on foreign investors and their countries of origin but also transmit their own interpretations and specific interests, thereby influencing the public debate and the acceptance of inward FDI.

Chinese FDI in the Media

Considering the portrayal of Chinese FDI in the media, Zhang (2014, 419) states that "China is now at the center of the media spotlight". One reason for this particular focus is that the media coverage surrounding Chinese FDI is determined by alarming stories and corresponding sensational headlines (Meunier et al. 2014, 110; Rosen and Hanemann 2011, 8). In the case of

China's growing presence in Africa for example, Mawdsley (2008) shows that the media accuse Chinese investors of exploiting Africa's resources and establishing poor labour conditions. In a study on Chinese FDI in the U.S., Rosen and Hanemann (2011, 62) observed that the media intuitively adopt a negative attitude towards Chinese investment proposals independently of whether they imply a real threat or not. These assessments follow general observations depicting China's rise as an economic threat rather than an opportunity (Kim et al. 2015, 2) and are also grounded in intuitive thinking about constructed images of China, combined with a lack of understanding of China's institutional environment (Hurst et al. 2012, 2). Becoming aware of these narratives, Meunier (2014, 157) criticises that there is little information on how much of this fear is genuine concern motivated by actual economic conditions or xenophobia produced by the media. Moreover, apart from various studies that emphasise examples of negative representations, limited research has been done to systematically address the images of Chinese investments conveyed by the media. In an earlier paper (Golinski and Henn 2015), we found that Chinese investors in Germany—other than one-sided negative characterisation—are either perceived as "imperialists", "spies", "moneymakers", "competitors", "rescuers" or "partners". Interestingly, also in the case of investments from other countries, the positions adopted by different (groups of) actors are largely rooted in country-specific ascriptions and images attributed to the investors' home country. The question, therefore, arises as to what extent othering as a process of constructing and identifying Chinese investors as deviating others is inherent to these media representations and how this might influence the social construction of specific public attitudes.

Research Design and Methodology

In order to grasp and analyse the images generated of direct investments from China in the German media, we use discourse analysis as a form of systematic content analysis (Gamson and Modigliani 1989; Gerhards 2006). In line with Ferree et al. (2002, 9), we regard the media discourse as a form of public communication on topics in which individual and collective actors publicly express their meanings and opinions to a general audience, thus contributing to the social construction of collective understanding (Bandelj 2008). Content analysis seems appropriate to access the subjective positions of the mediated actors in the texts as it allows to systematically count, assess and interpret different forms and content of communication (Brians et al. 2010, 195).

The material analysed included the press coverage of two national daily newspapers, *Frankfurter Allgemeine Zeitung* and *Handelsblatt*, published between 2004 and 2013. These two newspapers play an important role in the dissemination of news in Germany because of their high circulation—together approximately 385,000 per day (Statista 2015)—as well as their aspiration to provide high-quality reporting coupled with in-depth background information (Frankfurter Allgemeine Zeitung 2015; Verlagsgruppe Handelsblatt 2015).

In total, the empirical material consisted of 161 newspaper articles (*Frankfurter Allgemeine Zeitung* 80 articles, 49.7%; *Handelsblatt* 81 articles, 50.3%) identified by searching for logical strings[2] in the online archives of both dailies and by manually selecting relevant material (Bandelj 2008, 676).

Analysis relied on two main steps that combined quantitative and qualitative content analysis. First, we developed a systematic overview of the textual material (i.e. occasions of reporting, types of investments, names of firms and investors mentioned in the text) in order to explore typical structures and issues surrounding the newspaper discourse on Chinese investment. This provided a starting point for the second step, that is in-depth content analysis of selected texts focusing on rational contents as well as non-manifested meanings (e.g. Gerhards 2006, 308). Here we, first, analysed the significance of othering in German newspaper reports on Chinese investments and, second, explored and systematically classified thematic dimensions that construct and identify Chinese investors as deviating others.

Coverage of Direct Investments From China in German Daily Newspapers

The tremendous increase of Chinese FDI in Germany from €0.91 billion in 2004 to €1.18 billion in 2011 (OECD 2015) was paralleled by a strong growth of reports on these cross-border investments in the German newspapers analysed. Although in the first half of the period investigated (2004–2008) only 35 articles (21.7%) made Chinese investment a matter of discussion, newspaper coverage almost quadrupled between 2009 and 2013 (126 articles, 78.3%). More than half of all newspaper articles (89 articles, 55.3%) were published in the last two years under report (2012, 2013)—a period characterised by some important strategic takeovers by Chinese firms, for example the acquisitions of the German machine producers PUTZMEISTER CONCRETE PUMPS GMBH and KION Group AG. (Partial) takeovers emerge as the most prominent occasions for newspaper reporting, whereas greenfield investments were only occasionally reported on. This finding is remarkable as it contrasts with the actual situation. Although new firm foundations (445 companies, 84.0%) clearly dominate the entry strategy of Chinese institutional investors (e.g. industrial firms, banks), (partial) takeovers account for only 85 investment projects (16.0%; database MARKUS 2013, own investigation). This apparent paradox may be explained by the fact that greenfield investments do not usually attract the interest of nationwide newspapers due to their small employment effects (78.8% of all greenfield investments have less than ten employees) and that their activity fields are primarily limited to sales and other small-scale services.

Significance of Othering

The controversial portrayal of Chinese FDI in German daily newspapers is produced and reinforced by constantly constructing and interpreting Chinese investors as deviating others. The extent to which othering determines the newspaper discourse become clear when analysing the number and type of phrases that foster a literal and metaphorical distinction, resulting in the distinct treatment of Chinese investments. A distinction arises when actors in the press, journalists or extra-medial actors adopt and convey "egocentric" attitudes that judge Chinese investors with respect to their characteristics, identity and nationhood and simultaneously consider these as incompatible with the host economy and its national economic gains.

Our analysis reveals that around 40% of all newspaper reports (63 articles) view Chinese investors as deviating others. Rather than presenting short pieces of objective information, press reports othering investments usually provide relevant background information (e.g. FDI statistics), as well as statements of various actors such as (inter)national experts or business consultants. Over the period of analysis, two peaks of othering can be identified: first, the period from 2004 to 2006, when the press became aware of growing Chinese FDI both in Germany and on a worldwide scale. In that period, articles tended to focus more strongly on "the other Chinese" in the sense of a homogeneous group of invaders contesting the current balance of power on the world markets. During that time, Chinese investors were viewed as others in more than half of the newspaper articles; most emphasised the unpredictable, mysterious and uncontrollable consequences of investment:

> We must not be naive and believe these countries [China and Russia] are not up to something sinister [. . .]. Scientists, entrepreneurs, and politicians fear that state-controlled capitalists [. . .] will control key industries and exploit companies' knowledge. If state funds gain power, Germany will become vulnerable to political blackmail.
>
> (Hoffmann 2007)

In 2012, the newspaper discourse was dominated by a second peak of othering; this was when a certain number of noteworthy Chinese acquisitions took place. In this context, apparent technology- and knowledge-related differences between "us" (i.e. the putatively superior German firms worth protecting) and "them" were instrumentalised to justify the lukewarm reception of the Chinese investors: "By acquiring Western technology leaders they [Chinese companies] want to create the preconditions to out-compete their rivals in the world markets. [. . .] Firm acquisitions in the West are a warning signal" (Ziesemer 2012). Interestingly, serious concerns with respect to ongoing acquisitions were less important to the reports than the dynamic development of Chinese investments in Germany, in general. In this case, othering emerged from diffuse and abstract debates in which past negative experiences and demonised images were cyclically reproduced. Observations on current investments, in contrast, were not presented. Two groups of actors were revealed as instrumental in shaping the othering discourse on Chinese investors in the press: journalists and (inter)national experts working for banks, accountancy firms or other institutes. (Inter)national experts stand out because of their expertise on China's globalisation and the consequences this may have for the German industry; their knowledge is based on their observations of markets and empirical work. When experts are invited to explain Chinese investments in Germany, they usually recur to disparities between "our" and "their" economic, social, political or institutional backgrounds:

> After all, the [German and Chinese] cultures are different—and not every Chinese-German cooperation becomes a success story. 'The initial euphoria often vanishes quickly', says management consultant Helmut Hammer.
>
> (Spohr 2011)

Journalists, by contrast, often strategically distinguish between "us" and "them" to reinforce and amplify their reporting. Recalling a whole range of otherness enables them to convey certain information in a more dramatic way and thus attract broader attention, as the following headline suggests: "China goes shopping. The Chinese are tired of their cheap image. And they adorn themselves with world market leaders. At any price" (Ankenbrand 2012).

Dimensions of Othering

In-depth content analysis reveals three different thematic dimensions of othering in the German newspaper discourse. Chinese investors are framed as deviating others based on (1) their firm-specific knowledge and technological assets, (2) images and conceptions attributed to China's economic development and international geo-strategic objectives and (3) the political regime and cultural and institutional environment they originate from.

First, and perhaps most obvious, othering is reflected in the ascription of inferior firm-specific knowledge and technological assets. In this case, China's economy is typically associated with firms that lack technological capabilities, international competitiveness and advanced know-how. Against this background, the newspaper reports tend to reiterate Germany's past economic achievements, as suggested by phrases such as "the German art of engineering" (Giesen 2008) and "fantastic industrial base" (Wocher 2011). Chinese firms, in contrast, are viewed as representing a "low-cost location" (Hein 2005a) and "cheap mass-produced goods" (Prange 2012). Related to this is the tendency to accuse Chinese companies of espionage:

> The Chinese are hunting for [. . .] established brands which do not have the smell of China's cheap image, [and have] management structures,

> advanced information technology, worldwide distribution networks and [. . .] research and development.
>
> (Hein 2005b)

More positive elements were added to the newspaper discourse only recently when certain representatives of acquired German firms and some national experts reflected on Chinese strategic takeovers as "showpiece global transactions" (Preuß 2012) and characterised collaboration as one of equal partners. This shift in newspaper reporting mainly results from international observations that China's economy is becoming more competitive, from the first learning effects with Chinese investors (earlier reports still tended towards speculation), as well as the need to add this new understanding to a discourse still widely marked by stereotypes and prejudices. However, the perception of Chinese FDI is still widely determined by the view that "[h]igh-tech is produced by the German firm, simple and cheap goods are manufactured by the Chinese company" (Fröndhoff 2007). This view, which is cyclically reproduced, constructs a tendency to want to secure Germany's business leadership by avoiding close interconnections with Chinese firms.

Second, China's growing presence in the global markets is conveyed as a clear threat to the global North. By alluding to China's mere physical size, financial strength and rapid economic development, and by contrasting this with the financial crises and lacking dynamics faced by European countries, the articles portray China as a (future) superpower: "From the Far East a gigantic wave of money is spilling over to us. Government funds are making ready to hunt for European companies" (Hoffmann 2007). Moreover, articles appeal to public sentiments and reproduce prejudices by using metaphors such as "hungry for acquisitions" (Reuters News Agency 2012) or "Far Eastern economic wonderland" (Mayer-Kuckuk 2012). Some use a yellow background colour in reference to the historical notion of "Yellow Peril"[3] (Hein 2005b) or illustrations of a fire dragon (Rabe and Wiede 2005). Although the image of "China buying the world" is presented in considerable detail, the actual FDI positions are almost neglected. In fact, only very few newspaper articles mention that outward-bound direct investment to China from Germany and other countries continues to far exceed foreign capital flows from China to other world markets (e.g. Mayer-Kuckuk 2010). Through the portrayal of China as a mysterious country and imperialistic hunter for world power, Chinese investors can be rejected as incalculable others.

The third and last dimension of otherness stresses the deviating political systems, cultural nonconformities and the differing understanding of social or ethical norms. By these accounts, Chinese investors threaten the Western political and ethical regime and its core principles such as free market economies, the importance of labour laws, forms of good governance and measures of environmental protection. The following quotes reflect some of the arguments of the newspaper texts: "It is a cultural mission to explain to them [the Chinese] that five-year plans do not work outside of China" (Preuß and Paul 2013); "[i]n traditional Chinese firms, employees wait for instructions and implement them with consequence and diligence. In German firms, employees act more independently and advocate their opinion" (Oldekop 2012). Interestingly, such deviations are rarely associated with specific Chinese investments in Germany. Rather, media representations draw attention to images and stereotypes in order to construct an image of Chinese otherness with which Germans have nothing in common.

Conclusion

Our analysis of the representation of Chinese FDI in German daily newspapers finds that daily print media coverage clearly contributes to an othering of Chinese investments. We also observe that othering is less dependent on rational reporting on recent investment activities but largely results from surrounding discourses that imbue the mediated facts with specific images of the "other" Chinese. Journalists and (inter)national experts contribute to creating distance between Chinese investors ("them") and domestic firms ("us") by depicting the former as standing apart and outlandish. Representations of otherness reflect on Chinese investments not only from a purely economic perspective but also from an institutional, cultural, and social perspective. As a result, media coverage produces stigmatised images of otherness that are rooted in country-specific ascriptions rather than actual firm-specific behaviour. These constructions of otherness gain even more legitimacy when the dominance of domestic firms, and Germany as a favourable host country, is contrasted with the perceived deficits of Chinese firms and China generally. In this case, the daily press constructs a reality in which national interests have to be defended against pressures originating from China.

The power of the media is not restricted to the influence it exerts on its audience. It also shapes positions and interpretations within a broader social, political and economic framework. We, therefore, assume that othering is likely to reinforce the dissemination of economic subordination, social exclusion, and even cultural fears against investors originating from China. In this narrative, various perspectives portray Chinese direct investments in Germany as different and impossible to assimilate, evoking the prospect of economic threats to the host country as well as specific social and cultural problems. Such negative sentiments and responses towards multinational companies from China are likely to affect the investment climate, enhance protectionism and give rise to economic nationalism. In fact, the host country's reservations towards foreign investors might have direct or indirect impacts on (future) investment projects, for instance when governmental interventions or less investor-friendly policies—also in the light of future elections—aim to reduce the influx of foreign investment. This, however, carries the risk of losing favour with international investors. As a consequence, the economy might face long-term disadvantages in the global competition for international capital.

Further research is needed to shed light on the social, political and cultural embeddedness of cross-border economic transactions. In our context, this means clarifying to what extent the acceptance of foreign investors depends on the investors' countries of origin, and how the home and host countries' institutional distance influences the particular interpretation of foreign investors. This may enable policy-makers to come up with clear recommendations to create a favourable investment climate, and address the responsibility of foreign investors to utilise strategies to improve their public perception.

Acknowledgements

This chapter is based on results of the project BRICINVEST (www.bricinvest.de) funded by Hans Böckler Foundation. BRICINVEST was a joint project of Philipps-Universität Marburg, Leibniz-Institute for Regional Geography, Leipzig, and PCG Project-Consult GmbH, Essen. The authors would like to thank Martina Fuchs, Martin Franz, Vanessa Hünnemeyer, Lea Kvarantan, Susann Schäfer and Patrick Werner for their helpful comments on a previous version of this chapter.

Notes

1. In this volume, quotations from non-English sources are translated by the authors of the chapters.
2. The keywords include deutsch*, chin*, unternehme*/firm*, invest*/übernahme.
3. The term *Yellow Peril* is a colour metaphor that refers to the dangers Western societies and their living standards are supposedly exposed to in the face of immigration from eastern Asia (Von Petersdorff 2005).

References

Ankenbrand, H. 2012. "China kauft ein." *Frankfurter Allgemeine Zeitung*, May 6: 40.

Bandelj, N. 2003. "Particularizing the Global: Reception of Foreign Direct Investment in Slovenia." *Current Sociology* 51(3/4): 375–392.

Bandelj, N. 2008. "Economic Objects as Cultural Objects: Discourse on Foreign Investment in Post-Socialist Europe." *Socio-Economic Review* 6(4): 671–702.

Barlach, R., and L. L. Puerto Elizalde. 2010. "Volvo Sold to China: A Study on the Development in Representation of the Transaction." C-Thesis. Malmö University, Sweden.

Brians, C. L., Willnat, L., Manheim, J. B., and R. C. Rich. 2010. *Empirical Political Analysis: Quantitative and Qualitative Research Methods*. Boston: Pearson.

Caves, R. E. 1971. "International Corporations: The Industrial Economics of Foreign Investment." *Economica* 38(149): 1–27.

Collins, D. 2013. The BRIC States and Outward Foreign Direct Investment. Oxford: Oxford University Press.

D'Costa, A. P. 2012. "Capitalism and Economic Nationalism: Asian State Activism in the World Economy." In *Globalization and Economic Nationalism in Asia*, edited by A. P. D'Costa, 1–32. Oxford: Oxford University Press.

The Economist. 2010. "China Buys Up the World." *The Economist*, November 11. http://www.economist.com/node/17463473, accessed 2016, October 12.

Ferree, M. M., Gamson, W. A., Gerhards, J., and D. Rucht. 2002. *Shaping Abortion Discourse: Democracy and the Public Sphere in Germany and the United States*. Cambridge: Cambridge University Press.

Frankfurter Allgemeine Zeitung. 2015. "Qualität, Glaubwürdigkeit und Renommee." www.faz.media/medien/frankfurter-allgemeine-zeitung-fuer-deutschland/, accessed 2015, September 9.

Friebel, G., and M. Heinz. 2014. "Media Slant against Foreign Owners: Downsizing." *Journal of Public Economics* 120: 97–106.

Fröndhoff, B. 2007. "Experten erwarten weitere Zukäufe." *Handelsblatt*, October 29: 17.

Gamson, W. A., and A. Modigliani. 1989. "Media Discourse and Public Opinion on Nuclear Power: A Constructionist Approach." *American Journal on Sociology* 95(1): 1–37.

Gerhards, J. 2006. "Diskursanalyse als systematische Inhaltsanalyse. Die öffentliche Debatte über Abtreibungen in den USA und der Bundesrepublik Deutschland im Vergleich." In *Handbuch Sozialwissenschaftliche Diskursanalyse. Band II: Forschungspraxis*, edited by R. Keller, A. Hirseland, W. Schneider, and W. Viehöfer, 299–324. Wiesbaden: VS Verlag für Sozialwissenschaften.

Giesen, C. 2008. "Die Chinesen lassen uns alle Freiheiten." *Frankfurter Allgemeine Zeitung*, March 22: 11.

Golinski, S., and S. Henn. 2015. "Imperialisten, Spione oder Retter? Zur Charakterisierung von Direktinvestitionen aus Russland, Indien und China in deutschen Tageszeitungen." *Zeitschrift für Wirtschaftsgeographie* 59(1): 1–19.

Greer, C., and Y. Jewkes. 2005. "Extremes of Otherness: Media Images of Social Exclusion." *Social Justice* 32(1): 20–31.

Hanemann, T. 2014. "Chinese Direct Investment in the EU and the US: A Comparative View." *Asia Europe Journal* 12(1–2): 127–142.

Hanemann, T., and M. Huotari. 2015. "Chinesische Direktinvestitionen in Deutschland und Europa. Eine neue Ära chinesischen Kapitals." www.merics.org/fileadmin/user_upload/pdf/COFDI_Chinese_Foreign_Direct_Investment_DE.pdf, accessed 2015, August 25.

Hein, C. 2005a. "Angriff aus China." *Frankfurter Allgemeine Zeitung*, July 3: 38.

Hein, C. 2005b. "Chinas Griff nach der Industrie des Westens." *Frankfurter Allgemeine Zeitung*, June 21: 14.

Hoffmann, C. 2007. "Maos Erben rücken an." *Frankfurter Allgemeine Zeitung*, July 1: 33.

Hurst, L., Yuan Cai, P., and C. Findlay. 2012. "Chinese Direct Investment in Australia: Public Reaction, Policy Response, Investor Adaption." *EABER Working Paper Series 81*. Canberra: East Asian Bureau of Economic Research. http://www.eaber.org/sites/default/files/documents/Chinese%20direct%20investment%20in%20Australia%20-%20By%20Luke%20Hurst,%20Peter%20Yuan%20Cai%20and%20Cristopher%20Findlay.pdf, accessed 2017, March 29.

Jacobsen, J., and T. G. Jacobsen. 2011. "Economic Nationalism and FDI: The Impact of Public Opinion on Foreign Direct Investment in Emerging Markets, 1990–2005." *Society and Business Review* 6(1): 61–76.

Kang, Y., and F. Jiang. 2012. "FDI Location Choice of Chinese Multinationals in East and Southeast Asia: Traditional Economic Factors and Institutional Perspective." *Journal of World Business* 47(1): 45–53.

Kepplinger, H. M., and S. Glaab. 2007. "Research Note: Reciprocal Effects of Negative Press Reports." *European Journal of Communication* 22(3): 337–354.

Kim, S. Y., Meunier, S., and Z. Nyiri. 2015. "Yin and Yank? Public Opinion in Europe towards the U.S. and China." *Comparative European Politics*: 1–27. First online. Article not assaigned to any printed issue yet. DOI: 10.1057/s41295-016-0005-6).

Kulchina, E. 2014. "Media Coverage and Location Choice." *Strategic Management Journal* 35(4): 596–605.

Lipsey, R. E. 2004. "Home-and Host-Country Effects of Foreign Direct Investment." In *Challenges to Globalization: Analyzing the Economics*, edited by R. E. Baldwin, and L. A. Winters, 333–382. Chicago: University of Chicago Press.

Lohnson, J. L., Bottorff, J. L., Browne, A. J., Grewal, S., Hilton, B. A., and H. Clarke. 2004. "Othering and Being Othered in the Context of Health Sciences." *Health Communication* 16(2): 253–271.

Makin, T. 2008. "Capital Xenophobia and the National Interest." *Institute of Public Affairs: AOIF-Paper 8*. www.ipa.org.au/library/publication/1229298839_document_makin.pdf, accessed 2008, August 28.

Mawdsley, E. 2008. "Fu Manchu versus Dr Livingston in the Dark Continent? Representing China, Africa and the West in British Broadsheet Newspapers." *Political Geography* 27(5): 509–529.

Mayer-Kuckuk, F. 2010. "China: Übernahmen unter staatlicher Regie." *Handelsblatt*, September 3: 23.

Mayer-Kuckuk, F. 2012. "Der reichste Chinese geht einkaufen." *Handelsblatt*, January 31: 28.

Meunier, S. 2014. "A Faustian Bargain or Just a Good Bargain? Chinese Foreign Direct Investment and Politics in Europe." *Asia Europe Journal* 12(1): 143–158.

Meunier, S., Burgoon, B., and W. Jakoby. 2014. "The Politics of Hosting Chinese Investments in Europe: An Introduction." *Asia Europe Journal* 12(1): 109–126.

Oldekop, A. 2012. "Die Welle kommt." *Handelsblatt*, June 26: 63.

Organisation for Economic Co-operation and Development (OECD). 2015. "Foreign Direct Investment Position by Country." www.oecd-ilibrary.org/finance-and-investment/oecd-international-direct-investment-statistics-2014_idis-2014-en, accessed 2014, September 17.

Prange, S. 2012. "Mittelständler in chinesischer Hand." *Handelsblatt*, August 30.

Preuß, S. 2012. "Chinesische Sany übernimmt Putzmeister." *Frankfurter Allgemeine Zeitung*, January 30: 14.

Preuß, S., and H. Paul. 2013. "Sany hat große Pläne mit Putzmeister." *Frankfurter Allgemeine Zeitung*, February 22: 16.

Rabe, C., and T. Wiede. 2005. "Der Hunger des Drachen." *Handelsblatt*, June 24–26: 2.

Reuters News Agency. 2012. "Tochterfirma von Q-Cells geht an Chinesen." *Handelsblatt*, June 5.

Rosen, D. H., and T. Hanemann. 2011. "An American Open Door? Maximizing the Benefits of Chinese Foreign Direct Investment." *Special Report*. http://asiasociety.org/files/pdf/AnAmericanOpenDoor_FINAL.pdf, accessed 2015, February 12.

Serre, M. 2012. "Die Chinesen kommen! Europas Rettung oder Untergang?" *Arte F* (TV channel), 2014, January 31.

Servan-Schreiber, J.-J. 1967. *The American Challenge*. Paris: Edition Denoel.
Sinn, H.-W., and A. J. Weichenrieder. 1997. "Foreign Direct Investment, Political Resentment and the Privatization Process in Eastern Europe." *Economic Policy* 12(24): 177–210.
Spohr, F. 2011. "Chinesische Investoren gehen in Deutschland auf Einkaufstour.", *Handelsblatt*, September 8: 62–63.
Statista. 2015. "Verkaufte Auflage der überregionalen Tageszeitungen in Deutschland in 3. Quartal 2015." http://de.statista.com/statistik/daten/studie/73448/umfrage/auflage-der-ueberregionalen-tageszeitungen/, accessed 2015, November 11.
Tienari, J., Vaara, E., and I. Björkman. 2003. "Global Capitalism Meets National Spirit: Discourses in Media Texts on a Cross-Border Acquisition." *Journal of Management Inquiry* 12(4): 377–393.
Vaara, E., and J. Tienari. 2002. "Justification, Legitimization and Naturalization of Mergers and Acquisitions: A Critical Discourse Analysis of Media Texts." *Organization* 9(2): 275–304.
Van Houtum, H., and T. van Naerssen. 2002. "Bordering, Ordering and Othering." *Tijdschrift voor Economische en Sociale Geografie* 93(2): 125–136.
Verlagsgruppe Handelsblatt. 2015. "Fundierter und unabhängiger Qualitätsjournalismus." www.vhb.de/unternehmen/, accessed 2015, September 9.
Von Petersdorff, W. 2005. "Die 'gelbe Gefahr': Geschichte eines Schlagwortes." *Frankfurter Allgemeine Zeitung*, July 3: 38.
Wocher, M. 2011. "Chinesische Firmen gehen in Deutschland auf Shoppingtour." *Handelsblatt*, November 24: 25.
Wong, H. Y. 2013. "Foreign Market Entry Choice: Internal and External Perspectives." In *Cultural and Technological Influences on Global Business*, edited by B. Christiansen, E. Turkina, and N. Williams, 46–62. Hershey: IGI Global.
Zhang, A. 2014. "Foreign Direct Investment from China: Sense and Sensibility." *Northwestern Journal of International Law and Business* 34(3): 395–453.
Zhang, L. 2010. "The Rise of China: Media Perception and Implications for International Politics." *Journal of Contemporary China* 19(64): 233–254.
Ziesemer, B. 2012. "Auf Chinas Kaufrausch folgt ein Kassensturz." *Handelsblatt*, August 27: 10.

3 Behind the Scenes

Managers' Interpretations of Foreign Takeovers by Investors of Emerging Economies

Martina Fuchs and Martin Schalljo

Introduction

Currently, many Chinese and Indian firms are looking for opportunities to invest their capital in firms of the global North. Despite this trend, little research has been carried out on how the takeover process is construed by the managers involved in such cross-border acquisitions. This is surprising as the success of a takeover is significantly influenced by how managers interpret an M&A (Ghosh Ray and Ghosh Ray 2013, 114). This contribution focuses on how managers of acquired firms in Germany interpret, that is perceive and construe, takeovers by investors from China and India. In particular, the question is how managers' interpretation of their international counterparts in the takeover is shaped by "behind the scenes" sociocultural patterns that extend beyond immediate shared visions.

Portrayals in the media suggest a predominantly sceptic view of new Asian owners by German managers (Golinski and Henn 2015; see *Golinski* and *Henn* in this volume). This chapter shows that after the initial welcome, managers in cross-border acquisitions soon find themselves confronted with different organisational procedures and unfamiliar management styles in their foreign counterparts, leading them to distance themselves from the foreign investors. This can be explained through patterns of interpretation surrounding rational organisation and legitimate rule—patterns that are embedded in a typical "Western" and "Rhenish capitalist" professional management ethics.

Interpretation as a Topic of Geographical and Interdisciplinary Research

The relevance of interpretation, that is how actors perceive and construe their environment, has long been debated, often in relation to "rational" knowledge (Schütz 1943). Whilst bounded human rationality has become an important issue in economics, specifically in contributions on organisational decision-making (Simon 1957, 241–273), the humanities have been strongly influenced by the notion of "social construction of reality" (Berger and Luckmann 1966/1991). Since then, perception, stereotyping, prejudice, attribution and attitude have all become important topics of debate (Farr 1996;

Tindale et al. 2001, 2). In geography, interpretation has often been investigated from the perspective of mental maps (Downs and Stea 1977; Johnston 1972); behavioural and perception geography became established as broad disciplinary fields as a result (Bunting and Guelke 1979; Crawshaw 2013). Recently, imagination has become a focus of human geography (Daniels 2011; Gregory 2007) and spatial planning (Boudreau 2007; Wetzstein and Le Heron 2010, 1905–1906), where approaches extend far beyond the stimulus–response models of early perception geography and methods are provided that allow the reconstruction of actor's perceptions. Whilst research related to imagination is mostly concerned with actor-based perception and their visions of the world, interpretation more specifically relates to the reconstruction of reality through various symbolic systems, often with particular focus on the spoken language. Although the debate about knowledge and the knowledge base of regions has been advanced by investigating the construction of reality by economic actors, the particular case of managers has remained a rather unexplored topic in economic geography. Bathelt and Glückler (2011) and Fuchs (2014) take first steps in this direction, stimulated in particular by organisational studies on "shared visions".

Economic geography's interest in the mindsets of managers was also inspired by the notion of "psychic" or "cognitive" distance put forward by Johanson and Vahlne (1977). The concept was later advanced, with perspectives shifting to organisational and institutional distance (Boschma 2005; Torre and Rallet 2005). In this chapter, we address distance as part of the social construction of spatiality, which is often accompanied by ascriptions of identity and trust, othering and distancing oneself from counterparts (Cartwright and Cooper 2000, 79; Li 2005).

This understanding corresponds to conceptions of cross-border M&A in international management studies. Inspired by Hofstede (1980, 2001), advanced models were developed on sociocultural distance in organisations (Rottig et al. 2013; Teerikangas 2007; Weber and Drori 2008). Studies show that cognitive distance in M&A does not necessarily impair the success of the company; still, mutual understanding does facilitate processes (Gomes et al. 2013; Weber et al. 2011). Hence, M&A studies frequently prove a gradual mental rapprochement of business partners during the post-M&A development (Cartwright and Cooper 2001; Schweiger and Goulet 2005), or at least continuity in the perceived distance between them (Stahl and Voigt 2008). Our study indicates a different tendency, namely German managers distancing themselves from their foreign counterparts in the post-merger process.

Theoretical Concepts of Shared Visions and Patterns of Interpretation

Shared visions are the short-term and situational interpretations that managers have in common (Klimoski and Mohammed 1994, 421). As a close relative of immediate strategies, plans and practices, shared visions include perceptions, impressions, estimates, opinions, ideas and attitudes, all of which are transient.

Once the problem is solved, the "shared task representation" (Tindale et al. 2001, 13) is usually displaced by fresh problems and thus disappears.

Shared visions are influenced by normative sociocultural backstage rules, that is patterns of interpretation (Fuchs and Schalljo 2016). Patterns of interpretation are the commonly held, broadly distributed, normative and stable views and considerations of a (part of) society which direct how meaning and understanding is generated (Oevermann 1973/2001a, 2001b, 2001c). Even conscious neglect of such a rule (e.g. the rule of trust in business relations) implies reference to the rule. Patterns of interpretation are similar to the sociocultural "interpretive schemes" suggested by Giddens (1993, 113) or the sociocultural "frames" proposed by Goffman (1974) in that they lend structure to perception (Nooteboom 2012, 339). Usually they are "secret rules", tacit "everyday theories" and "scripts", becoming obvious only in critical situations (Oevermann 2001b, 36–38; Soeffner 2004). A takeover can be such a critical event.

The problem of identifying distinct and unambiguous rules of transformation between "deep structures", such as patterns of interpretation, and the "surface", such as shared visions has been debated since the 1980s (see Flick 2009, 19). We do not suggest there are clear and universal rules on how shared visions "represent" patterns of interpretation. Still, it has been shown that shared visions correspond to patterns of interpretation and vice versa (Ferreira et al. 2013, 58; see Figure 3.1). More precisely, patterns of interpretation help to explain the shared visions that occur. Our empirical insights illustrate the shared visions held by managers on organisational procedures and administrative order and how these shared visions are related to patterns of interpretation surrounding rational organisation and legitimate rule.

The patterns of interpretation found to occur in the interviews can be related to "Western" and "Rhenish" or "Teutonic" professional ethics in management (*Professionsethik*). Max Weber (1921/1922) described such ethics for a modern capitalist administration as early as the 1920s. Later in Germany, after the Second World War, such values corresponded to a "variety of capitalism"

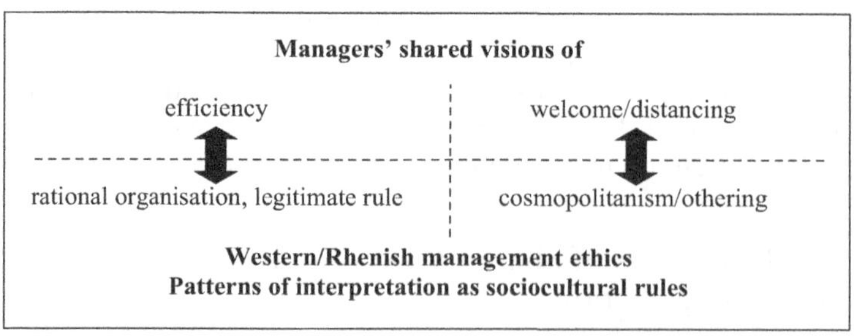

Figure 3.1 Heuristic concept of managers' shared visions and patterns of interpretation
Source: The authors.

which was based on linking profitability and social welfare, social partnership and co-determination and which was accompanied by particular standards of vocational education and training (Hall and Soskice 2001; Piore and Sabel 1984). Still, ideas surrounding particular management ethics are academic and heuristic constructs characterised by a certain fuzziness and vague boundaries. Obviously, there are no clear-cut or tangible management ethics that correspond to regional or national borders; hence, Western or Rhenish rules and norms can be said to describe a set of predominant general management principles that relate to widespread sociocultural values, such as cosmopolitan openness towards foreigners or more distancing attitudes.

Methodological Approach

In contrast to a broad range of quantitative modelling, current contributions often suggest qualitative measures for investigating intercultural differences in M&A (Rottig et al. 2013, 164; Rouzies 2013, 197) or narrative approaches (Cartwright and Magni 2009; Tarba et al. 2012, 80–81; Zhang and Stening 2013, 85–86), as does this contribution. To analyse "shared visions", qualitative content analysis is a proven method of choice (Flick 2009). Here we follow Soeffner's (2004) notion of methodologically controlled understanding, identifying relevant segments of the interviews and then carefully abstracting similar findings into common categories. To uncover "patterns of interpretation", the methodology uses Oevermann's (2001c) "structural hermeneutics", a method which has only partially arrived in the Anglophone discourse (Wagner et al. 2010). At its heart, Oevermann's method (2001c, 39–40) seeks to identify general sociocultural rules in interview material. Researchers look for the implicit essentials, that is the sociocultural backstage rules, rather than reconstructing the notional "facts" the interviewees are referring to (see Fuchs 2014, 60).

This contribution focuses on manager's interpretations in nine companies in Germany taken over by Chinese and Indian investors between 2010 and 2014. The cases refer to complete, majority-owned acquisitions of medium-sized and large companies. Interviews were conducted in 2014 and hence capture the early post-merger stage; a follow-up study was conducted in 2016. To better understand these cases, the project also included seven further takeovers by "Western" investors. All were cases of friendly takeovers. Interviewees generally expressed high esteem of the foreign firms and highlighted mostly positive aspects. However, the interviews also showed that behind the scenes, managers put some considerable distance between themselves and the new Asian owners when describing the early post-merger stage.

Empirical Findings

Shared visions of the new owners expressed by managers particularly related to organisational processes and hierarchical rules. Interviewees had shared visions about the administrative processes they were used to; these processes were not always adhered to by the Chinese or Indian investors. Examples of principles the German managers found lacking include the use of English as a common business language in international meetings; that meetings should have a clear agenda; that commitments, once entered into, are binding; and that responsibilities for particular activities are well defined. In the eyes of German managers work has to be foreseeable, predictable, resourceful and strategically oriented. If such rules are not adhered to, German managers begin a process of othering. Distance-marking expressions such as "they" and "them" (describing the new owners) were frequently found in the interviews. Even more notable is the view of German managers on "rational organisation", that is their normative expectation of how managers organise processes. In the eyes of the interviewees, Chinese and Indian executives often failed to apply such principles in the firms investigated. Interviewees stressed that Chinese executives sometimes did not speak fluent English and that they had the impression the new investors often did not follow Western management schemes such as introducing standardised processes or following clear lines of reporting. Also, particularly Chinese new owners were seen as too strongly focused on the influence of politicians. Indian investors were interpreted against their supposed background of a "caste mentality". Another frequent pattern of interpretation is related to legitimate rule. This was expressed by the shared vision that managers should meet—more or less—on a level playing field and that hierarchies are only legitimate when based on a functional logic, in other words when they lend pragmatic support to business. In their view, participation and the "voice" of subordinated management levels are not only allowed but also needed. In contrast to such norms, Indian and Chinese investors were often seen to adhere to formal hierarchies. In the words of one interviewee, "If the boss is at the table, nobody speaks." Another spoke of "lèse majesty" if somebody argued against their superior.

In this context, the autonomy of managers was also frequently addressed. Interviewees pointed to the general advantages resulting from their freedom in operational and (to some degree) financial decision-making, as—they argued—the investor has bought the complete firm, including its successful management and strategy.

Pragmatically, some interviewees appreciated the opaqueness that resulted from the lack of standardised organisational procedures and the complicated lines of reporting, taking them to be an advantage. In their view, this situation helped managers to continue with proven practices and protected the German company against rapid change after the takeover (see *Martin Franz, Kai Bollhorn* and *Reinhard Röhrig* in this volume). Not surprisingly, many interviewees expressed the shared vision that it was they who were primarily responsible for "the company" and "not the foreign cash investor". One manager stressed that the company had always been "profitable independently of the owner" and that management hence tried to "keep the investor out".

Such patterns of interpretation, which can be explained by the power of sociocultural conceptions of Western and Rhenish management, become even more evident when considering that most of the companies investigated are German not simply by virtue of having been established in Germany. Rather, they represent a type of company which has a long-standing tradition embedded in "Rhenish capitalism" and which happens to be based in Germany. Although managers' attitudes on this "variety of capitalism" are usually implicit and may differ in detail, the general appreciation of this economic model emerged as an important backstage rule. If such rules are not respected, managers are found to distance themselves from the new owners.

Obviously, such distancing is in conflict with the welcome the managers also expressed in the interviews. This relates to another Western backstage rule which states that managers should be open-minded, cosmopolitan and ready for ongoing change (see Fuchs and Schalljo 2016). For example, one of the companies in our sample—a "hidden champion" in Germany—started out as an independent medium-sized company. It was later taken over by a large German coal and steel company, then sold to a private equity investor and recently bought by a Chinese state-owned enterprise. The interviewee has worked for the company for many years and experienced the last two takeovers. He explained that in the beginning, he and the other executives had an optimistic shared vision of the Chinese investor. This openness resulted from the positive previous experiences of acquisitions, which showed that Rhenish-style routines could be protected. This optimistic view, however, began to gradually fade. Perceived differences did not decrease and were increasingly regarded as difficult. The interviewee expressed substantial distance to the new owners, reporting on how their instructions contradicted German law and labour relations and also civil society. There were similar findings in other cases. One interviewee stated that it was impossible to "bridge" the gap between the German company and the Chinese owner because a bridge would imply a degree of proximity between the business partners.

Our findings thus suggest that German managers do not distance themselves from the foreign investors from the outset. Later experiences, however, are sometimes interpreted as a challenge or even as endangering the achievements of the previous management model. Such shared visions relate to patterns of interpretation about rational organisation and legitimate rule, which are embedded in particular normative notions of Rhenish and Western management. The ultimate result is othering and distancing practices.

Conclusion

Our study demonstrates that not every acquisition leads to rapprochement. It can also lead to a distancing attitude. Managers generally start out with a shared vision that the new investors are welcome, corresponding to a pattern of interpretation of openness as part of professional management ethics. This, however, is pushed into the background in the post-merger process. Statements such as "being profitable independently of the owner" and "keep the investor out" show that German managers are distancing themselves from their foreign counterparts. Rhenish and Western professional management ethics obviously represent powerful backstage rules that influence how managers construe reality.

At the same time, our study only relates to a relatively "young" period in the history of particular takeovers. Results cannot simply be transferred to the future or to other kinds of international investors' relations. Additionally, it should be pointed out that our study only reconstructs the views of German managers. The corresponding shared visions and patterns of interpretations of the Chinese and Indian investors would constitute a promising research area.

Acknowledgements

We thank the German Scientific Foundation (FU 424/15–1) for supporting our research project. We also thank Ulrich Oevermann who inspiringly discussed interview extracts with us and supported us in tracing relevant patterns of interpretation.

For an extended conceptual discussion about patterns of interpretation, and an empirical basis also including private equity investments, see *Martina Fuchs* and *Martin Schalljo* (2016).

References

Bathelt, H., and J. Glückler. 2011. *The Relational Economy: Geographies of Knowing and Learning*. Oxford: Oxford University Press.

Berger, P. L., and T. Luckmann. 1966/1991. The Social Construction of Reality: A Treatise in the Sociology of Knowledge. London: Penguin.

Boschma, R. 2005. "Proximity and Innovation: A Critical Assessment." *Regional Studies* 39(1): 61–74.

Boudreau, J.-A. 2007. "Making New Political Spaces: Mobilizing Spatial Imaginaries, Instrumentalizing Spatial Practices, and Strategically Using Spatial Tools." *Environment and Planning A* 39(11): 2593–2611.

Bunting, T. E., and L. Guelke. 1979. "Behavioural and Perception Geography: A Critical Appraisal." *Annals of the Association of American Geographers* 69(3): 448–462.

Cartwright, S., and C. Cooper. 2000. *HR Know-How in Mergers and Acquisitions*. London: IPD.

Cartwright, S., and C. Cooper. 2001. Managing Mergers, Acquisitions and Strategic Alliances: Integrating People and Cultures. Oxford: Butterworth Heinemann.

Cartwright, S., and L. Magni. 2009. "The Value of Stories in Understanding the Past and Shaping the Future in Merged Organisations." *Advances in Mergers and Acquisitions* 8: 43–60.

Crawshaw, R. 2013. "Politics, Economics and Perception in Regional Construction." *Regional Studies* 47(8): 1177–1180.

Daniels, S. 2011. "Geographical Imagination." *Transactions* 36(2): 182–187.

Downs, R. M., and D. Stea. 1977. *Maps in Minds: Reflections on Cognitive Mapping*. New York: Harper and Row.

Farr, R. M. 1996. The Roots of Modern Social Psychology: 1872–1954. Oxford: Blackwell.

Ferreira, P., Vieira, E., and I. Neira. 2013. "Culture Impact on Innovation: Econometric Analysis of European Countries." In *Innovation in Socio-Cultural Context*, edited by F. Adam, and H. Westlund, 57–79. New York and London: Routledge.

Flick, U. 2009. An Introduction into Qualitative Research. London: Sage.

Fuchs, M. 2014. Worldwide Knowledge? Global Firms, Local Labour and the Region. Farnham: Ashgate.

Fuchs, M., and M. Schalljo. 2016. "'Western' Professional Ethics Challenged by Foreign Acquisitions: German Managers' Patterns of Interpretation Surrounding Chinese and Indian Investors." *Geoforum* 75(10): 20–28.

Ghosh Ray, K., and S. Ghosh Ray. 2013. "Cross-Border Mergers and Acquisitions: Modelling Synergy for Value Creation." *Advances in Mergers and Acquisitions* 12: 113–134.

Giddens, A. 1993. *New Rules of Sociological Method: A Positive Critique of Interpretative Sociologies*. 2nd Edition. Cambridge and Oxford: Polity Press and Blackwell.

Goffman, E. 1974. Frame Analysis: An Essay on the Organization of Experience. New York: Harper and Row.

Golinski, S., and S. Henn. 2015. "Imperialists, Spies or Rescuers? Characterization of Direct Investments from Russia, India and China in German Daily Newspapers." *Zeitschrift für Wirtschaftsgeographie* 59(1): 1–19.

Gomes, E., Angwin, D. N., Weber, Y., and S. Y. Tarba. 2013. "Critical Success Factors through the Mergers and Acquisitions Process: Revealing Pre-and Post-M&A Connections for Improved Performance." *Thunderbird International Business Review* 55(1): 13–35.

Gregory, D. 2007. "Imaginative Geographies." In *The Dictionary of Human Geography*, edited by D. Gregory, R. Johnson, G. Pratt, M. Watts, and S. Whatmore, 369–371. Oxford: Blackwell.

Hall, P. A., and D. W. Soskice. 2001. "An Introduction to Varieties of Capitalism." In *Varieties of Capitalism: The Institutional Foundations of Comparative Advantage*, edited by P. A. Hall, and D. W. Soskice, 1–70. Oxford: Oxford University Press.

Hofstede, G. 1980. Culture's Consequences: International Differences in Work Related Values. Newbury Park: Sage.

Hofstede, G. 2001. Culture's Consequences: Comparing Values, Behaviors, Institutions and Organizations across Nations. London and New Delhi: Thousand Oaks.

Johanson, J., and J. E. Vahlne. 1977. "The Internationalization Process of the Firm: A Model of Knowledge Development and Increasing Foreign Market Commitments." *Journal of International Business Studies* 8(1): 23–32.

Johnston, R. J. 1972. "Activity Spaces and Residential Preferences: Some Tests of the Hypothesis of Sectoral Mental Maps." *Economic Geography* 48(2): 199–211.

Klimoski, R., and S. Mohammed. 1994. "Team Mental Model: Construct or Metaphor?" *Journal of Management* 20(2): 403–437.

Li, L. 2005. "The Effects of Trust and Shared Vision on Inward Knowledge Transfer in Subsidiaries' Intra- and Inter-Organizational Relationships." *International Business Review* 14(1): 77–95.

Nooteboom, B. 2012. "Embodied Cognition, Organization and Innovation." In *Handbook of Knowledge and Economics*, edited by R. Arena, A. Festré, and L. Lazaric, 339–368. Cheltenham and Northampton: Edward Elgar.

Oevermann, U. 1973/2001a. "Zur Analyse der Struktur von sozialen Deutungsmustern (1973)." *Sozialer Sinn* 1(2): 3–33. www.digizeitschriften.de/dms/img/?PID=PPN598191607_0002llog6

Oevermann, U. 2001b. "Die Struktur von sozialen Deutungsmustern: Versuch einer Aktualisierung." *Sozialer Sinn* 1(2): 35–81. www.digizeitschriften.de/dms/img/?PID=PPN598191607_0002llog7

Oevermann, U. 2001c. *Strukturprobleme supervisorischer Praxis*. Frankfurt: Humanitas.

Piore, M., and C. F. Sabel. 1984. *The Second Industrial Divide*. New York: Basic Books.

Rottig, D., Reus, T. H., and Y. Tarba. 2013. "The Impact of Culture on Mergers and Acquisitions: A Third of a Century of Research." *Advances in Mergers and Acquisitions* 12: 135–172.

Rouzies, A. 2013. "Mixed Methods: A Relevant Research Design to Investigate Mergers and Acquisitions." *Advances in Mergers and Acquisitions* 12: 193–211.

Schütz, A. 1943. "The Problem of Rationality in the Social World." *Economica, New Series* 10(38): 130–149.

Schweiger, D. M., and P. K. Goulet. 2005. "Facilitating Acquisition Integration through Deep-Level Cultural Learning Interventions: A Longitudinal Field Experiment." *Organization Studies* 26(10): 1477–1499.

Simon, H. 1957. *Models of Man*. New York and London: Wiley.

Soeffner, H.-G. 2004. "Social Science Hermeneutics." In *A Companion to Qualitative Research*, edited by U. Flick, E. Kardoff, and I. Steinke, 95–100. London: Sage.

Stahl, G., and A. Voigt. 2008. "Do Cultural Differences Matter in Mergers and Acquisitions? A Tentative Model and Examination." *Organization Science* 19(1): 160–176.

Tarba, S. Y., Almor, T., and H. Benyamini. 2012. "A Comparative Anatomy of Two Cross-Border Acquisitions by Teva Pharmaceutical Industries." *Advances in Mergers and Acquisitions* 10: 75–102.

Teerikangas, S. 2007. "A Comparative Overview of the Impact of Cultural Diversity on Inter-Organisational Encounters." *Advances in Mergers and Acquisitions* 6: 37–75.

Tindale, R. S., Meisenhelder, H. M., Dykema-Engblade, A. A., and M. A. Hogg. 2001. "Shared Cognitions in Small Groups." In *Blackwell Handbook in Social Psychology: Group Processes*, edited by M. A. Hogg, and R. S. Tindale, 1–30. Oxford: Blackwell.

Torre, A., and A. Rallet. 2005. "Proximity and Localization." *Regional Studies* 39(1): 47–59.

Wagner, S., Lukassen, P., and M. D. Mahlendorf. 2010. "Misused and Missed Use: Grounded Theory and Objective Hermeneutics as Methods for Research in Marketing." *Industrial Marketing Management* 39(1): 5–15.

Weber, M. 1921/1922. *Wirtschaft und Gesellschaft*. Tübingen: Mohr/Siebek.

Weber, Y., and I. Drori. 2008. "The Linkages between Cultural Differences, Psychological States, and Performance in International Mergers and Acquisitions." *Advances in Mergers and Acquisitions* 7: 119–142.

Weber, Y., Tarba, S. Y., and A. Reichel. 2011. "A Model of the Influence of Cultural on Integration Approaches and International Mergers and Acquisitions Performance." *International Studies of Management and Organization* 41(3): 9–24.

Wetzstein, S., and R. Le Heron. 2010. "Regional Economic Policy 'In-the-Making': Imaginaries, Political Projects and Institutions for Auckland's Economic Transformation." *Environment and Planning A* 42(8): 1902–1924.

Zhang, X., and B. W. Stening. 2013. "Post-Acquisition Integration: A Two-Level Framework: Lessons from Integration Management of Cross-Border Acquisitions in the Global Automobile Industry." *Advances in Mergers and Acquisitions* 12: 75–111.

4 Industrial Relations and FDI From China and India in Germany

Martin Franz, Kai Bollhorn and Reinhard Röhrig

Introduction

When German concrete pump manufacturer PUTZMEISTER announced in 2012 that the company had been acquired by the Chinese corporation SANY, this resulted in a protest of 700 employees at the company's location in Aichtal near Stuttgart. The press published various articles on the acquisition that emphasised these protests and fears. As we will show later, this is not an isolated case of FDI from an emerging markets' firm resulting in workforce insecurity in the German target company. Employees and their collective agents (works councils and labour union representatives) fear job losses, a lowering of social standards and the weakening of existing co-determination rights. Such resentments "can partly be attributed to media reports that, by transporting distinct views and evaluations, influence recipients' perceptions, thus helping to shape public acceptance of foreign investors" (Golinski and Henn 2015, 1). Put differently, employees thus fear the repercussions of the perceived distance between them and the investor. Media reports foster this practice of othering (Reuter 2002) by emphasising the differences between Germany and the investors' country of origin (see *Sophie Golinski* and *Sebastian Henn* in this volume). Yet the practice of othering can also be related to real differences in the societal embeddedness of the foreign actors, such as different regulation of industrial relations in the investors' country of origin (institutional distance). Little is still known about the real impacts of such differences on industrial relations in the acquired companies. Existing work on the impacts of FDI on industrial relations (e.g. Bluhm 2001; Tholen 2007) has analysed investments from countries with higher standards in countries with lower standards, but few studies have analysed investments from countries with low standards in industrial relations in countries with higher standards. This chapter aims to close this research gap by focusing on the impact of such investments. It does so by analysing the influence of FDI on pre-existing co-determination rights, internal works agreements and collective pay agreements, as well as the communication between investors and collective agents of labour.

When we started our research in July 2013 we identified 530 companies in Germany with Chinese institutional investors and 302 companies with

Indian institutional investors in the database MARKUS. We targeted investors active in the production or service sector in their country of origin. This applied to 492 (92.8%) of the Chinese and 273 (90.4%) of the Indian FDI cases in Germany. To obtain quantitative data, for example on the financial situation of the acquired companies, managers or other high-level representatives of the acquired companies were interviewed on the telephone. Fifty-seven interviews were conducted with companies that have a Chinese investor (response rate, 11.6%) and 51 interviews with an Indian investor (response rate, 18.7%). In total, 40 of these interviews were conducted with companies that made a brownfield investment. Fifty-seven qualitative face-to-face interviews were conducted with managers and works council representatives of German companies acquired by a Chinese or an Indian company. In addition, 26 interviews with experts such as trade union representatives were conducted to obtain an external view of the acquisitions. Qualitative content analysis was used to analyse the interviews.

In the following, we provide, first, an introduction to FDI and, second, the consequences of FDI for labour. In the third part, the German system of co-determination is presented. This is followed by empirical results which are structured along the following four topics: (1) the situation of the German companies before acquisition and the reactions of workers, (2) the investors' prior knowledge of industrial relations in Germany, (3) day-to-day business with the new owner and (4) communication between the new owner and representatives of the works councils. Finally we present our conclusions.

FDI and Labour

Various authors have discussed the influence of national differences in industrial relations on the activities of multinational companies (e.g. Edwards et al. 2006; Ferner and Quintanilla 1998). Others have investigated whether transnational investments by multinational companies result in the convergence of industrial relations in different countries (e.g. Mueller 1992; Ortiz 1999). Although Mueller (1992) expects national differences in industrial relations to be eroded, strong national specificities persist (Edwards et al. 2006; Ortiz 1999). For example whilst there is no legislation in the USA that defines employee rights in M&As, German law stipulates that the employees of acquired companies keep their basic pay and conditions. Changes to pre-existing employment relations must be negotiated with the works councils that are compulsory in firms with more than five employees (Edwards et al. 2006). Differences in industrial relations and social standards can be a source of resentment among employees in the case of FDI. Employees may fear that the new foreign owner will not accept the pre-existing standards of industrial relations and social standards and attempt to undermine them. These fears are based on the cognitive, cultural, institutional and/or organisational distance—real or ascribed—between the investor as the "other" and the employees of the target company as the "we".

Distance is not only a potential source of fear but also important for establishing self-identity—a process of self-constituting othering (Reuter 2002). Different kinds of distance and proximity are relevant for analysing such relationships. Boschma (2005) differentiates proximity in terms of concepts and mental models (cognitive proximity), rules (institutional proximity), membership in organisational units and subunits (organisational proximity) and physical distance (geographic proximity). Other authors use the term *cultural proximity* (e.g. Gill and Butler 2003) which overlaps with Boschma's categories of cognitive and institutional proximity. Generally, real distance (e.g. institutional distance in terms of different laws) needs to be set apart from differences ascribed to the "other", such as (socially constructed) stereotypes. Knoben and Oerlemans (2006, based on Gertler 1995) point out that literature has two levels of analysis for cultural distance: (1) distance between geographical areas (continents, nations, regions as containers) in which organisations share the same culture and (2) distance between collaborating actors. The first level is particularly important when it comes to looking at the differences ascribed to actors from other continents, nations and regions. Actors may use a container view of culture and identify the "other" through stereotype imaginations. Here we use the term *cultural distance* to encompass attributes like values, beliefs and traditions ascribed to the "other" (see also the Introduction of this book). We regard types of ascribed cultural distance as crucial in the cases analysed.

Different perceptions based on distance at the level of management (see *Martina Fuchs* and *Martin Schalljo* in this volume) are not the only aspect influencing the acquisition process and ensuing activities. The various employees and their collective agents (works councils and trade unions) are also embedded in local, national or even transnational networks, regulations and traditions (e.g. Cumbers et al. 2008; Franz 2010) which influence their perceptions of distance and their subsequent reactions. How employees perceive an acquisition can be affected by factors that may not apply at the managerial level. These factors could include a lack of knowledge of ongoing processes and their impacts, as well as a lack of knowledge on the investor and their reputation, aims, values and strategies (which may foster othering on the basis of ascribed cultural distances). On the other hand, the investors potentially lack knowledge of the corporate culture in the acquired company and the institutional contexts in which it is embedded. These distances can result in wrong expectations, influence decisions and result in misunderstandings.

Co-Determination Rights in Germany

Labour co-determination on a corporate level is an essential aspect of the prevailing understanding of capitalism in Germany (Hall and Soskice 2001; see also *Martina Fuchs* and *Martin Schalljo* in this volume). Although co-determination in Germany is not without problems (e.g. Eichhorst and

Marx 2011; Whittall 2005), the model is still widely regarded as a major strength of the German economy (Jirjahn 2010; Reisenbichler and Morgan 2012). Cooperation between works councils (elected representatives of the employees) and the company's management is based on the Betriebsverfassungsgesetz (Industrial Constitution Act), which defines the rights and duties of the companies as well as those of the labour representatives. The regulations on co-determination in the Betriebsverfassungsgesetz go beyond the regulations in other European countries and in countries such as China and India.

Potential foreign investors aiming at acquiring a (majority) stake in a German company or full ownership must ensure their activities conform to German co-determination legislation and culture. As a minimum, they need to overcome institutional distances sufficiently to meet the necessary legal requirements. As the German system of industrial relations, however, is rooted in the values and expectations of German society, they also need to overcome cognitive and ascribed cultural distances if conflicts are to be avoided. From a German perspective, there often seems to be a lack of knowledge of co-determination rights, with investors seemingly underestimating the influence of co-determination on the process of acquisition and the later day-to-day business in a German company. In such cases, the behaviour of investors with regard to co-determination may result in conflicts. Empirical findings by Jirjahn and Müller (2009) show a negative correlation between the existence of a works council and ownership by a foreign investor, although the authors do not give an explanation for this.

Situation of Companies Before Acquisitions and Workers Reactions

From the perspective of the company managers surveyed, workers were insecure about the future of their company after the acquisition only in a minority of cases (see centre pie in Figure 4.1). Furthermore, active resistance against the acquisitions was only reported in 5% of the cases (see right-hand pie in Figure 4.1). Given the negative press reports about the future of acquired companies (see *Sophie Golinski* and *Sebastian Henn* in this volume), both of these figures appear very low. A potential explanation could be the financially unstable situation of the acquired companies. Among the interviewed companies with an investor from China and India, the majority had declared insolvency or were financially unstable before selling (see left-hand pie in Figure 4.1). However, another reason may be that this is the view of management only: all representatives of works councils interviewed stated that there had been insecurity on the part of the employees. As there are institutional distances (e.g. the labour standards in China and India are lower than those in developed economies) and perceived cognitive distances (e.g. the image of Chinese companies as undermining social standards and co-determination rights, as well as their supposed use of dishonest and corrupt business practices [Fehr 2009]), these insecurities seem justified.

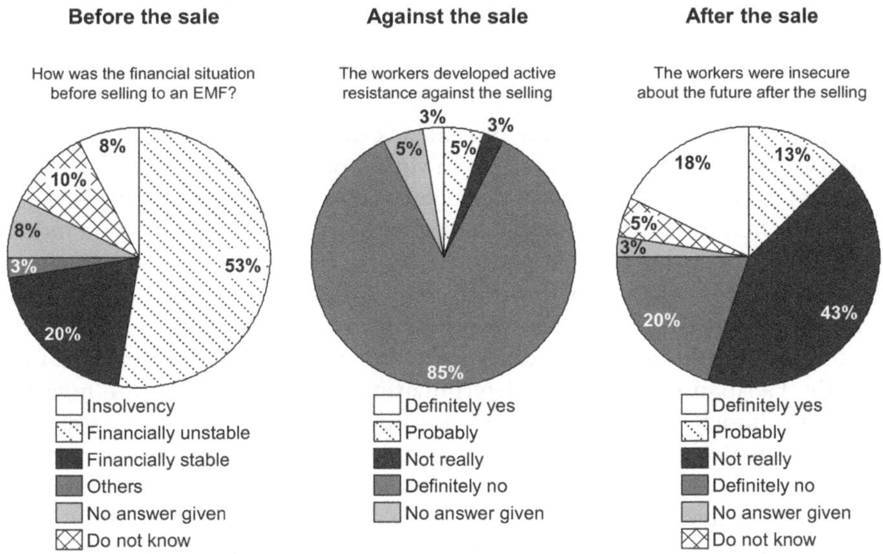

Figure 4.1 The financial situation of the companies before acquisition and workers' reaction to acquisition by a Chinese/Indian company

Source: Own data.

Note: n = 40. EMF = Emerging Market Firm.

Surprisingly, only two cases of acquisitions by Chinese and Indian firms were identified in which employee insecurity resulted in active resistance to the acquisition. These cases are the acquisition of the concrete pump producer PUTZMEISTER by China-based SANY and the acquisition of the plastics department of automotive supplier ZF, BOGE, by CHINESE TMT. In both cases, workers were not expecting their company or department to be sold to a foreign investor as they thought they were in a financially stable situation and did not see the need for new ownership.

Prior Knowledge of the Investor on Industrial Relations in Germany

In the vast majority of the cases analysed German actors perceived the investors to only have minor to no knowledge of the German system of industrial relations and co-determination prior to the acquisition. Only in exceptional cases did the investor have comprehensive knowledge of the topic beforehand.

> They don't know anything about co-determination. We observed this the first time we had contact with them. [. . .] In the acquisition negotiations

> nobody told them anything about co-determination culture or trade unions in Germany; thus they were presented with a fait accompli after the acquisition.
>
> (Interview with representative of a works council)

This example documents the typical lack of preparation on the investors' side. Only few cases document that the investors had a rudimentary knowledge of co-determination practices before investing in Germany. In such cases the investors often attempted to obtain detailed information on industrial relations during the first phase of negotiations with the previous owner. This especially applies in those cases in which the investor already had some experience from previous investments in Germany or other European countries. In addition, some cases were documented in which information on the German system of co-determination was provided to the investor by consultancies supervising the acquisition negotiations. Surprisingly, it seems that not every consultancy or previous owner considers this topic important. Only in very few cases did the investor establish direct contact to the works councils during the negotiation process to learn more about their role. In the majority of cases no direct contact was established between the investor and the works council or trade unions both during and after the acquisition (an aspect we will return to). In other words, no attempts were made to bridge the distances between the investor and works councils or trade unions.

Day-to-Day Business With the New Owner

Analysis of works council experiences with the new owners shows that normally, the new owners make no attempt at undermining pre-existing industrial relations. Rather, the Betriebsverfassungsgesetz seems to be accepted as a basis. In the majority of cases, the new owners acted neutrally towards pre-existing industrial relations. Similar results were obtained concerning the acceptance of internal works agreements and collective pay agreements. In the majority of cases, pre-existing agreements and existing practices of collective payment negotiations and raises in salary were accepted. In a few cases there were even attempts by the investors to exceed pre-existing agreements. Institutional distance (differences in industrial relations) and (ascribed) cultural distances therefore do not result in behaviour that challenges existing industrial relations.

In some interviews, an improved relationship was perceived between the works council and the new owner compared to the old owner, contributing to the positive development of labour relations in business practice: "Today we are much more involved than we were when it was a family-owned company as they [. . .] only did what they were obliged to by law and even for this we had to fight" (interview with representative of a works council). Although this particular perception is that of a works council representative, there are cases where the management of the acquired company also thought that relations between the works council and company had improved under the new owner: "Our new shareholders financially supported the plans we made with the works council as they were not interested in trouble" (interview with a German manager).

However, a few cases were identified in which the investor had a conflict-oriented approach with respect to existing industrial relations. "That was a red rag to him. He says '[. . .] Why do others want to decide with me? It is my company, I pay, I bring the money and others want to decide what happens with my money'" (interview with a German manager of a company). In some cases the investor cut back existing practices to the statutory minimum and attempted to renegotiate salaries, working time regulations and other agreements. This reinforced the distinction between "we" and "the other" and sometimes resulted in strong conflicts, for example in one company where the employees came out on strike for one month.

Negative attitudes towards existing industrial relations are proof of cognitive as well as institutional distances between the investor and the collective agents of labour in Germany. Although cognitive and ascribed cultural distances may persist, in most cases the investors seem to eventually accept pre-existing industrial relations because of their legally binding character. This at least was stated in many interviews. "We often had conflicts in which the Indian investor was shocked and said 'I do not understand why you Germans scare away the investors.' [. . .] So he is still against it, but because it is as it is and it works, he more or less agrees to it" (interview with a German manager of a company). In this case, the existing institutional distance (differences in industrial relations) matches the cognitive and cultural distance. The differences in how the situation is perceived by the German manager and the investor seem to be rooted in different values (ad personam which may be interpreted as cultural distance), as well as different experiences with industrial relations in India and Germany.

Communication Between the New Owner and Representatives of Labour

Generally, the level of communication between the new owner and representatives of labour was found to be low, depending on the individual approach of the actors on both sides. As stated before, the investor established direct contact to the works council during the negotiation process in only a few cases. Additionally, the level of communication between the new owner and the representatives of labour often decreases in day-to-day business. This lack of direct communication prevents a bridging of the perceived cultural, cognitive and institutional distances. However, the lack of communication is not always the fault of the new owner. In some cases, it was the works council that did not make any attempt to build or maintain direct contact with the owner: "We have no contact. Not at all. Zero. We do not want to have contact" (interview with a representative of a works council). This lack of communication seems to be related to two factors:

First, the essential role of the German management in day-to-day business remains: "So the main contacts for us are our managers here. And the investor is actually in the background; he intervenes very little as far as we notice" (interview with a representative of a works council). Normally, contact between the works council and the new owner only takes place through the German management which acts as an intermediary. A correlation was noted with the size of the investing company: often the investors are large corporations in which direct contact between the owner and the representatives of labour in individual affiliates is unusual. Contact with the works council is part of day-to-day business and thus the responsibility of local management—which is German in most of the cases analysed. These relationships also point to the low level of integration of the German subsidiary that was observed in most of the cases.

Second, the language barrier: in those cases in which the works council attempted to build direct contact with the new owner, language barriers often prevent successful communication: "Ultimately, language is the basis of a works council's work. And if you have to speak English unfortunately much gets lost. [. . .] In some circumstances you talk at cross purposes" (interview with a representative of a works council). Experiencing language barriers frustrates works council members and results in their giving up any attempts at establishing direct contacts. In such cases contact is only through intermediaries: "I do not speak English, I do not speak Indian and then there he is with his broken German. We ended up in communication with three degrees of separation" (interview with a representative of a works council). Strategies to overcome language barriers include the use of interpreters or the recruitment of German-Chinese persons. The latter strategy was used only by one works council.

Conclusion

Differences in industrial relations and social standards between an investor's country and the country in which the investor wants to acquire a company can be a source of resentment. Employees may fear that the investor will not accept existing standards but try to undermine them in order to align them with the situation in their home country. Such fears are based on perceived organisational, cultural and institutional distances between the investor and the employees of the targeted company. In many cases, however, the prejudiced imagination of the investors as the "other" was stronger than it proved to be in later interaction. The intensity of fears and their manifestation in the form of resistance seems to be related to the financial situation of the targeted company before acquisition. Among the companies interviewed the majority was financially unstable before the acquisition. Thus, employees may see the investor more as a saviour than as an aggressor (see *Sophie Golinski* and *Sebastian Henn* in this volume).

Analysis of the interviews showed that in many respects, investors from China and India cannot be thought of in black and white. It became clear that the origin of an investor does not allow verifiable conclusions on the degree to which he or she will follow German laws and habits of industrial relations. A conflict-oriented approach by the new owners was the exception within the companies analysed. Employees perceiving the target company as the "we" and the investor as the "other" is mostly not justified, as many investors make efforts to bridge the organisational, cognitive, cultural and institutional distances. Two kinds of bridging efforts can be identified: (1) obligatory bridging, where investors accept those parts of the German system of industrial relations that are defined by law, and (2) voluntary bridging, where investors accept or even encourage practices of industrial relations that exceed the legally binding regulations.

Generally, language barriers are a factor that negatively affects levels of communication, especially in the case of Chinese acquisitions. This is true irrespective of spatial distances—it does not matter if the investor is located in Germany or in his country of origin. However, the language barrier is not the sole reason for the low level of communication. In corporations, what seems to matter most are organisational structures, where direct contact between the owner and the representatives of labour in single-affiliated companies is unusual. It is this lack of direct contact due to organisational distance that prevents the bridging of (perceived) cultural, cognitive and institutional distances.

Acknowledgements

This chapter is based on results of the project BRICINVEST (www.bricinvest.de) which was funded by the Hans Böckler Foundation. BRICINVEST was a joint project of Philipps-Universität Marburg, Leibniz-Institute for Regional Geography, Leipzig, and PCG Project-Consult GmbH, Essen. The authors give thanks to the project team members Sophie Golinski, Sebastian Henn and Jörg Weingarten. Furthermore the authors wish to thank Inka Gersch, Sebastian Henn and Philip Müller for their comments on previous versions of the chapter.

References

Bluhm, K. 2001. "Exporting or Abandoning the 'German Model'? Labour Policies of German Manufacturing Firms in Central Europe." *European Journal for Industrial Relations* 7(2): 153–173.

Boschma, R. A. 2005. "Proximity and Innovation: A Critical Assessment." *Regional Studies* 39(1): 61–74.

Cumbers, A., Nativel, C., and P. Routledge. 2008. "Labour Agency and Union Positionalities in Global Production Networks." *Journal of Economic Geography* 8(3): 369–387.

Edwards, T., Coller, X., Ortiz, L., Rees, C., and M. Wortmann. 2006. "How Important Are National Industrial Relations Systems in Shaping Restructuring in MNCs?" *European Journal of Industrial Relations* 12(1): 69–88.

Eichhorst, W., and P. Marx. 2011. "Reforming German Labour Market Institutions: A Dual Path to Flexibility." *Journal of European Social Policy* 21(1): 73–87.

Fehr, M. 2009. "Wie chinesische Firmen ihr Deutschland-Geschäft managen." *Wirtschaftswoche*, 2009, October 14. www.wiwo.de/unternehmen/neue-studie-wie-chinesische-firmen-ihr-deutschland-geschaeft-managen/5238260.html, accessed 2016, December 5.

Ferner, A., and J. Quintanilla. 1998. "Multinationals, National Business Systems and HRM: The Enduring Influence of National Identity or a Process of 'Anglo-Saxonization'." *International Journal of Human Resource Management* 9(4): 710–731.

Franz, M. 2010. "The Potential of Collective Power in a Global Production Network: UNICOME and Metro Cash & Carry in India." *Erdkunde* 64(3): 281–290.

Gertler, M. S. 1995. "'Being There': Proximity, Organization, and Culture in the Development and Adoption of Advanced Manufacturing Technologies." *Economic Geography* 71(1): 1–26.

Gill, J., and R. J. Butler. 2003. "Managing Instability in Cross-Cultural Alliances." *Long Range Planning* 36(6): 543–563.

Golinski, S., and S. Henn. 2015. "Imperialists, Spies or Rescuers? Characterization of Direct Investments from Russia, India and China in German Daily Newspapers." *Zeitschrift für Wirtschaftsgeographie* 59(1): 1–19.

Hall, P. A., and D. Soskice. 2001. Varieties of Capitalism: The Institutional Foundations of Comparative Advantage. Oxford: Oxford University Press.

Jirjahn, U. 2010. *Ökonomische Wirkungen der Mitbestimmung in Deutschland: Ein Update*. Arbeitspapier 186. Düsseldorf: Hans Böckler Stiftung.

Jirjahn, U., and S. Müller. 2009. Nonunion Worker Representation, Foreign Owners and the Performance of Establishments in Germany. Working paper. Trier: University Press.

Knoben, J., and L. A. G. Oerlemans. 2006. "Proximity and Inter-Organizational Collaboration: A Literature Review." *International Journal of Management Reviews* 8(2): 71–89.

Mueller, F. 1992. "Flexible Working Practices in Engine Plants: Evidence from the European Automobile Industry." *Industrial Relations Journal* 23(3): 191–204.

Ortiz, L. 1999. "'Unions' Response to Teamwork: Differences at National and Workplace Level." *European Journal of Industrial Relations* 5(1): 49–69.

Reisenbichler, A., and K. J. Morgan. 2012. "From 'Sick Man' to 'Miracle': Explaining the Robustness of the German Labor Market during and after the Financial Crisis 2008–09." *Politics and Society* 40(4): 549–579.

Reuter, J. 2002. Ordnungen des Anderen. Zum Problem des Eigenen in der Soziologie des Fremden. Bielefeld: Transcript.

Tholen, J. 2007. Labour Relations in Central Europe: The Impact of Multinationals' Money. Aldershot: Ashgate Publishing Ltd.

Whittall, M. 2005. "Modell Deutschland under Pressure: The Growing Tensions between Works Councils and Trade Unions." *Economic and Industrial Democracy* 26(4): 569–592.

5 Cultural Frictions in Post-merger Integration Processes

A View on "Face" When Dealing With Asian Counterparts

Muriel Durand

Introduction

The cultural friction perspective offers a framework for investigating the contacts between individuals in post-merger integration processes in cross-border M&A. This contribution reconsiders the study of friction at the individual level, exploring "face" when dealing with Asian counterparts as one possible way of disentangling the friction concept. The chapter asks how middle managers interpret "losing face" in particular situations and how this produces cultural friction in cross-border acquisitions.

As stated by Drogendijk and Zander (2010) the notion of friction places a strong emphasis on the interaction of executives. Moreover, cultural friction posits that cultural differences may be either synergistic or disruptive (Luo and Shenkar 2011). Still, as such notions of cultural friction have not been operationalised because of their empirical complexity (Koch et al. 2016), it seems appropriate to specifically focus on friction in managers' interactions (Ambos and Håkanson 2014). This chapter puts forward grounded critical incidents as a methodological approach (Durand 2016) and offers a specific example of how to apply this in practice. Grounded critical incidents seem a suitable starting point for empirically capturing facets of intercultural friction in that they measure middle managers' own perceptions of cultural friction. This contribution intends to address the measurement gap from a novel perspective, capturing the impact of cultural differences or distances in global business and investigating managerial perceptions during intercultural interactions in cross-border acquisitions with a particular focus on "face saving and keeping".

The first section gives some theoretical background on the concepts of friction and face. Next, a selected example is discussed, emphasising the understanding or misunderstanding of face-saving as a facet of friction. The results, discussion and perspectives section highlights the relevance of "face" for research and the common practice of middle managers.

Cultural Friction

The friction metaphor provides a "superior representation of what is arguably the heart of the matter in international business studies, namely the interaction between viable entities" (Shenkar 2012a, 15). The cultural friction perspective offers a framework for investigating the relationships, or more precisely the contacts between individuals in intercultural encounters. Such encounters can occur in different nations, firms, or teams (Shenkar et al. 2008). Generally there are many meanings of the concept of friction in multicultural environments, such as misalignment (Rosen et al. 2008), collision (Buono and Bowditch 2003) or cultural dissonance (Irrman 2005). Shenkar et al.'s conception of friction, emphasising "contact", "interactions" and "cultural resistance", is appropriate when targeting individual encounters in cross-border settings (Luo and Shenkar 2011; Shenkar 2012a, 2012b; Shenkar et al. 2008). Luo and Shenkar (2011, 2) define cultural friction in international business as

> the extent to which two or more entities from different countries culturally resist with one another in real contact or interactions over the course of international business activities or transactions.

Friction, hence, focuses on the complexity of cultures and the interactions within (Drogendijk and Zander 2010), suggesting that cultural differences may be either synergistic or disruptive (Luo and Shenkar 2011).

Friction can result in positive outcomes and facilitate synergies. Hence, although conflict is sometimes regarded as dysfunctional it could be considered a normal process when managing across different sociocultural settings (Schotter and Beamish 2011). Empirical research indicates that synergies may emerge from cultural value differences (Koch et al. 2016), especially when the organisation is able to foster boundary-bridging managers who are able to generate "creative tensions" (Mudambi and Swift 2009; Schotter and Beamish 2011). Tensions emerging from those interactions are not necessarily "dysfunctional and disruptive" (Coser 1956, 23) but can have positive effects and create synergy (Shenkar et al. 2008). In a recent publication, Stahl and Tung (2014) highlight that traditional international business studies focusing on the effect of cultural differences tend to overemphasise the negative over the positive; the authors call for a more nuanced understanding of the multifaceted relationship between culture and international business processes and outcomes. Thus, there is growing evidence of the "double-edge sword" (Reus and Lamont 2009) of cultural diversity in that it can be both an asset and a liability in multicultural teams (Stahl et al. 2014). The following example shows a problematic situation of communication in a cross-border acquisition and explains the occurring friction.

Face Concerns as a Facet of Friction

To understand the nature of friction as one mechanism of cross-cultural encounters during post-merger integration, this contribution focuses a particular facet that underlies friction in grounded critical incidents: face concerns, that is face-giving, face-keeping and face-losing concerns as a core social value in Asian cultures (Hofstede, 2001). "Face" is a phenomenon in societies that are very conscious of social contexts. In that way, for Hofstede (2001) it is directly linked to "collectivism" as a fundamental cultural dimension. Face concern in a sense of dignity, respect and honour is a way to maintain harmony within the group in a "collectivist" culture. Causing someone to "lose face", even if done by accident, is an infraction rarely forgiven (Ho 1976). One may try to restore face using indirect and subtle communication, gift giving, honouring and complimenting. People concerned with face saving may not talk openly about a problem to avoid losing face and may not challenge their superior in front of others. "Gei mianzi", "Jiu mianzi" or "Xiexie gei mianzi" find an equivalent in "thank you for coming", to thank someone for accepting a dinner invitation for example, and would literally translate as "thank you for having given me face" (Hofstede 2001). Basically, face describes the proper relationship with one's social environment, which is essential to a person (or that person's family) as the front that is shown to the world. In a case study of the failed cross-border acquisition between Siemens and BenQ, Cheng and Seeger (2012) describe the face concern as a subtle cultural factor, illustrating how the directors at BenQ rejected chairman Lee's resignation to avoid his and the firm losing face and how they used an intermediary in a key role to reduce the loss of face towards the stakeholders.

Critical Incident Technique

Despite several attempts by Shenkar and colleagues to more rigorously conceptualise cultural difference (Luo and Shenkar 2011; Shenkar 2012a, 2012b; Shenkar et al. 2008), the notion of cultural difference has not gained the attention it deserves (Ambos and Håkanson 2014). Often, the term still remains at the metaphorical level. Shenkar (2012b) outlines the hidden assumptions behind the cultural "distance" construct, the challenges associated with it and its theoretical and methodological properties.

This study proposes an alternative grounded measure for obtaining information from individuals, designed to capture middle managers' perception of work-related issues during specific situations of the ongoing post-merger processes (see Harzing and Pudelko 2016; Stahl and Tung 2015). Critical incident methodology, based on managers' lived experience of cross-border acquisitions, is used to understand critical events by providing a grounded picture of the various challenges posed by M&As (Brookfield 1995). The use, the value and the relevance of the critical incident technique for studying managerial perception in post-merger integration has been discussed in an earlier paper (Durand 2016). The instrument developed and discussed in this study focuses on face as a key concern for the cultural interaction of middle managers in post-merger integration settings. The "face concern" is based on a preliminary grounded study that aimed at documenting middle managers' perceptions of cultural challenges, job changes and emotions during post-merger integration. The initial version of the questionnaire was based on issues identified during exploratory interviews and includes a pool of 22 critical incidents generated for the purposes of scale construction. To test the psychometric properties of the instrument, we followed the guidelines suggested by Hinkin (1998). The grounded scenarios were carefully built to simulate situations encountered by key informants. Later, a quantitative study followed to further refine the new scale. In total, 163 middle managers filled in the survey online, of which 142 responses were kept for data analysis (only those managers who had experienced at least one cross-border merger). The mean for the first alternative (strong order to leave) is 2.9648 on a 5-point Likert scale, which is just above the midpoint, and 3.2113 for the second alternative (sharing time and explain the policy), which is quite high. People in this case would have behaved the same way with someone from the same cultural background (m = 3.6056). From this we can infer that the frictional effect has been anticipated, as if it were the norm for the cross-border M&As experts (respondents) in these contexts.

The Case of "Losing, Giving, Keeping Face"

The following gives a specific example of "losing, giving, keeping face":

> **CI 1:** As an expert, you are sent to train people in a Corporate School abroad after a merger. You spend a lot of time at the workplace and it is like your new home in this foreign environment. One morning, one of the trainees arrives in the classroom together with five friends who are not with the company to have breakfast together.
>
> a: You strongly order them to leave, explaining that this is a private space reserved for people working here and not for others.
> b: You kindly explain the policy of the organisation but you allow them to stay, just this once, and share a cup of coffee/tea.

This critical incident is assigned to the label "privacy boundaries". The manager who experienced this event felt invaded at the workplace and asked people to leave the place (a place he considers "home" and one where he could find familiar elements). From a sociocultural perspective, the manager experienced friction and realised afterwards that he made a mistake in asking the trainee to leave the workplace, making him and his friends lose face. From the trainee's perspective it was natural to come to this workplace to share breakfast with his friends even though they were not part of the company. He felt insulted to be ordered to leave without understanding the reason why.

The manager could have accepted to spend this time with the group and developed a strong relationship and trust. Both are necessary ingredients for successful management in that they decrease perceived friction and prevent the group from losing face. The consequence of this loss of face is distrust, not only on the part of the trainee but also the whole group. It would require some strategies to repair the damaged relationship.

Understanding the friction that stems from face concerns adds information on the character of the cultural challenge managers have to confront. In the case described earlier, friction arises when a manager orders a trainee to leave the workplace and does not allow his friends to have breakfast there. The manager fails to see that in a collective context, such behaviour is the consequence of the values linked to strong group cohesion. At the same time, the manager feels troubled because the trainee does not show enough respect for his position as a manager; hence, he expected this disrespect to relate to his hierarchical position. This may be related to a "Western" management style (see *Martina Fuchs* and *Martin Schalljo* in this volume) and matches the insight of Cocroft and Ting-Toomey (1994) that U.S. respondents tend to use more direct conflict styles such as domination, whereas participants from "collectivist" cultures are more likely to use indirect, mutual face-saving conflict styles, such as according high importance to each other's face or face concerns (Cocroft and Ting-Toomey 1994). In the strategies proposed for successfully managing cross-border acquisitions, Rottig (2007) warns of using such a direct strategy of domination to control the acquired firm, especially in international alliances. Indeed, business practice has shown that in a large number of acquisitions, managers failed to treat this sensitive issue carefully, not treating the acquired workforce with the necessary deference (Rottig 2007).

Conclusion

The intent of this chapter was to shed light on cultural contacts, looking at cross-cultural frictions resulting from cross-border acquisitions from a grounded perspective. This is a contribution to the friction concept at the inter-individual level, revealing "face concerns" as one component of perceived friction in a specific context. Developing a novel method to operationalise the complexity of cross-cultural interactions at the inter-individual level is one possible answer to calls that researchers should focus on managers' actual problems rather than their own preconceived solutions (Harzing and Pudelko 2016; Stahl and Tung 2015). Managers may have difficulties finding the behaviour required by such situations, yet this can be decisive for developing synergies and managing long-term relationships with colleagues, partners and customers across international mergers (Brannen and Wilen 1998; Rottig 2007). Perceived friction as a result of face is a particularly sensitive aspect when the cultural backgrounds of the actors involve different work values and practices. In particular, a focus on Asian and Western middle managers could be inspiring for future research directions.

Acknowledgements

I am very grateful to Mikael Sondergaard for advising and encouraging me on this chapter. Many thanks to Mohammad Ahammad, Yipeng Liu, Marc Ohana, Mark Peterson and Shlomo Tarba for their guidance and insightful comments on the scale development.

References

Ambos, B., and L. Håkanson. 2014. "The Concept of Distance in International Management Research." *Journal of International Management* 20(1): 1–7.

Brannen, C., and T. Wilen. 1998. *Doing Business with Japanese Men: A Woman's Handbook*. Berkeley: Stone Bridge Press.

Brookfield, S. 1995. Becoming a Critically Reflective Practitioner. Thousand Oaks, CA: Sage.

Buono, A. F., and J. L. Bowditch. 2003. The Human Side of Mergers and Acquisitions: Managing Collisions between People, Cultures and Organizations. Washington, DC: BeardBooks.

Cheng, S. S., and M. W. Seeger. 2012. "Cultural Differences and Communication Issues in International Mergers and Acquisitions: A Case Study of BenQ Debacle." *International Journal of Business and Social Science* 3(3): 116–127.

Cocroft, B. A. K., and S. Ting-Toomey. 1994. "Facework in Japan and the United States." *International Journal of Intercultural Relations* 18(4): 469–506.

Coser, L. A. 1956. *The Functions of Social Conflict*. New York: Routledge.

Drogendijk, R., and L. Zander. 2010. "Walking the Cultural Distance: In Search of Direction beyond Friction." *Advances in International Management* 23: 189–212.

Durand, M. 2016. "Employing Critical Incident Technique as One Way to Display the Hidden Aspects of Post-Merger Integration." *International Business Review* 25(1): 87–102.

Harzing, A. W., and M. Pudelko. 2016. "Do We Need to Distance Ourselves from the Distance Concept? Why Home and Host Country Context might Matter More Than (Cultural) Distance." *Management International Review* 56(1): 1–34.

Hinkin, T. R. 1998. "A Brief Tutorial on the Development of Measures for Use in Survey Questionnaires." *Organizational Research Methods* 1(1): 104–121.

Ho, D. Y. F. 1976. "On the Concept of Face." *American Journal of Sociology* 81(4): 867–884.

Hofstede, G. 2001. Culture's Consequences: Comparing Values, Behaviors, Institutions and Organizations across Nations. Thousand Oaks: Sage Publications.

Irrman, O. 2005 "Communication Dissonance and Pragmatic Failures in Strategic Processes: The Case of Cross-Border Acquisitions." *Advances in Strategic Management* 22: 251–266.

Koch, P. T., Koch, B., Menon, T., and O. Shenkar. 2016. "Cultural Friction in Leadership Beliefs and Foreign-Invested Enterprise Survival." *Journal of International Business Studies* 47(4): 453–470.

Luo, Y., and O. Shenkar. 2011. "Toward a Perspective of Cultural Friction in International Business." *Journal of International Management* 17(1): 1–14.

Mudambi, R., and T. Swift. 2009. "Professional Guilds, Tension and Knowledge Management." *Research Policy* 38(5): 736–745.

Reus, T. H., and B. T. Lamont 2009. "The Double-Edged Sword of Cultural Distance in International Acquisitions." *Journal of International Business Studies* 40(8): 1298–1316.

Rosen, M. A., Wildman, J. L., Bedwell, W. L., Fritzsche, B., Salas, E., and C. S. Burke. 2008. "Diagnosing Friction Points in Multicultural Team Performance: A Rationale and Measurement Approach." *Proceedings of the Human Factors and Ergonomics Society Annual Meeting* 52(11): 753–757.

Rottig, D. 2007. "Successfully Managing International Mergers and Acquisitions: A Descriptive Framework." *International Business: Research Teaching and Practice* 1(1): 103–126.

Schotter, A., and P. W. Beamish. 2011. "Performance Effects of MNC Headquarters: Subsidiary Conflict and the Role of Boundary Spanners: The Case of Headquarter Initiative Rejection." *Journal of International Management* 17(3): 243–259.

Shenkar, O. 2012a. "Beyond Cultural Distance: Switching to a Friction Lens in the Study of Cultural Differences." *Journal of International Business Studies* 43(1): 12–17.

Shenkar, O. 2012b. "Cultural Distance Revisited: Towards a More Rigorous Conceptualization and Measurement of Cultural Differences." *Journal of International Business Studies* 43(1): 1–11.

Shenkar, O., Luo, Y., and O. Yeheskel. 2008. "From 'Distance' to 'Friction': Substituting Metaphors and Redirecting Intercultural Research." *Academy of Management Review* 33(4): 905–923.

Stahl, G. K., and R. L. Tung. 2015. "Towards a More Balanced Treatment of Culture in International Business Studies: The Need for Positive Cross-Cultural Scholarship." *Journal of International Business Studies* 46(4): 391–414.

6 Multiple Organisational Identities After M&As

Luca Giustiniano and Luigi De Bernardis

Introduction

This chapter focuses on the ambiguity of organisational identities (OIs) that might be triggered by M&As and the resulting mingling of a plurality of pre-existing identities. In contrast to the dominant literature and to common managerial perception, such plurality is considered a tolerable, if not completely normal, state that organisations can reach instead of a source of problems to be solved. The dominant literature on OI often provides methodologies and explication for creating a new OI (Gioia et al. 2013; Hatch et al. 2015; Ravasi and Schultz 2006). Yet these studies do not explain whether and how multiple OIs can be the right solution for an organisation. Here we provide evidence of a successful acquisition that has endured multiple identities. Generally speaking, extreme points would be to resist a new OI completely (people want to maintain the old identity) or to absolutely support the change (they fully "buy into" the new identity). Between these extremes are various combinations of multiple identities. The originality of our contribution lies in the consideration that these combinations may not be transitional but can represent a successful and organisationally sustainable solution. Although the extant literature considers the presence of multiple identities a temporary struggle that exposes the organisation to tensions, analysis of the sensemaking processes reported on here can be seen as (individual) tackling strategies that either resist or support the sensegiving "efforts" of top management[1].

In the following we first review the literature on the evolution of OI and multiple OIs before analysing the conditions that can allow the sensemaking process to succeed with respect to single or plural OIs.

Theoretical Background

Albert and Whetten (1985) defined OI in terms of centrality, endurance and distinctiveness. Recently, Foreman and Whetten (2012) argued that the concept of OI requires a deeper definition, adding recognisability and adaptability to the foregoing aspects. Furthermore, Gioia et al. (2013) identified four prevalent views on OI, namely the social constructionist view, social actor approach, institutionalism and population ecologist view. Among those approaches, the social constructionist approach is best placed to explain the dynamic evolution of OI because it does not consider OI in a static way. In line with this, the post-merger evolution of OI has recently been defined as a 'transitional identity', in other words an *interim sense* held by the members about what their organisation has become (Clark et al. 2010). It follows that M&As can increase the number of identities that characterise the combined organisation (Pratt and Corley 2007). Pratt and Foreman (2000) identified four ways of managing multiple OIs: deletion (one or more identities are removed), integration (OIs are fused into one), compartmentalisation (OIs are maintained, but separately), and aggregation (OIs are maintained, but linked). Aggregation is described as a strategy that maintains the old identities by creating some links between them. The authors explain that these links can take different forms, proposing hierarchy among identities as one such form, for example.

The social constructivist approach captures the natural instability of multiple identities. For instance, Gioia et al. (2010, 5) suggested that following its inception OI "is progressively, even continuously, negotiated by organisational members". Members of an organisation answer the question, "Who are we?" using identity labels, but each identity label can have multiple meanings associated with it (Corley and Gioia 2003). OI can also be considered a value system. Scholars have provided evidence of different value systems within a single firm whereby people can have conflicting objectives (Hayek 1945). The term *professional guild* has been used to refer to an association of people that are joined together by the common bonds of their profession (Mudambi and Swift 2009). Members of the organisation can belong to different professional guilds, offering a different way of considering multiple organisational identities. By introducing the possibility of meaning-based identity, a change in identity can be defined in terms of "sensegiving" and "sensemaking". Sensemaking represents the human act of constructing interpretations of ambiguous environmental stimuli (Weick 1995), whereas sensegiving is a deliberate attempt to shape the interpretations of others (Gioia and Chittipeddi 1991). Intentionality is central in defining the difference between sensemaking and sensegiving and is a fundamental part of the latter. In contrast to earlier studies, Ravasi and Schultz (2006) proposed an alternative framework to explain changes in identity which includes sensegiving. Dealing with post-M&A operational standards and procedures can thus be seen as an "enactment" of individual actions against the routines that ruled pre-M&A. This can threaten personal organisational identity when the "sense" made by the previously established practice breaks down (e.g. Weick 1990) and influences individual behaviours. In this state of ambiguity, the "giving" can be expressed as top management strategy, or be embedded, for example as artefacts in the IT solutions which may accompany M&As (e.g. De Bernardis 2012; Tyworth 2014). Thus, sensegiving can be associated with prescriptive efforts to promote the development of, or reinforcement of OI.

In the vein of sensegiving, Bartels et al. (2006) posited that organisational identification after a merger can be measured by considering the expected identification prior to the merger. More recently, Brown (2015, 24) introduced the concept of "identity work" as "the mutually constitutive processes whereby people strive to shape a relatively coherent and distinctive notion of personal self-identity" (Brown 2015, 24). This process seems to consider fragmentation and plurality in OI as a problem, with Brown arguing that successful identity work should increase coherence.

From the OI perspective, a cross-national M&A provides interesting opportunities to study organisations with multiple identities. Although previous studies have analysed the post-M&A evolution of OIs, they have mostly done so by considering singular identities only. The evolution of multiple identities has so far received comparatively little attention from OI researchers. Here we attempt to fill this gap by showing how the sensemaking process enables multinational companies to maintain multiple identities even after fully implementing the integration process (e.g. Hatch et al. 2015).

The evolution of OI can be studied using both qualitative and quantitative methods (Ravasi and Canato 2013). Our case makes use of qualitative methods (e.g. Hatch et al. 2015) and is based on a narrative analysis within a constructionist approach. It is a grounded study that attempted to identify relationships among "concepts". In line with previous contributions (Corley and Gioia 2004, 184; Gioia and Chittipeddi 1991, 444; Ravasi and Schultz 2006), we describe a two-step process: both an attempt at sensegiving (a deliberate strategy of identity aggregation) and a social process of sensemaking. The sensegiving in our case can be described by drawing on the aforementioned work of Pratt and Foreman (2000); both identity synergies and multiple OIs were apparent. In short, the managerial response was identified as "aggregation", that is the decision to maintain both identities and forge links between them (the creation of an identity hierarchy and/or the creation of new beliefs; Pratt and Foreman 2000). In our case study, the strategy of aggregation (producing a multiple identity) successfully passed the "sensemaking filter", making sense to and for the people in the acquired company. The framework proposed in the study can therefore contribute to explaining what happens after an M&A event from an organisational perspective. Although the existing literature considers this plurality of identities a normal situation that occurs within the lifetime of any company, it also considers it either a temporary condition or a constant source of trouble during the M&A integration process. Our study shows that the success of the sensemaking process depends on the resolution of four trade-offs that people solve together during the post-acquisition period. They are high versus low leadership appropriateness, ambiguity versus trust, the strength or weakness of the old identity and old values versus market needs. A previous publication shows that the companies in our study preserved their old identity while being integrated at the same time for the greater good (De Bernardis and Giustiniano 2015).

Methodology

Our study is a grounded model based on a case of M&A in the pharmaceutical industry, with a particular focus on the sense of "we". We used the following criteria to identify the case: a specific M&A goal, a successful merger, and an ongoing process of change. Several studies have proposed classifications of M&As based on reason-why criteria. Reason-why criteria are important here because the "specific M&A goal" is one of these reasons. If the acquisition aimed to destroy a competitor, for example, integration would not make sense in the first place. Qualitative data were collected through interviews with the managers and employees of the acquired company. Using the methodology adopted by Corley and Gioia (2004) for content analysis, we obtained first-order concepts which were grouped in second-order themes and then into aggregate dimensions. After uploading the transcripts of all of the interviews and the secondary data, we linked each sentence or paragraph to a node (a sort of concept). Paragraphs could be linked to one or more nodes. Hence, based on the grounded methodology, we formulated a model to describe the evolution of OIs.

Findings

Our case study describes the acquisition of OldCo by NewCo in the pharmaceutical industry. Based on content analysis, we first explain why this case is "extreme". We then describe the old OIs of the two companies and present a model for the sensemaking process.

Situating the Case

Usually, in M&As there is an *ex ante* power asymmetry between the acquirer and the target company. According to Cantwell and Mudambi,

> the ability of (acquired) subsidiary managers to exercise a voice within their new head office will tend to be weaker than those in (pre-existing) established subsidiaries whose ties and identification with the parent group go back longer. The managers that were part of an acquired group tend to be associated with a different corporate culture.
>
> (2005, 1115)

In our case study, this asymmetry is less important because it was two strong companies that merged and OldCo's power was conserved (e.g. giving relevance to the headquarters of OldCo and transforming OldCo into a biopharmaceutical business unit, see Table 6.1). Therefore, although the managers provided evidence of a high degree of ambiguity at the beginning of the acquisition, this M&A is an exceptional, extreme case. It underlines that the definition of "we" boundaries is central to understanding people's

Table 6.1 Case study rationale

Case study context	*Case study main contribution*
This case study is based on the acquisition of a pharmaceutical company (OldCo) by a multinational chemical-pharmaceutical group (NewCo). Both NewCo and OldCo have a long history in the pharmaceutical industry. In 2006, NewCo announced the acquisition of OldCo for more than €10 billion. The NewCo Group was then organised into pharmaceutical and chemical activities. After the acquisition, OldCo was combined with the ethical division within the pharmaceutical business sector of NewCo. The headquarters of this division was moved to the town where OldCo operated, creating a leading global supplier of biopharmaceutical products.	The case study provides evidence of the progressive reduction of ambiguity due to mindfulness in the management of change. Using the model, the managers of acquiring companies can understand whether their idea of OI evolution (defined in the sensegiving phase) can be socially shared in the sensemaking phase. Analysing reasons to change or commit (how trade-offs are "solved" by people), managers can be confident about the success of their OI evolution strategy after the sensemaking processes.

Source: De Bernardis and Giustiniano (2015, modified).

perceptions. For instance, the only manager (coming from the NewCo Italian subsidiary) who held on to his position in Italy after the acquisition said, "If the sense of 'we' is the former subsidiary of the acquiring company, we can say that our organisational identity has been extinguished?" Therefore, in this case, a sort of balance between two opposite asymmetries provided a sustainable multiple identity.

Old Identities—Unveiling the Sense of "We"

People perceived the old identity of OldCo as a "quick", specialised, leader-dependent company and the old identity of NewCo as a solid managerial company. The link between nationality and solidity was clear in people's narratives. However, the large size of the companies also had some negative connotations with respect to procedural bureaucracy. The process of OI evolution described by those interviewed leads us to consider the OI resulting from the acquisition as a multiple identity based on shared group values and singular local identities.

Our case study also highlights the different meanings assigned to the word *we*. Many interviewees used *we* only when referring to their own sites or departments. However, although respondents described the sub-identity to which they felt closest (e.g. department, site, company), a global identity was gradually being cultivated. This shows the importance of well-defined business boundaries for specifying which managerial response (aggregation or deletion) has been implemented (Marchegiani et al. 2012), as a global strategy of "identity aggregation" is sometimes needed to remove certain components of a local identity.

Sensemaking Process

The respondents described four trade-offs that occurred between resistance, on one hand, and support for change, on the other. They described the post-acquisition period as a moment of ambiguity when they had to decide whether to support the change or resist it. They described what they considered values and points of weakness in the old identity, making clear that their decision to support the change depended on the behaviour of the new managers towards these points. Leadership style appeared to be an ambiguous point, described simultaneously as a strength and as a limitation. In OldCo, the CEO's leadership was recalled by many interviewees to be linked to a lack of bureaucracy (the firm's "quickness") and his absolute control of the company.

The second point recalled by the respondents was the strength of the old identity. People in OldCo were convinced that NewCo would respect OldCo after the acquisition because of its well-known quality, reputation and quickness. On the other hand, before the acquisition, OldCo was already struggling with multiple identities that were diffused throughout the company. The opportunity to "modify something" to satisfy new market needs was a point recalled by many respondents as an enabler of change. After the acquisition, the employees were also exposed to a trade-off between the preservation of old values and responsiveness to market needs. For instance, the two companies shared common values but had different and complementary identities. Many of the respondents discussed these shared aspects in OldCo's and NewCo's identities. Both companies not only paid a lot of attention to their own histories but also shared the capability to anticipate change. According to many interviewees, this ability to simultaneously look to the past and to the future constituted a winning strategy. They also stressed that the two companies were strategically complementary and considered the change management process to be transparent and rational in that important decisions, such as whether to adopt the software solution already used by NewCo, were made mindfully. Interviewees successfully made sense of the new reality posed by the acquiring company because a multiple identity was proposed. They saw this solution as taking the best from each company and being able to meld two different business models and targeting strategies.

Lesson Learned

The results outlined suggest an answer to our research question of whether and how a multiple OI can be the right solution for an organisation. In this case, during the sensemaking process, people decided on whether or not to support the change. Their decision depended on their opinions of leadership appropriateness, the value of the old identity, the capacity to satisfy new market needs, and the behaviour that the new owners would adopt in dealing with these aspects. Generally speaking, possible outcomes would be (a) complete resistance to change (if people wanted to maintain the singular old identity), (b) a complete commitment to change (if people wanted to create an entirely new singular identity), or (c) the acceptance of a multiple identity based on the ability to make sense of the coexistence of diverse elements stemming from the respective OIs (i.e. if people wanted to take the "good" from each "side"). In this case study, the sensemaking process resulted in a multiple identity because two forces supported change (new market needs and ambiguity reduction) and two forces resisted it (CEO leadership and old identity value). In fact, despite the strength of the former CEO's leadership and the old identity, interviewees underlined that the acquisition was needed in order to satisfy new market needs (size of competitors, etc.). They also said they were confident in the new owners' competencies. Therefore, sensegiving (which proposes an "aggregation" strategy for OI) and sensemaking were coherent, as the success of the M&A can confirm.

Discussion and Conclusion

The evidence presented in the previous section can be generalised in order to answer our research question and to explain whether and how a multiple OI can be the right solution for an organisation. As many of the interviewees suggested, the sensemaking process can be described as a conflict between resisting and supporting the changes proposed in the sensegiving "efforts".

The resulting model is presented in Figure 6.1. This representation shares some commonalities with previous models proposed, for instance, the dual presence of sensegiving and sensemaking (Gioia and Chittipeddi 1991; Ravasi and Schultz 2006) and the balance between opposite forces (Clark et al. 2010). Nevertheless, it extends existing research by introducing the concept of multiple OIs as a possible output of the sensemaking process. In particular, the research here presented shows how the oscillation between different senses of "we" could allow the crystallisation of a multiple yet still internally consistent identity.

The framework shown in Figure 6.1 describes the post-M&A landscape of OIs as a sensemaking process that takes place when people interact. Once the other company is known, this sensemaking process enables people to appreciate the diversity of the mutual identity as a value rather than viewing it as a problem to solve.

The main conclusion of the findings presented here is that the output of this process can be single or multiple OIs. This output depends on both the appropriateness of the managerial response (sensegiving) and the success of the sensemaking process with respect to the four trade-offs (high/low leadership appropriateness, ambiguity versus trust, old identity's strengths versus weaknesses, old values versus market needs). The output is a continuum of multiple identities with two extreme points where the output is a singular identity, respectively (resistance to change versus commitment to change).

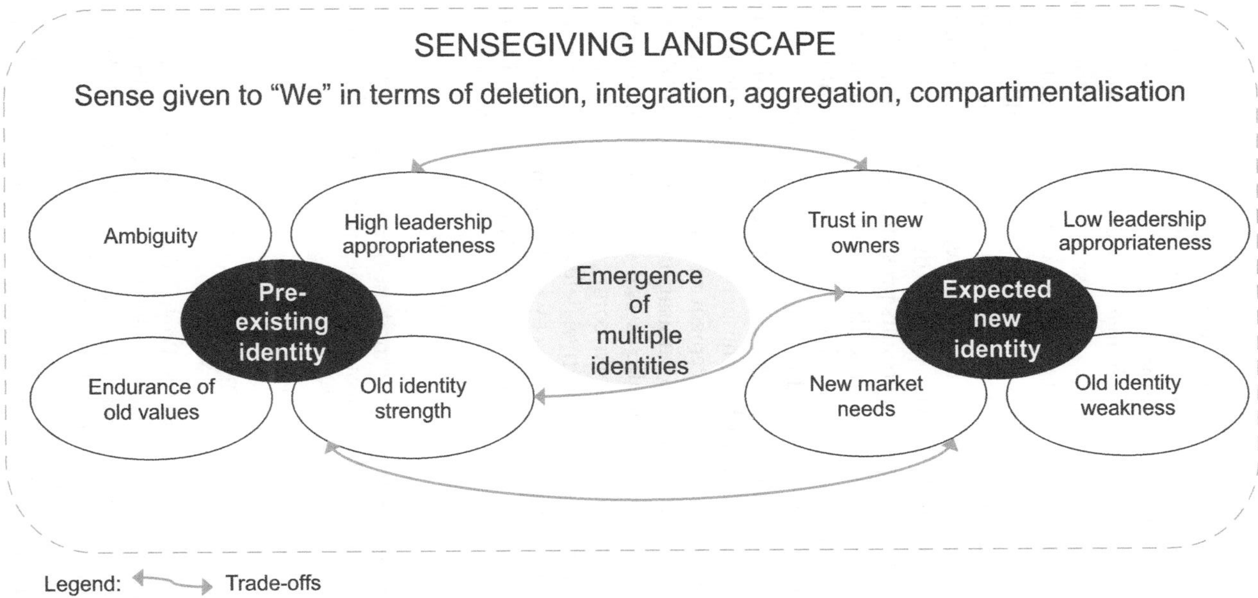

Figure 6.1 A model for the post-M&A evolution of multiple OIs

Source: The authors.

At one extreme, a singular identity is created by resolving all the trade-offs in favour of the decision to resist change. In this case, a managerial strategy to create a new identity will fail because people do not want to change. A strategy of compartmentalisation may be acceptable in this case. At the other extreme, people are completely committed to change. Once again, the resulting identity is singular because all the trade-offs are resolved in favour of the decision to embrace change. In this case, a strategy of deletion adopted by management will work because people want to change. Between these extremes, people will support change if they perceive that some aspects related to leadership appropriateness, new market needs and the value of the old identity are respected by the new owners. In such cases, the output will be multiple identities.

It is quite clear that the need to avoid failure should encourage managers of acquiring companies to select a suitable strategy for dealing with OIs (sensegiving) and to facilitate the social process of sensemaking that takes place through people's interactions. The results presented strongly imply that senior management should plan a response that takes account of multiple identities, in addition to literature suggesting that the evolution of OIs is a social, gradual, and continuous process. In short, the case of OldCo–NewCo shows that certain peculiar characteristics of the merging companies might allow not only the existence but, rather, the persistence of a multiple OI as well. This can also be seen as the achievement of a choir of different and diverse "voices", each recalling a specific organisational culture and OI (e.g. Cantwell and Mudambi 2005). In this specific case, it seems that the complementarity of the product portfolios of the two companies, and, therefore, of the distinctive competencies and competitive fields, have allowed the creation of conditions of tolerance and trust, thereby enabling the coexistence of the two "old" identities within a new hybrid one (e.g. Giustiniano and Bolici 2012).

Note

1. The views expressed in this chapter are those of the authors and are not intended to reflect the views of the Commissione Nazionale per le Società e la Borsa.

References

Albert, S., and D. Whetten. 1985. "Organizational Identity." *Research in Organizational Behavior* 7: 263–295.

Bartels, J., Douwes, De Jong M., and A. Pruyn. 2006. "Organizational Identification during a Merger: Determinants of Employees' Expected Identification with the New Organization." *British Journal of Management* 17(S1): S49–S67.

Brown, A. D. 2015. "Identities and Identity Work in Organizations." *International Journal of Management Reviews* 17(1): 20–40.

Cantwell, J., and R. Mudambi. 2005. "MNE Competence Creating Subsidiary Mandates." *Strategic Management Journal* 26(12): 1109–1128.

Clark, S. M., Gioia, D. A., Ketchen, J., and J. B. Thomas. 2010. "Transitional Identity as a Facilitator of Organizational Identity Change during a Merger." *Administrative Science Quarterly* 55(3): 397–438.

Corley, K. G., and D. A. Gioia. 2003. "Semantic Learning as Change Enabler: Relating Organizational Identity and Organizational Learning." In *Handbook of Organizational Learning and Knowledge Management*, edited by M. Easterby-Smith, and M. Lyles, 621–636. London: Blackwell.
Corley, K. G., and D. A. Gioia. 2004. "Identity Ambiguity and Change in the Wake of a Corporate Spin-Off." *Administrative Science Quarterly* 49(2): 173–208.
De Bernardis, L. 2012. "Social Dimension in ERP Adoption and Implementation: The Evolution of Organizational Identity after an M&A." *Journal of Information, Communication and Ethics in Society* 10(3): 156–186.
De Bernardis, L., and L. Giustiniano. 2015. "Evolution of Multiple Organizational Identities after an M&A Event: A Case Study from Europe." *Journal of Organizational Change Management* 28(3): 333–355.
Foreman, P., and D. Whetten. 2012. "The Identity Paradox and an Expanded Framework of Organizational Identity." Proceedings of the New Frontiers in Management and Organizational Cognition Conference, National University of Ireland, Maynooth, 2012 September 6–7, Maynooth.
Gioia, D. A., and K. Chittipeddi. 1991. "Sensemaking and Sensegiving in Strategic Change Initiation." *Strategic Management Journal* 12(6): 433–458.
Gioia, D. A., Patvardhana, S. D., Hamilton, A. L., and K. G. Corley. 2013. "Organizational Identity Formation and Change." *The Academy of Management Annals* 7(1): 123–193.
Gioia, D. A., Price, K. N., Hamilton, A. L., and J. B. Thomas. 2010. "Forging an Identity: An Insider-Outsider Study of Processes Involved in the Formation of Organizational Identity." *Administrative Science Quarterly* 55(1): 1–46.
Giustiniano, L., and F. Bolici. 2012. "Organizational Trust in a Networked World: Analysis of the Interplay between Social Factors and Information and Communication Technology." *Journal of Information, Communication and Ethics in Society* 10(3): 187–202.
Hatch, M. J., Schultz, M., and A. M. Skov. 2015. "Organizational Identity and Culture in the Context of Managed Change: Transformation in the Carlsberg Group, 2009–2013." *Academy of Management Discoveries* 1(1): 56–87.
Hayek, F. A. 1945. "The Use of Knowledge in Society." *American Economic Review* 35(4): 519–530.
Marchegiani, L., Giustiniano, L., Peruffo, E., and L. Pirolo. 2012. "Revitalising the Outsourcing Discourse within the Boundaries of Firms Debate." *Business Systems Review* 1(1): 157–177.
Mudambi, R., and T. Swift. 2009. "Professional Guilds, Tension and Knowledge Management." *Research Policy* 38(5): 736–745.
Pratt, M. G., and K. G. Corley. 2007. "Managing Multiple Organizational Identities: On Identity Ambiguity, Identity Conflict, and Member Reactions." In *Identity and the Modern Organization*, edited by C. Bartel, S. L. Blader, and C. Wrzesniewski, 99–118. New York: Psychology Press.
Pratt, M. G., and P. O. Foreman. 2000. "Classifying Managerial Responses to Multiple Organizational Identities." *Academy of Management Review* 25(1): 18–42.
Ravasi, D., and A. Canato. 2013. "'How Do I Know Who You Think You Are?' A Review of Research Methods on Organizational Identity." *International Journal of Management Reviews* 15(2): 185–204.
Ravasi, D., and M. Schultz. 2006. "Responding to Organizational Identity Threats: Exploring the Role of Organizational Culture." *Academy of Management Journal* 49(3): 433–458.

Tyworth, M. 2014. "Organizational Identity and Information Systems: How Organizational ICT Reflect Who an Organization Is." *European Journal of Information Systems* 23(1): 69–83.

Weick, K. E. 1990. "The Vulnerable System: An Analysis of the Tenerife Air Disaster." *Journal of Management* 16(3): 571–593.

Weick, K. E. 1995. *Sensemaking in Organizations*. Thousand Oaks, CA: Sage.

7 Becoming a National Champion yet Remaining a Global Player

The Acquisition of Volvo Car by Zhejiang Geely

Claes G. Alvstam and Inge Ivarsson

Introduction

The aim of this chapter is to demonstrate how the internal organisation and culture of a multinational company undergo dramatic change when acquired by an emerging market multinational enterprise. It also shows how the acquiring company needs to strike a fine balance between the ambition of becoming a "national champion"—that is using the takeover of a prestigious foreign consumer brand to create a platform for inward technology and knowledge transfer in order to build up domestic manufacturing of the acquired brand—while at the same time retaining the global reputation and commercial success of the acquired company.

Only a few examples demonstrate these effects to date; the most illustrative cases can be drawn from large emerging markets such as China and India. China is of particular relevance with respect to national business culture, characterised by strong national institutions and a dominance of state-owned enterprises meeting the global market economy and the growing role of private entrepreneurship. China's encounter with the outside world began with the increasing inflow of FDI which has recently been complemented by an equally dramatic growth of outward FDI. From a virtually zero level in the late 1970s, China had grown to become the world's second-largest FDI destination by the late 2000s. Outward FDI flows remained modest until the mid-2000s when they took off at an equally rapid pace and are now set to make up for stagnant inward flows. This rapid change can be interpreted as a result of China's shift from the "coming-in" policy that was typical for the 1990s and the early 2000s to the "going out" and "going global" strategies that have dominated the last ten years (Shambaugh 2013, 174ff). At the same time, the growing outward FDI from China is itself undergoing a transition. The initial resource-seeking activities are increasingly being replaced by the seeking of strategic assets with the aim of transferring cutting-edge technology and knowledge back to China. The aim is to build a solid and internationally competitive manufacturing platform for the domestic market in order to later upgrade exports from China. There is a vast and growing literature offering descriptive observations on changing geographical destinations, objectives of FDI activities, and the main actors involved. Attempts are also being made to interpret and explain the new patterns, and there are calls for revising existing theories of internationalisation in order to better account for emerging market multinational enterprises, in particular, those from China (Aharoni 2014; Berning and Holtbrügge 2012; Cuervo-Cazurra 2012; Deng 2012; Luo et al. 2010; Mathews 2006; Narula 2012; Rugman and Quyen 2014; Tsai 2013; Williamson 2014; Wu et al. 2012; Zhang et al. 2012). The shift to foreign strategic asset seeking by private and state-owned Chinese firms, expressed in acquisitions of well-known companies and brands, has affected a wide range of industrial and consumer-based sectors and encompassed manufacturing as well as services, for example LENOVO/IBM PC, DALIAN WANDA/AMC THEATERS and SHUANGHUI/SMITHFIELD FOODS. The most spectacular acquisitions, however, have so far taken place within the automotive industry.

The production of passenger cars is an illustrative example of a broad range of parallel manufacturing systems. Passenger car production has a Janus face in that it is a widely perceived branded consumer product, on one hand, but also represents a comprehensive production system, on the other, with thousands of input items including small-scale local suppliers and global specialised firms. This makes the passenger car an excellent case for active industrial policy in an emerging economy, first as a means of climbing the value chain in order to create "national champions" and, second, as an efficient instrument of regional development policy that can promote local employment and diversification in more remote regions. The "going global" of the Chinese automotive industry has been followed by a large number of Chinese and foreign researchers, giving rise to an extensive body of literature (Chu 2011; Ding and Akoorie 2013; Drauz 2013; Lee and Choi 2013; Rugraff 2012; Tang and Fitzsimmons 2013). However, new features and patterns are continuously emerging, calling for ongoing amendment and revision of the theories put forward to explain this dynamic and rapid process. One such recent phenomenon is the mix of public–private partnership in foreign acquisitions from emerging markets, designed with the specific purpose of creating national champions. This mix is important as it represents a new phenomenon not only in China's internationalisation process but increasingly also in other large emerging market economies in which the national/federal government exerts strong and active influence on investment policy. So far, the existing literature does not provide a full analytical context for this new feature, although several attempts have been made in this direction. In particular, we find it useful to adopt the "springboard" approach, as well as the liability of "foreignness", "outsidership" and "origin" literature because they touch upon the subtle interactions of domestic government supporting emerging market firms to go abroad in order to become stronger at home (Chen 2006; Luo and Tung 2007; Ramachandran and Pant 2010; Ramamurti 2012). In addition, literature on the role of the state, in general, and the business system of the home country, in particular, contributes to the understanding of the motives and financial capacity to support such a policy (Luo et al. 2010). It also highlights how multinational companies achieve a balance between their global geographical pattern of production and markets and their locations within the regional setting (Beugelsdijk and Mudambi 2013). Analysis of inward FDI at the subnational level is moreover relevant in order to understand the interaction between national and local priorities (Chadee et al. 2003; Lee and Choi 2013; Meyer et al. 2011). We have previously suggested the label "hybrid multinational enterprise" to illustrate the grey zone between being "foreign" and "local". In this regard, the national government symbolises the Janus face of being both home country for the outward FDI and host country for the acquired multinational enterprise. At the same time it is assumed that production by the acquired multinational enterprise will grow, both in the new home/host country and in its previous locations (Alvstam and Ivarsson 2014). In this context, it can be assumed that the host country government at different administrative and geographical levels may pragmatically shift its perspective towards the acquired multinational company, regarding it as foreign or local depending on what is most suitable in the specific situation. The next section gives an example of the ambiguity of such in-betweenness and how it further complicates the clash of organisational cultures between the acquirers and the acquired. For the empirical example, we have mainly adopted a longitudinal qualitative approach, consisting of frequent interviews and other forms of personal communication with key actors within the companies involved during the period of investigation, which ran from the acquisition in 2010 to September 2015.

The Takeover of Volvo Cars by Zhejiang Geely Holding Group and its Minority Partners

The Chinese passenger-car industry and its prime suppliers have long been dominated by inward FDI and various constellations of joint ventures between domestic state-owned enterprises and globally active private firms from the U.S., Europe, Japan and Korea. As indicated earlier, however, there has been a more recent trend during the last ten years to also go abroad through foreign acquisitions. The main motive was to not only further strengthen domestic production in terms of management and technology but also to pave the way for future exports. Early examples were SAIC/SSANGYONG, NAC/MG ROVER, the automotive part manufacturer WANXIANG's expansion into the United States and recently the CHEMCHINA purchase of the Italian tyre manufacturer PIRELLI. Another strategic measure has been to capture dominant minority stakes in global automotive companies within a network of mutual cross-ownership, for example DONGFENG, which acquired 14% of PSA PEUGEOT CITROËN, and the talks of BAIC to take a stake in German DAIMLER, which already has a 10% stake in BAIC. A novel type of a foreign acquisition, though, was the US$1.8 billion takeover of the originally Swedish company, VOLVO CAR CORPORATION, by ZHEJIANG GEELY HOLDING GROUP from

American Ford Motor Corporation in 2010. Whereas MG Rover was taken over by a state-owned firm after a bankruptcy, Volvo Car Corporation was a profitable company, acquired by a private entrepreneur with a holding group listed in Hong Kong and incorporated in the Caribbean Islands. Even though there were other parties involved in the negotiations with Ford, Zhejiang Geely Holding Group and its chairman, Li Shufu, was the only one from China, giving rise to speculations that his bid was unofficially supported by the National Development and Reform Commission, the powerful arm of the Chinese government, as well as enjoying the financial backing of China Development Bank rather than bids by the far larger state-owned enterprises, all of which were already involved in various joint ventures and cross-ownerships with foreign companies and at first glance would have seemed more suitable candidates for acquiring Volvo Car Corporation. Over 25 years Li had built a business empire and, since 1996, in car manufacturing under the umbrella name Geely, having nine plants in China, with the main production base in Zhejiang province and its headquarters in Hangzhou. He also acquired the London Taxi Company. Whereas Zhejiang Geely Holding Group represented 51% of the successful bid, two local public investment corporations became minority owners: Daqing State Asset Operation Corporation (37%) and Shanghai Jiaerwoo Investment Company in Jiading (12%; Alvstam and Ivarsson 2014, 227). During the last years in the Ford family, before the global financial crisis, Volvo Car Corporation reported an annual production of 400,000 to 450,000 cars, mainly at two plants—Gothenburg (Sweden) and Ghent (Belgium). In 2010 its main markets (around 65%) were in Western Europe, of which Sweden represented 14%, the U.S. 15% and the rest of the world 20%, of which in China 8% (VCC 2016). Now Volvo Car Corporation was set to undergo a huge transition to become China-owned, although still with a global reach. Could it be possible to combine the ambition to remain a global prestigious brand, reliant on a mantra of safety, quality and environmental responsibility, with building a new home base in a state-controlled emerging market, in close collaboration with a less-than-prestigious small local car brand such as Geely and with public investment corporations mainly aiming at using the Volvo brand as a tool for boosting local employment and industrial transformation?

Volvo Car—From Sweden to the U.S. to China

When Volvo Car Corporation was divested from Volvo Group in 1999 and sold to Ford, there was a long period of adjustment from a Swedish to an American management culture in which Volvo Car Corporation became integrated into the "Premier Automotive Group" together with a couple of other foreign high-end brands. Initially, Volvo Car Corporation was granted a certain degree of freedom, particularly because it delivered continuous profits to its principal, and it is notable that no decision was taken to move manufacturing capacity from Europe to North America. However, the demands of technical coordination in product development gradually became more apparent, and the opportunities to develop own new models on own platform technology were limited. It is widely held within the organisation that VOLVO CAR CORPORATION never became fully integrated with FORD during the decade of ownership.

Even though the price tag of US$1.8 billion for the takeover by the Chinese "triad" partners was low compared to the US$6.5 billion that FORD had paid ten years earlier, the financial commitments by both the majority and minority holders were many times greater, reflecting the open cooperation of the public and private actors. It was crucial for the majority owner to send a rapid and clear signal that the takeover should not imply any loss of VOLVO CAR CORPORATION's corporate identity and its position in Europe and North America. At the same time, impatient demands from the minority owners had to be satisfied who were looking to the acquisition to provide employment opportunities and a transfer of technology and knowledge to their respective local communities. The answer to these combined demands was large-scale investment for rapid expansion, mainly in China but also overseas, expressed by the mantra that it was "time to let the tiger out of the cage", to quote Chairman Li himself. The first ambitious investment commitment was to launch a completely new production platform (Scalable Product Architecture), independent from FORD, and to develop a new generation of engines (VOLVO Engine Architecture). These two projects have required at least US$10 billion during 2010 to 2015 and were moves that symbolised the new era of becoming a Chinese company yet still retaining its global reach. The main part of these projects was undertaken in Sweden—not in China—and enhanced the support of the new owners among Swedish industry circles, as well by the trade unions.

With the new model generation as a starting point, an ambitious expansion of production and market volumes in China became possible. Until then, VOLVO CAR CORPORATION had had a limited local presence with a total sales volume in 2010 of about 30,000 units, mainly from a joint assembly with FORD in Chongqing. A breathtaking plan was launched to double VOLVO CAR CORPORATION's global sales from 400,000 to 800,000 units per year in 2015, with a sales target of 200,000 in China alone. This target was unrealistic from the very beginning, but served as another symbol of the serious commitment by the new owners. It still remains the official target, but has gradually been pushed forward, at present to 2020. Already in 2014, however, China became the largest single market with 81,000 units, or 17% of global sales. The expansion plan was implemented through the decision to build two new integrated plants in China and later, in addition, a new engine plant but not to reduce capacity in Europe—on the contrary. The location decisions reflected the subtle balance between national and regional/local interests and the even more delicate arm's-length distance between the two brands, GEELY and VOLVO, where the often-repeated mantra by Chairman Li was "VOLVO is Volvo and Geely is Geely." The traditional mode of operation in the joint ventures between state-owned companies and foreign firms in China has been to keep the domestic and foreign brands apart while commencing a looser or deeper upstream cooperation in terms of suppliers, product development and production facilities. In the Volvo Car Corporation–Geely case, the prospect of cooperation was built on joint ownership at the Holding Group level but with no direct formal bonds. However, it was no coincidence that the first plant was located close to Chengdu in Sichuan Province, where Geely already operated a plant, owned the land and provided the necessary office space. The second plant was placed in Daqing, home of the 37% owner, while a management office for coordination of product development, purchasing and human resources was located in Jiading, the site of the 12% owner. The engine plant was located in Zhangjiakou, northwest of Beijing, halfway (1,600 km) between Chengdu and Daqing, with no visible direct links to Zhejiang Geely Holding Group but fulfilling the same criteria as the other plants, namely being part of a larger local and regional development and industrial transformation strategy, also prioritised at the national level. Thus, the three locations are far from optimal as seen from a supply-chain or distribution point of view but should be regarded from the perspective of the respective local interests, supported by national efforts to disperse high-technology industry and to achieve a more balanced economic growth. The Daqing location in northern Heilongjiang Province, 1,400 kilometres by road northeast of Beijing and until now a centre of oil production, is a particularly obvious example of the local impatience for rapid economic development and industrial transformation. Thus, a new level of organisational and cultural distance was created. Not only the distance between European and Chinese production and management cultures had to be contended with, but, too, did the an even larger distance between the centre and periphery in China. The cost of building and running a manufacturing plant in China is a fraction of the European average, as the degree of robotisation is still low. Land and infrastructural investment are provided at highly subsidised prices, and the costs of overcoming the geographical distance in the supply chain are concealed in opaque contracts with logistics providers.

Further strategic location decisions have stressed even more the subtle balancing between the priorities of the Chinese owners and the need to maintain Volvo Car Corporation's image as a global company. The most spectacular cooperation project between Volvo Car Corporation and Geely, "China Euro Vehicle Technology", owned and run by Zhejiang Geely Holding Group, with the mission to develop a new platform for small-sized cars called "Compact Modular Architecture" for both Volvo and Geely, was located to Gothenburg instead of China, and employs a mix of European and Chinese engineers. The new joint plant for the common platform will be located even more symbolically in Taizhou/Luqiao in Zhejiang Province, coincidentally the birthplace of Li Shufu. The plant is scheduled to open in autumn 2017 and will be owned by Geely but run and managed by Volvo Car Corporation. At the same time, production capacity in both Gothenburg and Ghent has expanded, with the additional decision taken in 2015 to open a plant in the U.S.—an extraordinary measure, given the fact that Volvo Car Corporation never took such a decision before neither under Swedish nor American ownership.

Finally, the organisation of management and control also illustrates the balancing between the organisational cultures of the acquirer and the acquired. From the very beginning, an important symbolic measure was that the 13 management board members should be recruited internationally. Even though Mr. Li Shufu is the formal chairman, for the first five years the board meetings were effectively led by the deputy chairman who is a Swedish Volvo "old-timer" and who also served as one of the vice presidents for Ford before the Chinese takeover. Moreover, the board consists of five Swedes/Europeans and three Chinese, and in addition three trade union representatives who are all from Sweden. The first CEO was German with long experience in the Japanese and American car industry. He was replaced in 2013 by a Swede who had previously been the CEO of German MAN. The executive management team, composed 13 members, is completely Swedish/European. At the mid-management level, the initial idea was to create a "matched pair" organisation for the China operations, in which every function was manned by one Chinese and one non-Chinese, mostly Swedish. This system was generally abandoned after the first years due to uncertainties regarding the ultimate decision-making power. The present trend is that the senior and mid-management team members are becoming more Chinese while the CEO of Volvo Cars China is still Swedish.

The experiences of Volvo Car Corporation after the transition to Chinese ownership correspond to the assumptions put forward in the "springboard" and "liability of foreignness/outsidership/origin" literature. The acquisition of a foreign brand with a global presence has explicitly been driven by the desire to build a broader manufacturing base at home and to boost the reputation of the existing domestic brand. In addition, the springboard contains a second dimension in the sense that the ambitions at the national level are leveraged through the strong influence of regional and local interests. Volvo Car Corporation still suffers from the liability of foreignness because it is, in many cases, treated as a foreign company competing with domestic rivals; it also exhibits a different style of corporate governance than foreign brands in joint ventures with domestic state-owned enterprises. Nevertheless, through its three owners, it is already deeply embedded in China's economic and industrial development policy.

Final Remarks

The experience of the takeover of formerly Swedish Volvo Cars from American Ford by a Chinese consortium illustrates how a multinational company continuously needs to adapt to abrupt changes in organisation and culture in cross-border acquisitions. The acquisition signalled the transformation from a global company with its main markets in Europe and North

America to a Chinese company, which—although still foreign—has China as its largest market and is rapidly expanding its manufacturing base in China. The acquisition needs to be seen within the larger context of Chinese outward FDI, which is directed at seeking strategic assets and generally aims to speed up the transfer of technology and knowledge to China. From this perspective, outward FDI is seen as a road to inward FDI as well as increasing domestic investment, leading to the build-up of a diverse high-technology industry at home. In addition, in cases where the financial backup of a foreign acquisition is to a larger extent sourced from public investment funds at the local level, often in remote regions or regions under rapid industrial transformation, inward FDI to China should be seen as an instrument for promoting a better economic balance between regions. In this context, organisational and cultural distance is not only a concern at the cross-border level but also between centre and periphery within the same country. The example illustrates the subtle balancing act between the ambition to remain a global actor, with a reputation built on quality, prestige and environmental responsibility, and being viewed as more domestic than other foreign brands. It remains to be seen whether this "hybrid" situation is a temporary transitory stage before becoming a fully fledged domestic company or whether the balancing act between parallel organisational cultures can continue.

References

Aharoni, Y. 2014. "Theoretical Debates on Multinationals from Emerging Economies." In *Understanding Multinationals from Emerging Markets*, edited by A. Cuervo-Cazurra, and R. Ramamurti, 15–30. Cambridge: Cambridge University Press.

Alvstam, C. G., and I. Ivarsson. 2014. "The 'Hybrid' Emerging Market Multinational Enterprise: The Ownership Transfer of Volvo Cars to China." In *Asian Inward and Outward FDI: New Challenges in the Global Economy*, edited by C. G. Alvstam, H. Dolles, and P. Ström, 217–242. Basingstoke: Palgrave Macmillan.

Berning, S. C., and D. Holtbrügge. 2012. "Chinese Outward Foreign Direct Investment: A Challenge for Traditional Internationalisation Theories?" *Journal für Betriebswirtschaft* 62(3/4): 169–224.

Beugelsdijk, S., and R. Mudambi. 2013. "MNEs as Border-Crossing Multi-Location Enterprises: The Role of Discontinuities in Geographic Space." *Journal of International Business Studies* 44(5): 413–426.

Chadee, D. D., Qiu, F., and E. L. Rose. 2003. "FDI Location at the Subnational Level: A Study of EJVs in China." *Journal of Business Research* 56(10): 835–845.

Chen, T. J. 2006. "Liability of Foreignness and Entry Mode Choice: Taiwanese Firms in Europe." *Journal of Business Research* 59(2): 288–294.

Chu, W.-W. 2011. "How the Chinese Government Promoted a Global Automobile Industry." *Industrial and Corporate Change* 20(5): 1235–1276.

Cuervo-Cazurra, A. 2012. "How the Analysis of Developing Country Multinational Companies Helps Advance the Theory: Solving the Goldilocks Debate." *Global Strategy Journal* 2(3): 153–167.

Deng, P. 2012. "The Internationalization of Chinese Firms: A Critical Review and Future Research." *International Journal of Management Reviews* 14(10): 408–427.

Ding, Q., and M. E. M. Akoorie. 2013. "The Characteristics and Historical Development Path of the Globalizing Chinese Automobile Industry." *Journal of Technology Management in China* 8(2): 83–104.

Drauz, R. 2013. "In Search of a Chinese Internationalization Theory: A Study of 12 Automobile Manufacturers." *Chinese Management Studies* 7(2): 281–309.

Lee, K.-P., and J.-H. Choi. 2013. "Automobile Industry, Guanxi, and Social Networks in China."*Chinese Management Studies* 7(2): 155–171.

Luo, Y., and R. L. Tung. 2007. "International Expansion of Emerging Countries Enterprises: A Springboard Perspective." *Journal of International Business Studies* 38(4): 481–498.

Luo, Y., Xue, Q., and B. Han. 2010. "How Emerging Market Governments Promote Outward FDI: Experiences from China." *Journal of World Business* 45(1): 68–79.

Mathews, J. A. 2006. "Dragon Multinationals: New Players in 21st Century Globalization." *Asia-Pacific Journal of Management* 23(1): 5–27.

Meyer, K. E., Mudambi, R., and R. Narula. 2011. "Multinational Enterprises and Local Contexts: The Opportunities and Challenges of Multiple Embeddedness." *Journal of Management Studies* 48(2): 235–252.

Narula, R. 2012. "Do We Need Different Frameworks to Explain Infant MNEs from Developing Countries?" *Global Strategy Journal* 2(3): 188–204.

Ramachandran, J., and A. Pant. 2010. "The Liabilities of Origin: An Emerging Economy Perspective on the Costs of Doing Business Abroad." In *Advances in International Management*, edited by T. M. Devinney, T. Pedersen, and L.-T. Tihanyi, 231–265. New York: Emerald.

Ramamurti, R. 2012. "What Is Really Different about Emerging Market MNEs?" *Global Strategy Journal* 2(1): 41–47.

Rugman, A. M., and T. K. N. Quyen. 2014. "Modern International Business Theory and Emerging Market Multinational Companies." In *Understanding Multinationals from Emerging Markets*, edited by A. Cuervo-Cazurra, and R. Ramamurti, 53–80. Cambridge: Cambridge University Press.

Rugraff, E. 2012. "The New Competitive Advantage of Automobile Manufacturers." *Journal of Strategy and Management* 5(4): 407–419.

Shambaugh, D. 2013. *China Goes Global: The Partial Power*. Oxford: Oxford University Press.

Tang, L.-H., and B. Fitzsimmons. 2013. "The Converging Divergence of Labor Relations in Automobile Industry: The Case of China." *Competitiveness Review* 23(2): 175–188.

Tsai, H.-T. 2013. "Towards a Guanxi-Based Theory of Internationalization: Chinese, Taiwanese and Evolving MNEs." *Chinese Management Studies* 7(1): 111–126.

VCC. 2016. "Financial Reports 2011–2016Q3." www.volvocars.com, accessed 2016, November 24.

Williamson, P. J. 2014. "The Global Expansion of EMNCs: Paradoxes and Directions for Future Research." In *Understanding Multinationals from Emerging Markets*, edited by A. Cuervo-Cazurra, and R. Ramamurti, 155–168. Cambridge: Cambridge University Press.

Wu, X., Ding, W. L., and Y. J. Shi. 2012. "Motives and Patterns of Reverse FDI by Chinese Manufacturing Firms." In *Chinese International Investments*, edited by I. Alon, M. Fetscherin, and P. Gugler, 107–121. Aldershot: Ashgate.

Zhang, Y., Duysters, G., and S. Filippov. 2012. "Chinese Firms Entering Europe: Internationalization through Acquisitions and Strategic Alliances." *Journal of Science and Technology Policy in China* 3(2): 102–123.

8 Asymmetric Effects of Cultural Distance

A Comparison of German and Austrian Inbound and Outbound Cross-border Transactions and the Diverging Effect of Integration of Wholly Owned Target Firms

Lucas Huter, Mai Anh Dao, Daniel Degischer, Florian Bauer, Yvonne Stockhammer and Manuel Erlacher

Introduction

M&A are an important strategic pathway for organisational development and growth. Cross-border acquisitions, in particular, are triggered by the motive to exploit a firm's intangible assets such as patents or marketing skills to maximise stock performance (Morck and Yeung 1991). Since the 1990s the popularity of cross-border M&A has increased dramatically (Shimizu et al. 2004) because acquisitions are a vehicle for speeding up expansion across national boundaries (Nadolska and Barkema 2014). After a recent stagnation in global M&A activity following the global financial crisis, cross-border M&A by multinational enterprises have reached a net value of more than US$400 billion, constituting the most prominent way for multinational enterprises to engage in FDI (UNCTAD 2015). In contrast to their popularity, the success rates of acquisitions in general and in cross-border activities specifically are rather low. Failure rates between 40% and 60% are regularly reported (Homburg and Bucerius 2005, 2006). Other authors find different success rates for developed and emerging markets with acquirers gaining positive abnormal returns in China or India, suggesting that the acquisition of emerging economy firms is on average beneficial for the acquiring firm (Gaur et al. 2013). However, there is only little academic knowledge and understanding of the cross-border M&A phenomenon in general (Shimizu et al. 2004). Cross-border acquisitions differ from domestic M&A regarding the complexity deriving from business activities in different national cultural and institutional environments (Xu and Shenkar 2002). The formal and informal institutional environment of a country such as the legal framework and standards of conduct influence the success of cross-border M&A (Dikova et al. 2010). Likewise, national cultures have a strong impact on behavioural patterns of individuals and, thus, acquisition activities and their outcomes (Weber 1996). Consequently, national cultural differences are commonly cited to be a major challenge and held responsible for acquisition failure (Björkman et al. 2007).

Similar to the different theoretical arguments for positive and negative effects, empirical results are mixed (Stahl and Voigt 2008) and range from positive (e.g. Morosini et al. 1998) to negative (e.g. Slangen 2006). Even though many authors argue that more empirical research is needed on the relationship of cultural differences (e.g. Slangen 2006), we argue that a further step is required, namely expanding the cultural distance hypothesis by considering direction (Weber et al. 1996). Hence, we argue for a rejection of the implicit assumption that cultural distance is symmetric (Håkanson and Ambos 2010). This idea was derived from the similar, yet different, concept of psychic distance (Dow and Karunaratna 2006) which was first introduced by Beckerman (1956) and has been developed further since. Scholars have identified different macro-level stimuli such as geographic, political, economic and cultural factors as antecedents of psychic distance (Håkanson and Ambos 2010). Taking these factors into consideration, psychic distance captures the subjectively perceived differences between two countries as experienced by a certain individual (Sousa and Bradley 2008). Moreover, psychic distance constitutes an asymmetric measure of differences which depends on the direction of analysis (Håkanson and Ambos 2010). Hence, under a psychic distance lens, the distance from Austria to China does not necessarily equal the distance from China to Austria (Sousa and Bradley 2008). We take this idea of asymmetry and transfer it to the concept of cultural distance, which is less dependent on individual perceptions and, hence, less subjective. Thus, we argue that cultural differences have asymmetric effects (Weber et al. 1996). Nonetheless, we do not suggest a direct effect, even though cultural differences may have an impact on the whole acquisition process in either a positive or negative way. We hold that they might become most critical during post-merger integration (Slangen 2006) of low-tech targets, as in this phase many people have to interact with each other to create value (Grotenhuis 2001). The post-merger phase is decisive for value creation (Haspeslagh and Jemison 1991), which is particularly true for acquisitions within the low-tech industry. Transactions within low-tech industries are driven by motives such as synergy realisation and efficiency gains through integration, whereas high-tech acquisitions are motivated by the interest of getting access to R&D (research and development) resources, for which structural integration is not always the best solution (Puranam et al. 2009). Nonetheless, there are only few empirical studies on the interplay of cultural differences and integration (e.g. Bauer et al. 2016; Morosini et al. 1998; Slangen 2006). Against this background, our study makes two contributions.

First, inspired by the asymmetry of psychic distance, we hold that similar cultural distance can have different effects depending on the direction of the transaction. As a consequence, we separate our empirical analysis of wholly owned cross-border transactions within low-tech industries in inbound and outbound transactions to demonstrate the diverging effects. Second, we interconnect cultural differences with post-merger integration and argue that under specific conditions the negative effect of cultural differences can be bridged with post-merger integration.

The outline of our chapter is as follows: in the next section we review the literature on cultural differences and post-merger integration and develop our theoretical model. We then describe our methodological approach before we present the empirical results of our study followed by discussion.

Theoretical Framework and Model Development

The term *culture* is often used without any clear specification, as culture can be seen from different levels—for instance national, industrial, organisational, functional or professional culture (Björkman et al. 2007). Consequently, attributing failures in M&A to cultural issues might lead to confusion because of its all-embracing nature (Angwin and Vaara 2005). Our unit of analysis is culture and cultural distances in terms of national contexts. Culture is the "collective programming of the mind that distinguishes one group or category of people from another" (Hofstede 1991, 5). Consequently, national culture is a geographical social environment from which specific value systems emanate and which affects the way people interact with each other (Hofstede 1991). In M&A, differences in national culture between acquirer and target constitute a potential source of conflicts as well as benefits. When companies acquire entities abroad, cultural fit is an important determinant of M&A success and failure (Bauer et al. 2016).

On one hand, the encounter between different national values and practices of acquirer and target can cause tensions, negative feelings and attitudes among involved parties. This not only results in poor collaboration (e.g. Brock 2005) but also gives rise to the attitude that cross-border acquisitions generally are a cultural risk (David and Singh 1994). This is intensified in cross-cultural communication when misunderstandings are inevitable (Adler 1991), resulting in problematic interactions or even feelings of hostility (Chatterjee et al. 1992) which lead to increased employee turnover (Krug and Hegarty 1997) and a decrease in shareholder value (Larsson and Lubatkin 2001).

On the other hand, on a macro-level, some findings (e.g. Lane and Lubatkin 1998) support assumptions of the resource-based view (Barney 1991), arguing that diversity in national cultures can be a source of competitive advantage. A positive relationship between increased cultural distance and M&A performance has been observed (e.g. Morosini et al. 1998), pointing to the facilitating effect of complementarity on M&A success. Moreover, cultural differences can positively influence an acquisition if the buying firm favours the target's values and ways of doing business (Very et al. 1997). This positive effect has been reported in complementary knowledge backgrounds of top management teams (Krishnan et al. 1997), or knowledge transfer through cultural integration activities (Sarala and Vaara 2010). However, there is no certain outcome of how the organisations involved will respond to an acquisition. Both positive and negative effects might happen simultaneously (Teerikangas and Very 2012) or might be highly influenced by the variables chosen. Due to these conflicting results, we state that

> H1a: Cultural distance has a negative effect on M&A performance.
> H1b: Cultural distance has a positive effect on M&A performance.

In the following we postulate that these inconclusive results may depend upon whether the target organisation is integrated into the buying company or not, that is bringing together both companies to create competitive advantage by leveraging external resources with substitution and complementary relationships amongst both firms involved (King et al. 2008). Thereby, reducing costs and/or improving productivity through combining systems and procedures of the merged firms can help to homogenise and standardise work processes (Shrivastava 1986). Consequently, the greatest potential of synergy realisation can be attained by increasing interaction and coordination amongst acquirer and target (Larsson and Finkelstein 1999). Integrating new business entities is a long and complex process that determines the success of the acquisition (Haspeslagh and Jemison 1991). Thus, the post-merger integration has an impact on M&A performance (Zollo and Singh 2004), while cultural fit determines the effectiveness of the integration process in a cross-border setting (Weber 1996). One could argue that cultural differences do not directly affect the acquisition until integration takes place, which connects the different cultures and urges both entities to encounter each other (Shenkar 2001). Moreover, culture is perceived to be learnt in a socialisation process (Hofstede 1980). Consequently, without post-merger integration, which demands that both sides learn to work together and cooperate in the transfer of strategic capabilities during an interactive and gradual process (Birkinshaw et al. 2000), no synergies can be realised for fruitful, cross-organisational and particularly cross-cultural cooperation (Stahl and Voigt 2008). Aligning organisations with two different national backgrounds requires that beliefs, assumptions and values of the previously independent workforces form a jointly determined culture (Larsson and Lubatkin 2001), a unified organisational frame. The result of this process depends mainly on how the acquiring company manages the integration process as well as the extent to which conflicts are resolved—this encompasses for example the amount of coordination and socialisation mechanisms, or the degree of social control (Cartwright 2005). Weber et al. (2011) state that higher integration effectiveness is achieved if the integration approach emphasises the interest in the specific characteristics of an acquisition regarding synergy potential and cultural differences. So, integration efforts with increased employee involvement can avoid cultural clashes (Cartwright 2005). Nonetheless, Slangen (2006) found that integration moderates the effect of cultural distance on performance. National cultural distance has a negative effect on M&A performance at high levels of integration and a positive impact at low levels of integration (Slangen 2006). Thereby, post-merger integration mechanisms such as the implementation of transition teams, senior management involvement, temporary personnel exchange and rotation (Larsson and Lubatkin 2001) and rich communication across organisational boundaries (Ranft and Lord 2002) seem to be most effective to achieve acculturation. Deep-level cultural learning interventions, which involve an on-going dialogue of both firms' employees, cultural awareness, and introspection are necessary to build a common cultural identity based on cultural understanding, commitment, and cooperation (Schweiger and Goulet 2005). Thus, integration can mitigate cultural risks (David and Singh 1994). We therefore believe that under certain conditions post-merger integration positively moderates the effect of cultural distance on M&A performance; that is post-merger integration has the potential to intensify positive effects of cultural distance, on one hand, and to mitigate negative effects of cultural distance, on the other hand:

> H2: Integration positively moderates the effect of cultural distance on M&A performance.

Cultural distance literature has mostly treated national cultural distances by a simple distance measure, calculating the absolute delta (Björkman et al. 2007), and omitting asymmetries covered by the cultural dimension (Weber 1996). However, due to mixed empirical findings, Weber et al. (2011) call for an extended framework that also considers directions of cultural distances. The reason is that simple distance measures implicitly suppose that a German firm acquiring a Chinese target will be confronted with the same challenges and obstacles as a Chinese company when purchasing a German target (Shenkar 2001). In this context, the related psychic distance concept suggests asymmetric effects (Sousa and Bradley 2008), meaning that the German company might be more distant to China than vice versa. Although psychic distance not only covers the subjective interpretation of national cultural aspects but is also influenced by several other aspects such as political and economic factors (Håkanson and Ambos 2010), these asymmetric effects also apply to the concept of cultural distance. Drawing on this idea of asymmetry, the effects of cultural distance are potentially positive in one direction while negative in the other (Bauer et al. 2016). This is already implied by findings which indicate asymmetries depending on the direction of cultural distance. We follow the preceding suggestion and differentiate between inbound and outbound cross-border acquisitions, postulating that the direction of the transaction does matter. Hence, we expect to find differences between inbound and outbound acquisitions. Although we, a priori, expect to find negative effects of cultural distance in inbound transactions because of potential organisational resistance of the German or Austrian target firm towards the foreign acquirer, we expect less organisational resistance and, hence, positive or less negative effects of cultural distance in outbound transactions.

Methodology

Sample and Data

To test the hypotheses we used secondary M&A data retrieved from the Zephyr database. This study focused on completed cross-border M&A in which German or Austrian firms were involved either as an acquirer or as a target company. We chose German and Austrian firms as they have a strong international focus and because they have been relevant targets for international acquirers over the last years. The respective counterparts to the German and Austrian firms were companies based in Australia, Brazil, China, Denmark, Finland, India, the Netherlands, Norway, Russia, Sweden, UK and the U.S. Although M&A with acquirers from Germany and Austria are defined as outbound acquisitions, the reverse case (German and Austrian target companies) is called inbound. This approach allowed us to make a comparison between inbound and outbound transactions to examine possible asymmetric effects of national cultural distances and the moderating impact of integration.

The sample comprised 284 transactions. It focused on deals concluded by stock-listed acquirers in certain sectors of the manufacturing and service industry which led to full ownership after closure of the deal, aiming to exclude minority shareholdings that are mainly driven by financial, rather than strategic, purposes. Furthermore, an industry focus was necessary as industries act as an important context for acquisition motives (Teusler 2008) which in turn usually impact on the implementation of the acquisition (Ranft and Lord 2002). Therefore, we focused on low-tech industries only, as their integration approaches are not comparable with high-tech industries. In high-tech industries, such as the IT or the biotechnology sector, acquirers frequently substitute in-house R&D efforts with M&A (Bower 2001) and often refrain from structural integration of the target firm to preserve its innovation capabilities (Puranam et al. 2009). On the other hand, acquirers in more stable low-tech industries tend to use M&A for market extension, resource sharing, or efficiency gains (Bower 2001), all of which require a certain degree of integration effort. A sample period between 1 January 2008 and 31 December 2012 was considered appropriate as it ensured a sufficiently large sample and at the same time avoided sampling distortions as this period falls after the peak of the last M&A wave. Additionally, this sample period guaranteed that the transactions were at least in the final phase of integration at the time of the study (Homburg and Bucerius 2006).

Measurement Development

Dependent Variable

Following prior studies (Ferreira et al. 2014), we used M&A performance as a dependent variable. Whereas some previous studies applied stock market measures (Haleblian and Finkelstein 1999), others used accounting-based measures to record M&A performance (Ellis et al. 2011; Zollo and Singh 2004). Yet others asked key informants to assess the performance of transactions (Homburg and Bucerius 2006).

We follow Morosini et al. (1998) and define M&A performance as the sales growth rate. Sales growth rate is a backward-looking accounting measure which reflects realised performance; at the same time, it is not subject to accounting regime biases (He and Wong 2004). It can be considered a performance measure at the downstream end of a firm's value chain (Mudambi 2008). As our focus is on low-tech industries which are typically characterised by comparatively high marketing intensity and low R&D intensity, a downstream performance measure seems appropriate (Hitt et al. 2006). To compute the average sales growth rates, we collected the annual revenues from the acquirers' annual reports. The percentage growth rate was calculated for the periods before and after the deal and then averaged out.

Independent Variable

For cultural distance, we applied the Kogut and Singh Index (1988). Based on Hofstede's (2011) six cultural dimensions we computed the deltas between the acquirer country and the target country for each dimension and corrected the deltas for variance differences of the respective dimensions. Finally, the corrected deltas were averaged out to have one cultural distance measure for each country pair. Even though Hofstede's dimensions have been criticised by researchers (e.g. Tung and Verbeke 2010) we used them for two major reasons. First, they have been applied across many different management disciplines (Kirkman et al. 2006) and second, there is empirical evidence indicating that Hofstede's measures highly correlate with other measures such as Globe (Sarala 2010).

Moderating Variable

We consider post-merger integration to have a moderating effect on the negative impact of high cultural distance on M&A performance. We followed Puranam et al. (2009) and analysed press releases published up to one month before and one month after the deal announcement on corporate websites and websites of financial service providers to measure post-merger integration and post-merger autonomy as a dummy variable. This procedure aimed at assessing the post-deal organisational status of the target firm within the newly combined corporation. If the target firm's function in the organisation is that of a wholly owned subsidiary, we can assume that the target firm's operations will be fully integrated into the existing operations of the acquirer. If, however, the function exercised by the target firm is that of a separate unit, we can assume independent operations and thus structural autonomy of the target firm within the group (Graebner 2004). Such autonomy may emanate from various sources, including the control over pivotal knowledge intangibles (Cantwell and Mudambi 2005), and can give the target firm stronger capacity to forge solid external network relationships in the host country (Birkinshaw et al. 1998). However, to realise the target firm's potential to become a centre of excellence for the whole group, factors such as location dynamism, cross-fertilisation of competences between target firm and the rest of the group, as well as the extent of support by the parent firm or headquarters for the target must additionally be taken into consideration (Frost et al. 2002). To measure the degree of post-merger integration and post-merger autonomy we screened two to three press articles per transaction with a keyword search for the phrases "wholly owned subsidiary" and "separate unit" (Puranam et al. 2009, 318). If the press releases explicitly mentioned the structural autonomy of a target firm, integration was considered to have not taken place, whereas in the absence of such indication structural integration was considered to have taken place. As this measure was also used in previous research and demonstrated reliable overlaps with other measures of integration and autonomy, we confidently applied it to our study (Puranam et al. 2009).

Control Variables

Acquisition experience, institutional distance and acquirer size were used as control variables due to their potential effect on M&A outcome (Bauer and Matzler 2014). The experience variable was measured as the number of deals conducted by an acquirer (Haleblian and Finkelstein 1999) in the preceding years. Institutional distance was operationalised with the competitiveness index provided by the World Economic Forum. The three categories of this index (basic requirements, efficiency enhancers and innovation and sophistication) were consolidated to calculate the delta between the acquirer country and the target country. Last, acquirer size was defined as the number of employees.

Results

Table 8.1 presents the descriptive statistics of the sample.

Hypothesis Testing

We used ordinary least-squares regression analysis to test the hypotheses. To check for asymmetric effects of cultural distance and integration, we

Table 8.1 Descriptive statistics of the sample

SAMPLE DESCRIPTION					
Acguiring Countries	**#**	**%**	**Types of Transaction**	**#**	**%**
Austria	18	6.3	Inbound	184	64.8
Australia	6	2.1	Outbound	100	35.2
Brazil	1	0.3		284	100.0
China	13	4.6			
Denmark	1	0.3			
Finland	9	3.2	**Post-merger Integration**	**#**	**%**
Germany	82	28.9			
India	2	0.7	Integration	145	51.0
Netherlands	12	4.2	No integration	128	45.1
Norway	3	1.1	Missing	11	3.9
Russia	2	0.7		284	100.0
Sweden	24	8.5			
United Kingdom	25	8.8			
United States	86	30.3	**Acquisition Experience**	**#**	**%**
	284	100.0			
			No experience	107	37.7
			1–5 prior deals	91	32.1
			6–10 prior deals	47	16.5
			> 10 prior deals	39	13.7
				284	100.0

Source: The authors.

applied these three models to the entire sample as well as to the subsamples of inbound transactions and outbound transactions. The results of the regression analysis are illustrated in Table 8.2.

The results for model 1 reveal that acquirer size is the only control variable that has a significant effect on M&A performance, however, only in the case of the overall sample ($\beta = -0.258$; $p = 0.007$) and outbound transactions ($\beta = -0.302$; $p = 0.007$).

Model 2 (overall) shows that cultural distance has a negative impact on the dependent variable ($\beta = -0.220$; $p = 0.010$). Moreover, a finer-grained analysis of model 2 proves that the negative effect of cultural distance on M&A performance is even stronger for inbound transactions ($\beta = -0.414$; $p = 0.005$), whereas there is no significant impact in the case of outbound transactions ($\beta = -0.043$; $p = 0.689$). Hence, the results confirm hypothesis 1a in the case of inbound, but not for outbound, acquisitions, thereby suggesting asymmetric effects of cultural distance.

In model 3 the moderating effect of integration has a significant positive effect in the overall sample ($\beta = 0.249$; $p = 0.003$). For the subsamples, however, model 3 draws a different picture as the moderating effect of integration is not established for inbound transactions ($\beta = 0.245$; $p = 0.109$). In the case of outbound transactions, however, integration positively moderates

Table 8.2 Results of the regression analysis

OVERALL	*Model 1*	*Model 2*	*Model 3*
Cultural Distance		–0.220**	–0.195*
Integration		–0.060	–0.059
Cultural Distance × Integration			0.249**
Acquisition Experience	–0.015	0.006	0.019
Institutional Distance	0.028	0.049	0.068
Acquirer Size	–0.258**	–0.312***	–0.369***
F-Value	2.918	3.238	4.382
R^2	0.062	0.110	0.168
Adjusted R^2	0.041	0.076	0.130
INBOUND	*Model 1*	*Model 2*	*Model 3*
Cultural Distance		–0.414**	–0.329*
Integration		–0.039	–0.013
Cultural Distance × Integration			0.245
Acquisition Experience	–0.100	–0.142	–0.136
Institutional Distance	0.046	0.118	0.120
Acquirer Size	–0.200	–0.328*	–0.382*
F-Value	0.825	2.291	2.428
R^2	0.051	0.207	0.253
Adjusted R^2	–0.011	0.116	0.149
OUTBOUND	*Model 1*	*Model 2*	*Model 3*
Cultural Distance		–0.043	–0.058
Integration		–0.126	–0.138
Cultural Distance × Integration			0.204+
Acquisition Experience	0.075	0.074	0.093
Institutional Distance	–0.052	–0.052	–0.027
Acquirer Size	–0.302**	–0.322**	–0.328**
F-Value	2.599	1.839	2.213
R^2	0.086	0.102	0.142
Adjusted R^2	0.053	0.047	0.078

Source: The authors.

+ Significant at $p < 0.10$; *Significant at $p < 0.05$; **Significant at $p < 0.01$; ***Significant at $p < 0.001$.

the impact of cultural distance on M&A performance (β = 0.204; $p = 0.056$). Hence, hypothesis 2 can only be approved for outbound transactions. The interaction between cultural distance and integration in the case of inbound and outbound acquisitions is illustrated in Figure 8.1.

All in all, the results provide empirical evidence for the asymmetric effects of cultural distance and post-merger integration for wholly owned cross-border transactions within low-tech industries.

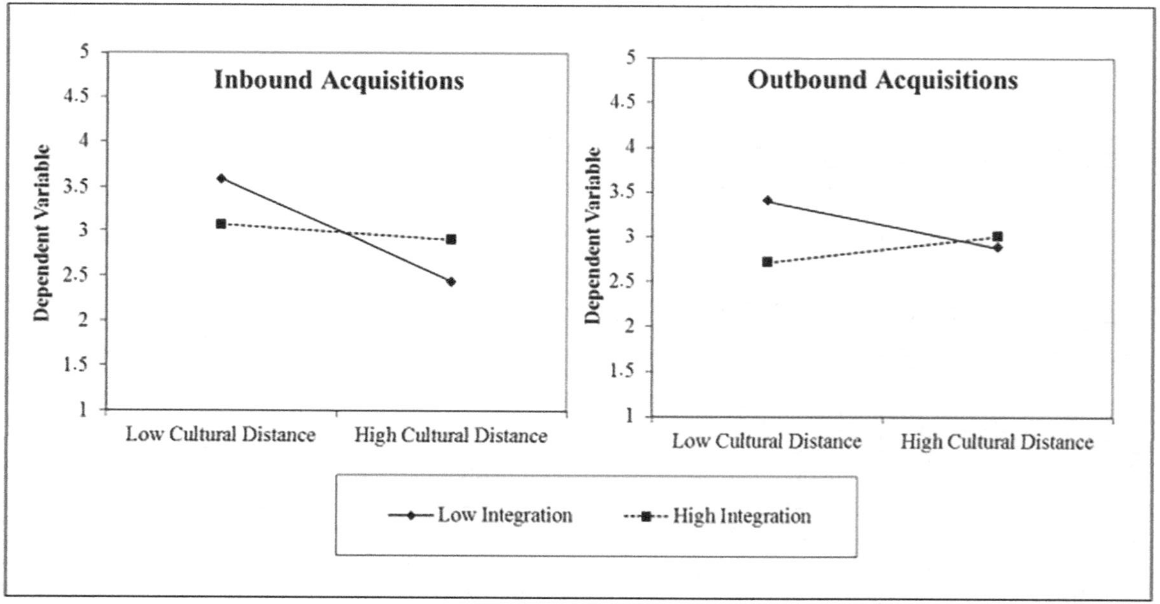

Figure 8.1 Interaction between cultural distance and integration in the case of inbound and outbound acquisitions
Source: The authors.

Discussion and Implications

Limitations

Our study is not free of limitations. First, we ignore organisational culture and its possible interplay with national culture. Although national culture "represents a deeper layer of consciousness" (Stahl and Voigt 2008, 165), "double layer integration" has been shown to be important (Barkema et al. 1996). Second, we rely on secondary data that generally oversimplifies the concepts employed, which is particularly evident in terms of post-merger integration. Thus, finer-grained measurement and analysis of integration would be necessary to confirm our results. Furthermore, the secondary data allowed us to only implement a one-dimensional cultural distance measure as the independent variable. Future research could refine our results through primary data research which allows the application of the more comprehensive psychic distance concept. Third, there is growing recognition that integration and autonomy are not the opposing ends of a single scale but rather coexist. It would be highly relevant to understand the interplay of national culture and the area of conflict between integration and autonomy within different layers of integration. Fourth, our assessment of integration is rather static. Future research would benefit from considering integration as a dynamic process with many interrelated tasks (Meglio and Risberg 2010). A fifth limitation results from our sampling approach as we implemented three foci in our sample—a geographic focus, an industry focus and a focus on wholly owned M&A—which might limit the extent to which our results can be generalised. Last, we use the sales growth rate as a dependent variable to measure M&A performance. As this constitutes a downstream performance measure of the value chain, we thereby neglect important insights stemming from employing upstream performance measures such as R&D output in the form of for example patent registrations (Mudambi 2008; Szücs 2014). Future research should therefore also consider the additional application of upstream performance measures.

Theoretical Implications

We firstly found empirical evidence that cultural distance matters in cross-border acquisitions. Although the overall results suggest a negative effect of cultural distance on M&A performance, we only find this effect in inbound and not in outbound acquisitions. One reason for these diverging effects may be our sampling. As Germany and Austria have high technological standards and economic prosperity and, hence, enjoy a high national standing, acquisitions by German and Austrian acquirers may be more positively or at least neutrally perceived by foreign target companies than the other way around. Moreover, Austrian and German targets might have more difficulty to accept new influences, as they are less tolerant of acquirer dominance (Stahl et al. 2012). Particularly when acquirers come from developing and targets from highly developed countries, acquisitions are likely to be surrounded by patriotic, sometimes even xenophobic attitudes of both the target companies' employees and the public towards the acquirer (see *Sophie Golinski* and *Sebastian Henn* in this volume; Hope et al. 2011). This indicates that cultural distance has asymmetric effects.

Second, M&A integration literature has mainly focused on the discussion of absorption, on one hand, and the need for autonomy, on the other (Zaheer et al. 2013). The empirical evidence on integration is not unequivocal and ranges from positive (Larsson and Finkelstein 1999) to negative (Puranam et al. 2009). We found that the separation of inbound and outbound acquisitions acts as an important determinant as perceived cultural distances are not symmetrical. Integration efforts rather depend on the national cultural context with respect to the respective position (being either the acquirer or the target organisation). This supports Goulet and Schweiger's argument that "acquirers may be culturally predisposed in the way they approach integration, and that targets may be culturally predisposed in the way they respond to integration" (2006, 410). Following up on Stahl et al. (2012) we can credibly support this observation providing empirical evidence across 14 different countries (see Franke and Richey [2010] for a study on international generalisations). Future research could investigate the integration efforts of companies in the context of cultural distance research and may implement other context-related variables.

Third, we found that the size of the acquirer negatively impacts on M&A performance. Ranft and Lord (2002) found that relative size and prior performance are indicators for relative standing. Our results suggest that an acquirer's size is an indicator of relative standing and power. Bigger acquirers may be associated with stricter rules, hierarchies, bureaucracy, loss of autonomy and radical and ruthless change and thus lead to greater organisational resistance within the target firm. This is particularly critical when the target firm possesses key resources such as knowledge intangibles that are of strategic importance to the acquirer. Being the gatekeeper to such key resources increases the intra-firm bargaining power of the target (Mudambi and Navarra 2004), thereby enabling the target to resist the acquiring firm's integration plans. As this effect occurs in both inbound and outbound acquisitions, we believe that size is a potential source for in-group and out-group biases (Lakshman 2011). The independence of this effect from cultural backgrounds could be a valuable future research direction.

Managerial Implications

Our study holds several implications for managers. First, managers should be aware of cultural differences. However, they should draw a finer-grained picture of these differences. In the case of inbound acquisitions, cultural differences may have a negative impact on M&A performance whereas in the case of outbound acquisitions, there is a neutral effect. Nonetheless, post-merger integration can be a vehicle for achieving synergies. However, the beneficial or detrimental effects of post-merger integration depend on inbound and outbound settings. Although managers could beneficially transfer their systems and structures in outbound acquisitions, post-merger integration has no significant effect in the case of inbound acquisitions. Managers from firms that plan to acquire in Germany and Austria should know that cultural differences can cause direct dramatic problems.

Additionally, managers should be aware of in-group and out-group biases deriving from the acquirer's size. Before a feeling of fear and suppression can occur, managers should foster communication and trust building among the organisation's members to avoid negative effects of this bias. A last conclusion stems from the insignificance of acquisition experience (control variable). Although commonly cited as an important success factor it did not show significant effects in our study. Here managers should avoid the misapplication and generalisation trap and consider commonalities and differences in their acquisitions.

References

Adler, N. J. 1991. "Communicating across Cultural Barriers." In *International Dimensions of Organizational Behavior*, edited by N. J. Adler, 63–91. Boston, MA: PWS-KENT Publishing Company.

Angwin, D. N., and E. Vaara. 2005. "Introduction to the Special Issue: 'Connectivity' in Merging Organizations: Beyond Traditional Cultural Perspectives." *Organization Studies* 26(10): 1445–1453.

Barkema, H. G., Bell, J. H. J., and J. M. Pennings. 1996. "Foreign Entry, Cultural Barriers, and Learning." *Strategic Management Journal* 17(2): 151–166.

Barney, J. 1991. "Firm Resources and Sustained Competitive Advantage." *Journal of Management* 17(1): 99–120.

Bauer, F., and K. Matzler. 2014. "Antecedents of M&A Success: The Role of Strategic Complementarity, Cultural Fit, and Degree and Speed of Integration." *Strategic Management Journal* 35(2): 269–291.

Bauer, F., Matzler, K., and S. Wolf. 2016. "M&A and Innovation: The Role of Integration and Cultural Differences: A Central European Targets Perspective." *International Business Review* 25(1): 76–86.

Beckerman, W. 1956. "Distance and the Pattern of Intra-European Trade." *The Review of Economics and Statistics* 38(1): 31–40.

Birkinshaw, J., Bresman, H., and L. Håkanson. 2000. "Managing the Post-Acquisition Integration Process: How the Human Integration and Task Integration Processes Interact to Foster Value Creation." *Journal of Management Studies* 37(3): 395–425.

Birkinshaw, J., Hood, N., and S. Jonsson. 1998. "Building Firm-Specific Advantages in Multinational Corporations: The Role of Subsidiary Initiative." *Strategic Management Journal* 19(3): 221–241.

Björkman, I., Stahl, G. K., and E. Vaara. 2007. "Cultural Differences and Capability Transfer in Cross-Border Acquisitions: The Mediating Roles of Capability Complementarity, and Social Integration." *Journal of International Business Studies* 38(4): 658–672.

Bower, J. L. 2001. "Not All M&As Are Alike: And That Matters." *Harvard Business Review* 79(3): 93–101.

Brock, David M. 2005. "Multinational Acquisition Integration: The Role of National Culture in Creating Synergies." *International Business Review* 14(3): 269–288.

Cantwell, J., and R. Mudambi. 2005. "MNE Competence-Creating Subsidiary Mandates." *Strategic Management Journal* 26(12): 1109–1128.

Cartwright, S. 2005. "Mergers and Acquisitions: An Update and Appraisal." *International Review of Industrial and Organizational Psychology* 20: 1–38.

Chatterjee, S., Lubatkin, M. H., Schweiger, D. M., and Y. Weber. 1992. "Cultural Differences and Shareholder Value in Related Mergers: Linking Equity and Human Capital." *Strategic Management Journal* 13(5): 319–334.

David, K., and H. Singh. 1994. "Sources of Acquisition Cultural Risk." In *The Management of Corporate Acquisitions: International Perspectives*, edited by G. von Krogh, A. Sinatra, and H. Singh, 251–292. London: Macmillan.

Dikova, D., Sahib, P. R., and A. van Witteloostuijn. 2010. "Cross-Border Acquisition Abandonment and Completion: The Effect of Institutional Differences and Organizational Learning in the International Business Service Industry, 1981–2001." *Journal of International Business Studies* 41(2): 223–245.

Dow, D., and A. Karunaratna. 2006. "Developing a Multidimensional Instrument to Measure Psychic Distance Stimuli." *Journal of International Business Studies* 37(5): 578–602.

Ellis, K. M., Reus, T. H., Lamont, B. T., and A. L. Ranft. 2011. "Transfer Effects in Large Acquisitions: How Size Specific Experienca Matters." *Academy of Management Journal* 54(6): 1261–1276.

Ferreira, M. P., Santos, J. C., Ribeiro de Almeida, M. I., and N. R. Reis. 2014. "Mergers & Acquisitions Research: A Bibliometric Study of Top Strategy and International Business Journals, 1980–2010." *Journal of Business Research* 67(12): 2550–2558.

Franke, G. R., and R. G. Richey. 2010. "Improving Generalizations from Multi-Country Comparisons in International Business Research." *Journal of International Business Studies* 41(8): 1275–1293.

Frost, T. S., Birkinshaw, J. M., and P. C. Ensign. 2002. "Centers of Excellence in Multinational Corporations." *Strategic Management Journal* 23(11): 997–1018.

Gaur, A. S., Malhotra, S., and P. Zhu. 2013. "Acquisition Announcements and Stock Market Valuations of Acquiring Firms' Rivals: A Test of the Growth Probability Hypothesis in China." *Strategic Management Journal* 34(2): 215–232.

Goulet, P. K., and D. M. Schweiger. 2006. "Managing Culture and Human Resources in Mergers and Acquisitions." In *Handbook of Research in International Human Resource Management*, edited by G. K. Stahl, and I. Björkman, 405–426. Cheltenham and Northampton: Edward Elgar Publishing Limited.

Graebner, M. E. 2004. "Momentum and Serendipity: How Acquired Leaders Create Value in the Integration of Technology Firms." *Strategic Management Journal* 25(8/9): 751–777.

Grotenhuis, F. D. J. 2001. "Marriages between Asian, American, and Dutch Corporations: A Matter of Cultural Fit?" *Review of Pacific Basin Financial Markets and Policies* 4(2): 203–220.

Hakanson, L., and B. Ambos. 2010. "The Antecedents of Psychic Distance." *Journal of International Management* 16(3): 195–210.

Haleblian, J., and S. Finkelstein. 1999. "The Influence of Organizational Acquisition Experience on Acquisition Performance: A Behavioral Learning Perspective." *Administrative Science Quarterly* 44(1): 29–56.

Haspeslagh, P. C., and D. B. Jemison. 1991. *Managing Acquisitions*. New York: The Free Press.

He, Z.-L., and P.-K. Wong. 2004. "Exploration vs. Exploitation: An Empirical Test of the Ambidexterity Hypothesis." *Organization Science* 15(4): 481–494.

Hitt, M. A., Franklin, V., and H. Zhu. 2006. "Culture, Institutions and International Strategy." *Journal of International Management* 12(2): 222–234.

Hofstede, G. 1980. Culture's Consequences: International Differences in Work-Related Values. Newbury Park: SAGE Publications.

Hofstede, G. 1991. Cultures and Organizations: Software of the Mind. London: McGraw-Hill.

Hofstede, G. 2011. "Dimensionalizing Cultures: The Hofstede Model in Context." *Online Readings in Psychology and Culture* 2(1): 1–26.

Homburg, C., and M. Bucerius. 2005. "A Marketing Perspective on Mergers and Acquisitions: How Marketing Integration Affects Postmerger." *Journal of Marketing* 69(1): 95–113.

Homburg, C., and M. Bucerius. 2006. "Is Speed of Integration Really a Success Factor of Mergers and Acquisitions? An Analysis of the Role of Internal and External Relatedness." *Strategic Management Journal* 27(4): 347–367.

Hope, O.-K., Thomas, W., and D. Vyas. 2011. "The Cost of Pride: Why Do Firms from Developing Countries Bid Higher?" *Journal of International Business Studies* 42(1): 128–151.

King, D. R., Slotegraaf, R. J., and I. Kesner. 2008. "Performance Implications of Firm Resource Interactions in the Acquisition of R&D-Intensive Firms." *Organization Science* 19(2): 327–340.

Kirkman, B. L., Lowe, K. B., and C. B. Gibson. 2006. "A Quarter Century of Culture's Consequences: A Review of Empirical Research Incorporating Hofstede's Cultural Values Framework." *Journal of International Business Studies* 37(3): 285–320.

Kogut, B., and H. Singh. 1988. "The Effect of National Culture on the Choice of Entry Mode." *Journal of International Business Studies* 19(3): 411–432.

Krishnan, H. A., Miller, A., and W. Q. Judge. 1997. "Diversification and Top Management Team Complementarity : Is Performance Improved by Merging Similar or Dissimilar Teams?" *Strategic Management Journal* 18(5): 361–374.

Krug, J. A., and W. H. Hegarty. 1997. "Postacquisition Turnover among US Top Management Teams: An Analysis of the Effects of Foreign vs. Domestic Acquisitions." *Strategic Management Journal* 18(8): 667–675.

Lakshman, C. 2011. "Postacquisition Cultural Integration in Mergers & Acquisitions: A Knowledge-Based Approach." *Human Resource Management* 50(5): 605–623.

Lane, P. J., and M. Lubatkin. 1998. "Absorptive Capacity and Interorganizational Learning." *Strategic Management Journal* 19(5): 461–477.

Larsson, R., and S. Finkelstein. 1999. "Integrating Strategic, Organizational, and Human Resource Perspectives on Mergers and Acquisitions: A Case Survey of Synergy Realization." *Organization Science* 10(1): 1–26.

Larsson, R., and M. Lubatkin. 2001. "Achieving Acculturation in Mergers and Acquisitions: An International Case Survey." *Human Relations* 54(12): 1573–1607.

Meglio, O., and A. Risberg. 2010. "Mergers and Acquisitions: Time for a Methodological Rejuvenation of the Field?" *Scandinavian Journal of Management* 26(1): 87–95.

Morck, R., and B. Yeung. 1991. "Why Investors Value Multinationality." *The Journal of Business* 64(2): 165–187. www.jstor.org/stable/2353061

Morosini, P., Shane, S., and H. Singh. 1998. "National Cultural Acquisition Distance and Cross-Border Acquisition Performance." *Journal of International Business Studies* 29(1): 137–158.

Mudambi, R. 2008. "Location, Control and Innovation in Knowledge-Intensive Industries." *Journal of Economic Geography* 8(5): 699–725.

Mudambi, R., and P. Navarra. 2004. "Is Knowledge Power? Knowledge Flows, Subsidiary Power and Rent-Seeking within MNCs." *Journal of International Business Studies* 35(5): 385–406.

Nadolska, A., and H. G. Barkema. 2014. "Good Learners: How Top Management Teams Affect the Success and Frequency of Acquisitions." *Strategic Management Journal* 35(10): 1483–1507.

Puranam, P., Singh, H., and S. Chaudhuri. 2009. "Integrating Acquired Capabilities: When Structural Integration Is (Un)necessary." *Organization Science* 20(2): 313–328.

Ranft, A. L., and M. D. Lord. 2002. "Acquiring New Technologies and Capabilities: A Grounded Model of Acquisition Implementation." *Organization Science* 13(4): 420–441.

Sarala, R. M. 2010. "The Impact of Cultural Differences and Acculturation Factors on Post-Acquisition Conflict." *Scandinavian Journal of Management* 26(1): 38–56.

Sarala, R. M., and E. Vaara. 2010. "Cultural Differences, Convergence, and Crossvergence as Explanations of Knowledge Transfer in International Acquisitions." *Journal of International Business Studies* 41(8): 1365–1390.

Schweiger, D. M., and P. K. Goulet. 2005. "Facilitating Acquisition Integration through Deep-Level Cultural Learning Interventions: A Longitudinal Field Experiment." *Organization Studies* 26(10): 1477–1499.

Shenkar, O. 2001. "Cultural Distance Revisited: Towards a More Rigorous Conceptualization and Measurement of Cultural Differences." *Journal of International Business Studies* 32(3): 519–535.

Shimizu, K., Hitt, M. A., Vaidyanath, D., and V. Pisano. 2004. "Theoretical Foundations of Cross-Border Mergers and Acquisitions: A Review of Current Research and Recommendations for the Future." *Journal of International Management* 10(3): 307–353.

Shrivastava, P. 1986. "Post-Merger Integration." *The Journal of Business Strategy* 7(1): 65–76.

Slangen, A. H. L. 2006. "National Cultural Distance and Initial Foreign Acquisition Performance: The Moderating Effect of Integration." *Journal of World Business* 41(2): 161–170.

Sousa, C. M. P., and F. Bradley. 2008. "Cultural Distance and Psychic Distance: Refinements in Conceptualisation and Measurement." *Journal of Marketing Management* 24(5/6): 467–488.

Stahl, G. K., Chua, C. H., and A. L. Pablo. 2012. "Does National Context Affect Target Firm Employees' Trust in Acquisition?" *Management International Review* 52(3): 395–423.

Stahl, G. K., and A. Voigt. 2008. "Do Cultural Differences Matter in Mergers and Acquisitions? A Tentative Model and Examination." *Organization Science* 19(1): 160–176.

Szücs, F. 2014. "M&A and R&D: Asymmetric Effects on Acquirers and Targets?" *Research Policy* 43(7): 1264–1273.

Teerikangas, S., and P. Very. 2012. "Culture in Mergers and Acquisitions." In *The Handbook of Mergers and Acquisitions*, edited by D. Faulkner, S. Teerikangas, and R. J. Joseph, 392–430. Oxford: Oxford University Press.

Teusler, N. 2008. Strategische Stabilitätsfaktoren in Unternehmenskooperationen. Wiesbaden: Gabler Verlag.

Tung, R. L., and A. Verbeke. 2010. "Beyond Hofstede and GLOBE: Improving the Quality of Cross-Cultural Research." *Journal of International Business Studies* 41(8): 1259–1274.

UNCTAD [United Nations Conference on Trade and Development]. 2015. *World Investment Report 2015*. Geneva: United Nations Publication. http://unctad.org/en/PublicationsLibrary/wir2015_en.pdf

Very, P., Lubatkin, M., Calori, R., and J. Veiga. 1997. "Relative Standing and the Performance of Recently Acquired European Firms." *Strategic Management Journal* 18(8): 593–614.

Weber, Y. 1996. "Corporate Cultural Fit and Performance in Mergers and Acquisitions." *Human Relations* 49(9): 1181–1202.

Weber, Y., Shenkar, O., and A. Raveh. 1996. "National and Corporate Cultural Fit in Mergers/Acquisitions: An Exploratory Study." *Management Science* 42(8): 1215–1227.

Weber, Y., Tarba, S. Y., and Z. R. Bachar. 2011. "Mergers and Acquisitions Performance Paradox: The Mediating Role of Integration Approach." *European Journal of International Management* 5(4): 373–393.

Weber, Y., Tarba, S. Y., and A. Reichel. 2011. "A Model of the Influence of Culture on Integration Approaches and International Mergers and Acquisitions Performance." *International Studies of Management and Organization* 41(3): 9–24.

Xu, D., and O. Shenkar. 2002. "Institutional Distance and the Multinational Enterprise." *The Academy of Management Review* 27(4): 608–618.

Zaheer, A., Castaner, X., and D. Souder. 2013. "Synergy Sources, Target Autonomy, and Integration in Acquisitions." *Journal of Management* 39(3): 604–632.

Zollo, M., and H. Singh. 2004. "Deliberate Learning in Corporate Acquisitions: Post-Acquisition Strategies and Integration Capability in U.S. Bank Mergers." *Strategic Management Journal* 25(13): 1233–1256.

9 Brownfield Investments in the German Automotive Parts Industry

Private Equity as a Door Opener

Christoph Scheuplein

Introduction

FDI are undertaken by a variety of different types of investors (Dicken 2011). In the past decade, private equity (PE) firms have become a new type of investor in this market segment in every part of the world. In the mid-2000s, UNCTAD (2006, 19) estimated the total value of PE investments to be about one fifth of all cross-border investments. Since the slump in investments during the global financial and economic crisis, this value has increased to almost a quarter (UNCTAD 2015, 15). Owing to the typically short holding periods in this area, PE investments used to be regarded as purely financial portfolio investments. With the rise in the global economy of institutional investors that make large long-term investments, this business model has changed, and the line between PE and direct investment has blurred (Dunning and Dilyard 1999, 24–25). In the standard business model of PE, funds have a finite life, so sooner or later, the question of selling arises. With the emergence of this new type of investor, a new aspect also presents itself on the side of the sellers of direct investments: whereas in other areas, the sale of a company is usually motivated by its economic performance or by specific circumstances affecting its owners, in this case, it is a feature of the business model. Naturally, this makes the portfolio companies of PE firms potential targets for FDI.

This chapter focuses on FDI made after the exit of the PE firms previously involved (referred to hereafter as "exit FDI") and examines whether such sale offers attract specific types of buyers and whether there are clear, consistent differences between the target companies and the FDI of other owners. Because other sellers usually are strategic investors—that is sellers that work in the same branch as the target company—this FDI is referred to "strategic FDI". The scope of this chapter is limited to incoming FDI made in the automotive parts industry in Germany in the 2009–2014 period.

The second section introduces the business model of PE and describes the range of PE activities in Germany. The following section gives a brief overview of the automotive industry in Germany. The fourth section develops the focus of the research question, formulates some hypotheses and explains the sample composition. The next section takes a closer look at the structures of exit FDI, and the final section provides some conclusions for further research into exit FDI.

Private Equity in Germany and FDI in the Automotive Industry

The term *private equity*, as used in this chapter, refers only to acquisitions of established companies (buyouts), not to investments in new companies or in companies in the foundation phase (venture capital; for a general discussion of buyouts, see Cumming 2012; Talmor and Vasvari 2011). PE first came to prominence in the U.S. in the 1960s in the form of investments made on behalf of banks, insurance companies and private lenders (Kaplan and Strömberg 2009). In most cases, its business model involves setting up a fund whose capital the PE firm invests to acquire companies, which are sold before the end of the fund's life, usually within ten years. The profits are then distributed to the investors, with the PE firm receiving management fees and a share in the profits.

In Germany, it was not until the late 1990s that PE was used on a larger scale (Jowett and Jowett 2011, 52–75). This development was facilitated by the withdrawal of the 1950s founders' generation, the privatisation of state-owned enterprises and the 2002 tax exemption for capital gains from the sale of corporations (Bessler et al. 2010). It was around that time that American and British PE firms first started to make considerable investments and open subsidiaries in Germany. 2007 and 2008 saw record-breaking investments in the German PE market; however, this was after the most extensive buyout activities in the automotive parts industry had been recorded, in 2005 and 2006 (Scheuplein 2012, 55). The financial and economic crisis that began in September 2008 put an immediate stop to this trend (Achleitner et al. 2010). Since then, the number and volume of investments have remained at a stable high level (EVCA 2015; Preqin 2014; Scheuplein 2015).

The rise of PE has also been one of the consequences of the financialisation of the economies in the industrialised countries (Haves et al. 2014). In Germany, this financialisation is not nearly as pronounced as it has been in the U.S. and the UK. Their larger funds have allowed PE firms from these two countries to dominate the buyout market in Germany because they started to increase their activities in that country in 2000. As of 2013, the ten PE firms with the largest investments in the German market as measured by transaction volume had their headquarters in either the U.S. or the UK (Scheuplein 2015, 153). These firms have substantial funds of more than €1 billion that allow them to engage in major deals and cover large areas of the market. The majority of the American–British PE firms operate on at least two continents. Very large firms such as KKR, Permira and Blackstone have between 15 and 20 subsidiaries in countries across the globe, including the newly industrialised countries in Asia, which enables them to observe the market for corporate control in every major economic region and to activate their global network even for highly specialised industry niches.

The vast majority of German PE firms were founded after 2000 and have smaller funds (rarely more than €300 million). These firms specialise in small and medium-sized companies and usually limit their activities to the German market. In addition, there seem to be significant cultural differences between German and Anglo-Saxon PE firms, particularly when it comes to industrial relations (Lippert and Jürgens 2012). During the boom years from 2005 to 2008, private equity firms active in the German market simply adopted the business practices that had already been widely used in the Anglo-Saxon sphere (see Appelbaum and Batt 2014). In contrast, German PE firms emphasise their loyalty to the domestic small and medium-sized companies, especially in the automotive industry (Frick and Krug 2010). In the aftermath of the global economic crisis of 2008/09, private equity firms, including those from the Anglo-Saxon countries, began to adapt some of their business practices to the German model (Haves et al. 2014). From today's perspective, adjustments to the Anglo-Saxon market-based system of industrial relations were not very significant (Beck and Scherrer 2015, 168).

Overall, the introduction of PE has led to an internationalisation of the German economy. First, the introduction of PE has required an external impulse. Second, many companies are temporarily owned by foreign PE firms due to their financial strengths. However, in the industry under study in this chapter—the automotive parts industry—PE is only one of several actors involved in FDI.

The automotive industry is geographically dispersed and highly fragmented, with an oligopolistic group of original equipment manufacturers (OEM) assembling the vehicles in areas close to the buyers' markets and sourcing parts from a highly differentiated group of high-wage and low-wage suppliers (Freyssenet et al. 2002). The increase in value creation at the parts suppliers, technical changes and the rise of OEM in the newly industrialised countries have led to a constant global restructuring of the automotive industry (Amighini and Gorgoni 2014; Bailey et al. 2010), with the result that the major parts suppliers—also known as tier 1 suppliers—and the OEM are now almost equal players. This means that not only are there several reasons for engaging in FDI, but there are also a large number of potential buyers besides the PE investors that have a background in the industry.

The value of an acquisition often depends on the company's position in the supply pyramid. Automotive suppliers can be divided into three categories of importance according to the degree of technological expertise involved, with suppliers of standardised parts (e.g. screws) being on the lowest level (tier 3), suppliers of components (e.g. headlamps) on the medium level (tier 2) and suppliers of systems (e.g. car seat systems) on the highest level (tier 1; Frigant 2011; Womack et al. 1990). In addition, automotive suppliers can be classified according the product segment they serve, so that for example a manufacturer of electronic systems is of greater importance because of its technological expertise than a manufacturer of plastic components for car interiors.

In Germany, the automotive industry is by far the most important industry in the manufacturing sector. This has enabled the German companies to make major FDI in the international market (Klodt and Christensen 2007), whereas incoming FDI in Germany have been relatively limited (Bundesbank 2015, 67; ZEW and NIW 2009, 87–88). The economic development agency Germany Trade & Invest has estimated that 3% of all investments in the German automotive industry are direct investments (Bochow 2007; GTAI and ZVEI 2014, 1).

Research Question, Hypotheses and Sample

This chapter seeks to improve our knowledge of the seller side in FDI. Such information is highly relevant, particularly in cases where a large portion of FDI are the result of M&A, which might make the involvement of certain potential investors a matter of economic and sociopolitical concern, an example being the direct investments from the BRIC (Brazil, Russia, India and China) countries, which accounted for one third of all FDI made in Germany in the past few years (GTAI and ZVEI 2014, 1). Many of these investors were Chinese firms (Zhang 2015), which also made the most substantial direct investments of all newly industrialised countries. The potential and actual risks of such involvement have been critically discussed in studies on the national economic structures (Golinski and Henn 2015), the employment effects of such involvement (Bollhorn 2015) and the management practices used (Fuchs and Schalljo 2016).

If the role of the seller side in FDI is examined (Gentile-Lüdecke 2014), the ownership structures of sellers can be studied as a factor influencing the internationalisation of portfolio companies. For this purpose, two hypotheses are proposed:

> H1: An increasing number of FDI in the automotive parts industry in the German market are investments in which PE firms act as sellers.
> H2: Foreign multinational PE firms have played a significantly more important role in this increase than have domestic PE firms that focus on small and medium-sized companies.

Given that the foreign direct investors are from industrialised and newly industrialised countries, this chapter also examines this differentiation both in relation to the target companies and in relation to the selling PE firms. A reasonable assumption is that the international relations of the PE firms, along with their unfiltered focus on generating returns on investment, make these firms more open to all market participants than strategic actors. This may accommodate potential buyers from newly industrialised countries and leads to the third hypothesis:

> H3: Exit FDI makes market entry easier for firms from the newly industrialised countries than does strategic FDI.

Also relevant here is a target company's position in the supply pyramid and the product segment referred to earlier, which is addressed by the fourth hypothesis:

> H4: Target companies that are acquired by investors from the newly industrialised countries are at a lower level in the supply pyramid and/or serve product segments of relatively lower value than is the case for companies acquired by investors from industrialised countries.

The sample used to test these hypotheses was based on a review of the M&A databases of DealNews/Majunke Consulting and Zephyr/Bureau van Dijk for the period 2009–2014. In addition, the data concerning 2009 and 2010 were cross-checked against the M&A Review database. The sample included all FDI in companies in the automotive parts industry that had their headquarters in Germany. The sample consisted of 169 direct investments. Of these, 42 were made by PE firms; these investments will be referred to in the following as "PE-FDI" (private equity FDI). However, the focus of this chapter is on exit FDI in which companies were removed from the portfolios of PE firms. This exit FDI was contrasted with cases of M&A investments in which a strategic investor acquired a company from an owner that was not a PE firm.

Because a number of suppliers had gone into administration as a result of the global economic crisis of 2008/09, a decision had to be made whether or not to regard these insolvencies as "exits" of PE investors. In such cases, the FDI in question was assigned to the respective owner prior to going into administration: insolvent companies that were owned by a strategic investor prior to going into administration were regarded as "strategic FDI", and companies that were owned by a PE firm were regarded as "exit FDI".

FDI and the Long-term Influence of Private Equity

PE has come to play a major role in FDI in the automotive parts industry in the past few years. In addition to the 42 PE-FDI made by foreign PE firms between 2009 and 2014, 35 exit FDI were derived from the data.

The following is a comparison of the 35 exit FDI and the 92 strategic FDI. In total, these 127 FDI affected 91,000 employees and involved revenues of €8.0 billion. The companies affected by an exit FDI were significantly larger in terms of total numbers of employees and revenues. The number of exit FDI and strategic FDI increased from 13 cases in 2009 to 29 cases in 2014, with 2013 being the only year a smaller number (20) was recorded. The number of employees affected by such FDI also increased in that period, from 5,900 to 15,600. The largest proportion of exit FDI was observed in 2011 (31%), and the largest proportions of employees affected by an exit FDI in that same period were observed in 2011 and 2012 (48%). This was followed by a decrease, and by 2014, exit FDI represented 13 % of all FDI and affected 29% of all employees. These results indicate that the large proportion of exit FDI in the period in question corresponds with the 2005/06 wave of target company buyouts. This cyclical investment behaviour of PE also puts into perspective the role exit FDI may play in the future: in the next few years, the proportion of exit FDI will probably remain at an even lower level.

The next step of the analysis was to test hypothesis 2 by examining the previously mentioned differentiation into highly capitalised, primarily globally oriented foreign PE firms and domestic PE firms that focus on small and medium-sized companies. The results show that, having been involved as sellers in 57% of the entire exit FDI under study, the global foreign PE firms did indeed play a more important role than did the domestic firms. In addition, the exit FDI by the foreign PE firms affected about 70% of all employees and involved 73% of the total revenue of the target companies. Whereas target companies sold by a German PE firm had an average of about 1,000 employees, target companies sold by a British or American PE firm had at least twice as many. A similar ratio was observed for the revenue generated by the target companies. Thus, the exits of global foreign PE firms were a major force behind the cross-border acquisitions considered here.

The third step of the analysis was to determine whether the PE firms, in their role as owners, preferred buyers from particular regions of origin. In view of the important role the newly industrialised countries have come to play in FDI in the past few years, the question is whether these countries have increasingly been able to acquire their companies by means of FDI (Hypothesis 3). To test this hypothesis, each of the buyouts under study was assigned to one of three categories ("triad countries", "newly industrialised countries", and "other countries") depending on the country in which the buyer had its headquarters. The "triad countries" included the countries of North America, the countries of Western Europe and Japan, where the major centres of the automotive industry were located during the second half of the 20th century. Of the more recent centres of the automotive industry that have developed over the past 20 years, only companies from China, India, Mexico and Turkey were assigned to the group of the "newly industrialised countries", because only companies from these four countries acted as buyers in the FDI studied here.

Table 9.1 shows that the proportion of companies previously owned by PE that were acquired by firms from newly industrialised countries is significantly larger than that of companies previously owned by strategic investors (42% versus 20%). Buyers from the triad countries made up 46% of all exit FDI but as many as 70% of all strategic FDI. Buyers from newly industrialised countries acquired a proportion of employees working for companies acquired by means of an exit FDI (50%) that was even larger than that of employees working for companies owned by strategic investors (37%). For revenues this proportion is reversed (45% from exit FDI versus 52% from strategic FDI).

Table 9.1 Exit FDI and strategic FDI by number of target companies, numbers of employees and revenues in the target companies of the German automotive parts industry, 2009–2014

	Target companies		*Employess*		*Turnover*	
	Number	*Share*	*Thousand*	*Share*	*Mio. €*	*Share*
Exit FDI						
Newly industrialised countries	15	42.9	25.1	49.6	1,991	44.9
Triad countries	16	45.7	23.7	47.0	2,392	53.9
Other countries	4	11.4	1.7	3.4	51	1.2
Total	35	100.0	50.6	100.0	4,434	100.0
Strategic FDI						
Newly industrialised countries	18	19.6	15.2	37.0	1,896	52.1
Triad countries	64	69.6	22.4	54.3	1,333	36.6
Other countries	10	10.9	3.6	8.8	411	11.3
Total	92	100.0	41.2	100.0	3,640	100.0
Total Exit FDI and Strategic FDI	127		91.9		8,074	

Source: Calculated based on data provided by DealNews/Majunke Consulting and Zephyr/Bureau van Dijk.

Overall, the results confirm that the proportion of companies acquired by means of an exit FDI by a buyer from a newly industrialised country was larger than that of companies acquired by an investor from either of the other two groups of countries. Thus, in this somewhat lessened form, PE represented a door opener for firms from the newly industrialised countries that sought to gain access to the German market. But how important were the companies that had been acquired in this way? The previously mentioned distinction of three levels of technological expertise (tiers 1, 2 and 3) was used to categorise the companies affected by a cross-border acquisition during the 2009–2014 period. Of these companies, 109 were identified as tier 3 suppliers, 50 as tier 2 suppliers and 10 as tier 1 suppliers.

The results indicate that the proportion of tier 1 companies acquired by firms from the newly industrialised countries was the same as that of companies acquired by firms from the triad countries (6%). In fact, the proportion of tier 2 companies acquired by firms from the newly industrialised countries was slightly larger than that of companies acquired by firms from the triad countries (35% vs 30%). Of these, PE firms sold a larger proportion of target companies with a higher technological level (e.g. over 50% of all tier 2 companies, whereas other investors sold only about 20%).

The final step of the analysis was to determine the structure of the cross-border acquisitions on the basis of ten product segments of the automotive industry commonly used in the research literature (e.g. engine, drivetrain and chassis). Of these ten segments, up to three segments could be assigned to each company. The results show that the investors from the newly industrialised countries invested in similar segments than did investors from "triad countries", meaning that hypothesis 4 was not confirmed.

Conclusion

This chapter examined the owner structure of the sellers involved in cross-border acquisitions. The owner type of PE firms, which did not engage in buyout activities on a broader scale in Germany until about 15 years ago, shows business practices that set it apart from other types of owners. Its exit-oriented business model made PE a major driver of FDI in the German automotive parts industry in the period 2009–2014. Overall, PE firms sold a larger number of companies with a larger total number of employees through cross-border acquisitions than did any other of the owner types under study. This trend was driven primarily by the global foreign financial investors that have imported PE to Germany in the past few decades. However, the cyclical investment behaviour of PE investors (with the peak of investments having been reached in 2011/12) appears to be reflected in the sales.

Quantitatively, the buyers from the newly industrialised countries benefited more from this access to the automotive parts supplier market. Qualitatively, investors from newly industrialised countries bought target companies that were in a similar position in the supplier pyramid and that served similar product segments as did investors from "triad countries".

These results clearly show that a seller's owner structure influences the scope and structure of cross-border acquisitions. As yet, it is impossible to tell what consequences this owner pluralisation in the automotive industry will have in the long run. Will the German production model be enhanced through new expertise and new market entries being integrated, or is the expertise being transferred to the new centres of the automotive industry in the newly industrialised countries?

References

Achleitner, A.-K., Metzger, G., Reiner, U., and M. Tchouvakhina. 2010. "Beteiligungs markt nach der Krise: Optimistischer Ausblick, aber Angebotslücke im Wachstums kapital wird grösser.", https://www.kfw.de/Download-Center/Konzernthemen/Research/PDF-Dokumente-Sonderpublikationen/Beteiligungsmarkt-nach-der-Krise-LF.pdf, accessed 2017, March 28.

Amighini, A., and S. Gorgoni. 2014. "The International Reorganisation of Auto Production." *World Economy* 37(7): 923–952.

Appelbaum, E., and R. Batt. 2014. *Private Equity at Work: When Wall Street Manages Main Street*. New York: Russel Sage Foundation.

Bailey, D., De Ruyter, A., Michie, J., and P. Tyler. 2010. "Global Restructuring and the Auto Industry." *Cambridge Journal of Regions, Economy and Society* 3(3): 311–318.

Beck, S., and C. Scherrer. 2015. "Varieties of Capitalism: Beyond Simple Dichotomies." In *Financial Cultures and Crises Dynamics*, edited by B. Jessop, B. Young, and C. Scherrer, 162–175. Abingdon and New York: Routledge.

Bessler, W., Holler, J., and M. Seim. 2010. "Venture Capital and Private Equity in Germany." In *Private Equity: Fund Types, Risks and Returns, and Regulation*, edited by D. Cumming, 511–554. Hoboken: Wiley.

Bochow, A. 2007. Ausländische Direktinvestitionen in der Automobilzulieferindustrie: Eine empirische Analyse Ostdeutschlands. Berlin and Munich: poli-c-books.

Bollhorn, K. 2015. "Acquisitions of German Companies by Chinese and Indian Corporations: A Threat to Employment and Knowledge Retention?" *Die Erde* 146(1): 16–20.

Bundesbank. 2015. "Bestandserhebung über Direktinvestitionen." https://www.bundesbank.de/Redaktion/DE/Downloads/Veroeffentlichungen/Statistische_Sonderveroeffentlichungen/Statso_10/2015_bestandserhebung_direktinvestitionen.pdf?__blob=publicationFile, accessed 2017, March 28.

Cumming, D. 2012. *The Oxford Handbook of Private Equity*. Oxford: Oxford University Press.

Dicken, P. 2011. Global Shift: Mapping the Changing Contours of the World Economy. London: Sage.

Dunning, J., and J. R. Dilyard. 1999. "Towards a General Paradigm of Foreign Direct and Foreign Portfolio Investment." *Transnational Corporations* 8(1): 1–52.

EVCA [European Private Equity and Venture Capital Association]. 2015. "2014 European Private Equity Activity. Statistics on Fundraising, Investments and Divestments." www.investeurope.eu/media/385581/2014-european-private-equity-activity-final-v2.pdf, accessed 2016, July 28.

Freyssenet, M., Shimizu, K., and G. Volpato. 2002. *Globalization or Regionalization of the European Car Industry?* Basingstoke: Palgrave Macmillan.

Frick, S., and V. Krug. 2010. "Finanzierung, Konsolidierung, M&A und Strategie: Zulieferer in einem sich drastisch wandelnden Umfeld." In *Money vs. Technology: Materialien zur Automobilindustrie* 42, edited by Verband der Automobilindustrie, 23–85. Berlin: VDA.

Frigant, V. 2011. "Egyptian Pyramid or Aztec Pyramid: How Should We Describe the Industrial Architecture of Automotive Supply Chains in Europe?" *Cahiers du GREThA* 27. http://ideas.repec.org/p/grt/wpegrt/2011-27.html.

Fuchs, M., and M. Schalljo. 2016. "'Western' Professional Ethics Challenged by Foreign Acquisitions: German Managers' Patterns of Interpretation Surrounding Chinese and Indian Investors." *Geoforum* 75: 20–28.

Gentile-Lüdecke, S. 2014. "Selling to Chinese Firms: A Seller's Perspective: Empirical Evidence from the German Automotive Industry." In *Multinational Enterprises, Markets and Institutional Diversity*, edited by A. Verbeke, R. van Tulder, and S. Lundan, 71–96. Bingley: Emerald Group Publishing Limited.

Golinski, S., and S. Henn. 2015. "Imperialisten, Spione oder Retter? Zur Charakterisierung von Direktinvestitionen aus Russland, Indien und China in deutschen Tageszeitungen." *Zeitschrift für Wirtschaftsgeographie* 59(1): 119.

GTAI [Germany Trade & Invest], and ZVEI [German Electrical and Electronic Manufacturers' Association]. 2014. *Foreign Direct Investment*. www.zvei.org/Publikationen/ZVEI_Direktinvestionen_2014_Englisch.pdf, accessed 2016, August 17.

Haves, J., Vitols, S., and P. Wittke. 2014. "Financialization and Ownership Change: Challenges for the German Model of Labour Relations." In *Financialization, New Investment Funds, and Labour: An International Comparison*, edited by H. Gospel, A. Pendleton, and S. Vitols, 148–175. Oxford: Oxford University Press.

Jowett, P., and F. Jowett. 2011. *Private Equity: The German Experience*. Basingstoke: Palgrave Macmillan.

Kaplan, S., and P. Strömberg. 2009. "Leveraged Buyouts and Private Equity." *Journal of Economic Perspectives* 23(1): 121–146.

Klodt, H., and B. Christensen. 2007. "Home Market Effects of Foreign Direct Investment: The Case of Germany." *Außenwirtschaft* 62(1): 63–76.

Lippert, I., and U. Jürgens. 2012. Corporate Governance und Arbeitnehmerbeteiligung in den Spielarten des Kapitalismus: Pfade der Unternehmensentwicklung in der Automobilzulieferindustrie in Deutschland, Schweden und den USA. Berlin: Sigma.

Preqin. 2014. "Private Equity Spotlight: 2014 in Review." www.preqin.com/spotlight, accessed 2015, March 22.

Scheuplein, C. 2012. "Industrial Restructuring by Financial Investors? Buy-and-Build Strategies in the German Automotive Supplier Industry from 2000 to 2010." In *Industrial Transition: New Global-Local Patterns of Production, Work, and Innovation*, edited by M. Fromhold-Eisebith, and M. Fuchs, 49–64. Farnham and Burlington: Ashgate.

Scheuplein, C. 2015. Private Equity Monitor 2013: Eine aktuelle Bestandsaufnahme zur Übernahmetätigkeit von Private Equity Investoren in Deutschland. Mitbestimmungsförderung Report, 7. Düsseldorf: Hans-Böckler-Stiftung.

Talmor, E., and F. Vasvari. 2011. *International Private Equity*. Chichester: Wiley.

UNCTAD [United Nations Conference on Trade and Development]. 2006. *World Investment Report 2006*. New York and Geneva: United Nations Publications.

UNCTAD [United Nations Conference on Trade and Development]. 2015. *World Investment Report 2015*. New York and Geneva: United Nations Publications.

Womack, J., Jones, D., and D. Roos. 1990. *The Machine That Changed the World*. New York: Rawson Associates.

ZEW [Centre for European Economic Research] and NIW [Lower Saxony Institute for Economic Research]. 2009. *Die Bedeutung der Automobilindustrie für die deutsche Volkswirtschaft im europäischen Kontext*. Hanover and Mannheim: ZEW and NIW.

Zhang, H. 2015. China's Outward Foreign Direct Investment: Theories and Strategies. Hong Kong: Enrich Professional Publishers.

10 Reactions to China's Cross-border Investment and International Investment Law

Karl P. S. Sauvant and Michael D. Nolan

Introduction

China is now one of the world's most important outward investors. The salient features of the country's cross-border direct investments include that its FDI has grown rapidly, that state-owned enterprises play a dominant role and that outward investment takes place within an elaborated regulatory framework. Not surprisingly, the rapid rise of China's outward FDI—and especially the M&As increasingly used as the principal mode of entry into foreign markets—has received considerable, often sceptical, attention on the part of host countries' newspapers, the business community and governments—warranting trust-building endeavours from stakeholders. China needs to adapt to these developments, not only in its national policies but also in its approach to its international investment agreements, in the framework within which Chinese firms invest abroad.

Salient Features of China's Outward FDI and Policy Issues Related Thereto

China has become a major player in the world FDI market. The country's outward FDI flows grew from US$7 billion in 2001 to US$116 billion in 2014, for an accumulated stock of US$730 billion (UNCTAD STAT n.d.). In terms of outflows, this made China the single most important *home* country among *all emerging markets* (UNCTAD 2014, 7) and the third-largest among *all* home countries. In fact, China's outward FDI flows have almost caught up with China's inward FDI flows: in 2001, the percentage of outward FDI flows as compared to inward FDI flows was 15%; in 2013, it was 90% (UNCTAD STAT n.d.).

By the end of 2012, China's 16,000 multinational enterprises had established about 22,000 foreign affiliates in 179 countries and territories (MOFCOM 2013). Chinese firms have invested substantially in both developed and developing countries, increasingly using M&As as a mode of entry. Chinese's FDI distribution across sectors and geographic regions is, however, difficult to ascertain, as more than two-thirds of China's non-financial sector outflows are channelled via financial centres and tax havens (MOFCOM

2012); consequently, the countries and sectors in which they are ultimately invested is unknown. It seems likely, however, that services and natural resources are the most important sectors.

At the same time, these figures should not disguise that, globally, China's average share in world FDI outflows averaged only 5% from 2010 to 2012 while its share in the world's outward FDI stock was 2% in 2012 (UNCTAD STAT n.d.).

Apart from its speedy rise, there are two other features that characterise China's outward FDI. The first is that, in contrast to virtually all other major outward investors, state-owned enterprises account for a substantial share of China's outward FDI flows and stock. By the end of 2011, the 113 central state-owned enterprises controlled by the State-owned Assets Supervision and Administration Commission (SASAC n.d.) alone accounted for 66% of China's non-financial FDI outflows and 76% of China's non-financial outward FDI stock in 2011. This raises the question of whether China's outward FDI serves purposes other than commercial ones (Sauvant et al. 2012). As discussed in the following, these concerns have led to the creation or strengthening of regulatory review processes of incoming M&As, especially for certain sensitive industries. Obama's September 2012 veto of a Chinese windmill project near a military base in Oregon—the first such veto in 22 years—is emblematic of these concerns (Inside U.S. Trade 2012).

The second feature relates to China's relatively sophisticated regulatory framework dealing with outward FDI. This framework has moved, within two decades, from restricting to encouraging (Sauvant and Chen 2013, 141–163). Embedded in an overall development strategy, China's "going out" strategy has two principal purposes: (1) to facilitate and support outward FDI to create globally competitive Chinese firms and (2) to encourage outward FDI that contributes directly to China's development, especially by obtaining natural resources, promoting exports or strengthening China's technological base. The government has put in place an institutional structure and various instruments ("home country measures") for this purpose.

Although a number of government institutions participate in outward FDI, the principal ones are the National Development and Reform Commission and the Ministry of Commerce. In 2006, these and other institutions established a "sector direction policy" that provides guidance for specific promotional measures on the basis of investment that is encouraged, allowed and prohibited (Sauvant and Chen 2013, 141–163). The specific instruments used to encourage outward FDI include various subsidies (including financial and fiscal support), priority rights (e.g. access to loans, to foreign exchange or to overseas financing), expedited approval and tax rebates on (or waivers for) the export of goods. Within the formal regulatory framework, these home country measures appear equally available to both state-owned enterprises and private enterprises.

Finally, a network of 128 bilateral investment treaties as of 1 June 2013 (UNCTAD 2013), as well as a number of other international investment agreements, provides protection to China's outward investors. Although these treaties were originally concluded with inward FDI in mind, they have evolved over time to reflect China's evolution as an outward investor.

Yet, although China's regulatory framework for outward FDI appears sophisticated, the approval process is complex and cumbersome. With further growth of outward FDI, this approval process must be simplified, if not replaced by mere notifications: given the growing number of Chinese outward investors and their foreign affiliates, examining and approving each individual investment decision might simply overwhelm the authorities. Broader reform efforts seem to foreshadow such revamping: as of May 2014, only deals valued at more than US$1 billion require official approval, as compared to the previous value threshold at more than 100 million (NDRC n.d.). It would also be more efficient to create a "one-stop shop" for the measures available to qualifying outward investors. The combination of both approaches would lead to control measures regarding outward FDI being replaced by incentives to support the government's broader economic development goals. This would make home country measures even more important, to encourage outward FDI that contributes as much as possible to the country's development.

With China becoming a net outward investor, the government's interest in protecting its outward investments may trump its interest to protect its own firms from inward FDI in certain sectors. This, in turn, likely will have implications for China's policy stance on international investment agreements. In July 2013, China and the United States reached a watershed accord to continue their negotiations of a bilateral investment treaty on the basis of pre-establishment national treatment and the negative list approach to exceptions from such treatment (Li 2014), which pinpoints the shift in emphasis in the country's perspective from a host country to a home country.

Furthermore, China is not the only country that has used home country measures to promote national objectives regarding the outward FDI of its firms. Virtually all developed countries pursue similar policies and support them through appropriate instruments (Sauvant et al. 2014). Hence, if home country measures become an object of international negotiations, a number of countries would be directly affected.

For some developed countries, however, it is undesirable to help firms investing abroad, as investors from emerging markets, and especially state-owned enterprises from China, have become significant outward investors. Home country measures have been seen as giving special advantages to state-owned enterprises, distorting the competitive outward FDI landscape in the markets in which they invest. Based on the concept of "competitive neutrality" (OECD 2005) no entity in an international market should have undue competitive advantages vis-à-vis its competitors. Thus, measures to help firms in their outward FDI, even when available equally to both public and private entities, may be evaluated in terms of their impact on competitive neutrality.

To date, international discussions have focused on advantages enjoyed by state-owned enterprises, despite the fact that (1) home country measures are available to both public and private firms and (2) there is no systematic evidence that home country measures provide state-owned enterprises with competitive advantages, regardless of whether state-owned enterprises are based in developed economies or emerging markets (Sauvant et al. 2014). A recent study of the OECD (Organisation for Economic Co-operation and Development) concluded the same, noting that "[e]xisting information on such advantages is often either anecdotal or limited to individual cases" (Kowalski et al. 2013).

The competitive neutrality discussion continues in the OECD, but has also gained traction in the negotiations of the Trans-Pacific Partnership Agreement, with a view toward imposing discipline on state-owned enterprises. Depending on the outcome of these negotiations, the support that China's state-owned enterprises obtain when investing abroad may become a difficult policy issue.

The Perception and Reception of China's Outward FDI in Host Countries

China's outward FDI faces considerable attention and rising scepticism (see *Martina Fuchs* and *Martin Schalljo*, and *Sophie Golinski* and *Sebastian Henn* in this volume). This scepticism stems from the speed with which this investment has grown, the leading role of state-owned enterprises in China's outward FDI, potential negative effects associated with FDI (such as foreign control over critical resources and industries, the delocalisation of research and development capacities, a reluctance to process natural resources in host countries, poor working conditions, adverse environmental effects and uncompetitive advantages and behaviour), the fear that host countries do not benefit fully from this investment, perceived unfair competition, the negative image of the home country in some host countries and the fear that China's outward FDI might compromise national security (see *Susan M. Walcott* and *Ingo Liefner* in this volume). A review of important host countries among developed countries and emerging markets for China's outward FDI sheds more light on these matters[1]. Chinese greenfield investment, however, is generally welcome (as opposed to M&As), notwithstanding concerns regarding FDI in natural resources and telecommunications.

In most of the host countries to Chinese FDI, *newspapers* tend to represent a more critical constituency—albeit unevenly (Gallagher 2013). National security concerns are particularly salient in the U.S., France and the UK. Chinese FDI receives attention in natural resource-rich countries, such as Australia, Canada, Kazakhstan and Zambia. The fear is that, when critical resources are controlled from abroad, the benefits associated with such projects may not be equitably distributed between foreign investors and host countries, including environmental concerns (Pheakdey 2013) and fear of imported labour and poor working conditions (Zoljarga 2013). The business press in some countries, however, are more neutral in tone. In the U.S. for example, Chinese investments in depressed areas, such as Detroit, were positively commented on (Chen 2010).

The *business community* itself is not strongly engaged in the public debate on this subject. Big businesses typically support an open international investment regime that provides strong protections for investors and investments and access to markets. Moreover, China is an important export market and host country for many firms, which renders enterprises reluctant to advocate restrictive policies. Given perceived competitive threats, however, firms and business associations may lobby the government to take action, as the arrival of new competitors is rarely welcome. In the case of FDI by state-owned enterprises, concerns regarding possible competitive advantages are more acute (BCTT n.d.).

Finally, *governments* reflect the conflicted attitude of other stakeholders. On balance, however, government *executives* maintain a welcoming attitude, both towards incoming FDI, in general, and from China, in particular. Chinese FDI was especially welcome in European countries affected by the euro crisis, as a means to forestall the bankruptcy of domestic firms and re-launch economic growth. Some countries introduced regulations to facilitate such investment. For example Ireland introduced new regulations simplifying visa processes (Ireland Houses of the Oireachtas 2012). In Russia and Kazakhstan, authorities welcome Chinese FDI, although there are also fears that China's role might become too strong (Panibratov 2014). Southeast Asian countries are closely linked with China through regional value chains, and governments therefore regard Chinese FDI as a positive factor for their development.

Government executives also have concerns, however, and are subject to pressure from their *legislatures*, or individual members of such bodies. Concerns relate to various issues but typically focus on national security and the role of state-owned enterprises in China's outward FDI. Security concerns are particularly pronounced in the U.S., where the CFIUS (Committee on Foreign Investment in the United States)—consisting of members of various Departments of the United States government—reviews and, depending on the outcome of the reviews, investigates M&As by foreign companies in the country. If the CFIUS finds that the national security of the U.S. is negatively affected by a particular M&A, it can require mitigation measures or, ultimately, recommend to the president of the U.S. that the transaction be vetoed. Although the CFIUS regularly reviews M&As, only twice in that institution's history did it recommend vetoing a transaction. Most recently (in 2012), this involved the purchase by Ralls Corporation, a wholly owned U.S. subsidiary of Sany Group (a Chinese heavy-machinery manufacturing company), of four limited liability companies previously formed to develop wind farms in northern-central Oregon; the assets of these companies were located in close proximity to a military base. Ralls had to divest itself fully from the companies involved (Schlager et al. 2014).

In Australia and Canada, governmental concerns focus more on the control of natural resources and the net benefits associated with their exploitation, although other tests are employed as well. The discussions surrounding the takeover of Australia's LYNAS (Domain-b.com 2009) and the acquisition of Canada's NEXEN (Austen 2012) exemplify this. In the first case, Australia's Investment Review Board disallowed the transaction out of concern that it would threaten supplies of rare earths to non-Chinese customers (Sydney Morning Herald 2011). The second transaction was approved by Canadian regulators, as well as the CFIUS, whose approval was needed as NEXEN had assets in the U.S. (Rocha 2013). In India, questions relating to Chinese FDI and security were raised in parliament (Satyanand 2015). Perhaps the best-known parliamentary reaction towards Chinese FDI in general was a 2005 resolution adopted by the U.S. House of Representatives overwhelmingly condemning the attempted takeover of the U.S. firm UNOCAL by CNOOC of China (U.S. Congress 2005).

These various pressures are reflected in the fact that a number of countries have strengthened or established review mechanisms for incoming FDI, focused on M&As by state-owned enterprises. Countries must walk a fine line between mitigating concerns and maintaining an attractive investment climate for Chinese multinational enterprises. These mechanisms focus on national security and net benefits for the host country, including concerns about state-owned enterprises being advantaged by subsidies.

Although the competitive advantage concern is now discussed in international negotiations, many countries have strengthened their mechanisms to review incoming M&As to ensure that such transactions are in their national interest. In the U.S., the Foreign Investment and National Security Act, adopted in 2007, strengthened the role of the Committee on Foreign Investment in the United States in reviewing incoming M&As. Among other things, it requires that incoming M&As by state-owned enterprises be notified and subjected to investigations. In December 2012, Canada issued guidelines to clarify the investment process applicable to acquisitions of a certain size by state-owned enterprises, stating that

> [e]ach case will be examined on its own merits; however, given the inherent risks posed by foreign state-owned enterprise acquisitions in the Canadian oil sands the Minister of Industry will find the acquisition of control of a Canadian oil sands business by a foreign state-owned enterprise to be net benefit to Canada on an exceptional basis only.
>
> (Government of Canada 2012)

In February 2008, Australia announced a new policy requiring the Treasurer to examine specific issues when considering applications for investments by foreign governments and their agencies, including notions of independence and security (Australian Government Foreign Investment Review Board 2010).

The measures taken by these three countries create the tools to block, if necessary, undesirable M&As—both from China and other countries. It is noteworthy, however, that these actions occurred in reaction to China's rapid rise in outward FDI, and the screening mechanisms are particularly strong for M&As by state-owned enterprises. From China's perspective, government activities impacting Chinese (state-owned enterprise dominated) outward FDI through host country review mechanisms are, not surprisingly, of concern.

In sum, the perception and reception of China's growing outward FDI in China's principal host countries have been decidedly mixed regarding both the entry strategies of Chinese multinational enterprises into host countries and the reactions to such investment by various host country constituencies. As recently stated by the governor of China's Central Bank, "[d]ifferent entities have behaved differently. There may have been some phenomena of Chinese investors [that were] not so good, not so satisfactory" (Blas 2014). As China's outward FDI grows, it may well be that scepticism towards such investment will continue to grow. The question then becomes, "What can be done to deal with the reaction to China's outward FDI in order to avoid a backlash and build trust?"

At the national level, state-owned enterprises—as the main outward investors—have a responsibility to make sure that their investments abroad are well planned, prepared and received. This is particularly important when investments take the form of M&As and are in sensitive industries or involve iconic targets. Once established, state-owned enterprises must make additional efforts to be, and be recognised as, good corporate citizens. This can be achieved for example by sourcing from local suppliers, employing nationals in high corporate positions, becoming members of local associations and engaging in various corporate social responsibility activities. Additionally, affiliates could support the Group of 7 initiative of establishing a global facility that helps developing countries negotiate large-scale contracts with multinational enterprises. In its June 2014 Summit, the Group of 7 announced "a new initiative on Strengthening Assistance for Complex Contract Negotiations" (European Commission 2015).

China's government also has a role to play. For example, it could more closely enforce the various instruments already in place to guide the behaviour of its foreign investors abroad. More ambitiously, China could complement its "going-out" strategy with a systematic and broad-based "going-in" strategy (Sauvant and Chen 2014) to maximise not only the benefits of the country's outward FDI for China but also for the development of host countries in which Chinese firms invest—in short, embody the characteristics of sustainable FDI. Such a "going-in" strategy would not only enforce the current regulatory framework for the behaviour of Chinese multinational enterprises abroad but also monitor its implementation, expand it to focus on emerging sustainability issues (e.g. CO_2-neutral foreign affiliates), make voluntary guidelines mandatory or condition the availability of certain support measures for outward FDI on the observation of rules of corporate social responsibility. Adoption of a "going-in" strategy by China along these lines could serve as a model for other home countries, both developed and developing.

Most important, the mixed perception and reception of China's outward FDI in host countries strengthen China's interest in international investment agreements that protect China's outward FDI and help secure access to markets. At the same time, China would want to protect its "going-out" strategy and the various instruments it has put in place in the context of this strategy.

China's Changing Approach to International Investment Agreements

As mentioned earlier, China's international investment agreements programme, which was entirely focused on inbound investment since its inception in 1982, now keenly reflects on China's positioning as an outward investor.

Indeed, in its first generation of bilateral investment treaties, concluded between 1982 and 1998, China took a restrictive approach to foreign investment protection, notably concerning dispute resolution. China was then a predominantly capital-importing country and had little incentive to place its trust in a dispute-resolution mechanism that could impinge its sovereignty, which is why these first bilateral investment treaties only allowed investors to commence arbitration proceedings against a host state for "disputes involving the amount of compensation for expropriation" (China-Mongolia BIT 1991, Art. 8, 3). In later generations of bilateral investment treaties, China broadened its consent to arbitrate "any disputes concerning investments" (China-Germany BIT 2003, Art. 9). This broadened consent to arbitration at the turn of the century coincided with an impending announcement of China's "going-out" strategy and the subsequent 50-fold rise in outward investment (UNCTAD STAT n.d.).

At the same time, China adopted standards of protection of foreign investment similar to those prevalent in Western countries, such as provision of fair and equitable treatment "in accordance with customary international law" (China-Peru FTA 2009, Art. 132) or ensuring full protection and security in accordance with "commonly accepted rules of international law" (China-New Zealand FTA 2008, Art. 143). It also departed from its position not to grant national treatment to foreign investors equal to that afforded to its own citizens when it agreed in July 2013 to granting national treatment at the pre-establishment stage of any investment (except if made in a prohibited sector contained in an exhaustive negative list; Li 2014).

All the while, China made sure that its state-owned enterprises (accounting for more than half of total FDI) would fall within the ambit of bilateral treaty protections through the insertion of language such as "public institutions" (China-Korea BIT, Art. 1(2)b) or "governmentally owned or controlled" (China-Mexico BIT 2008, Art. 1; China-New Zealand FTA 2008, Art. 11) investors.

In practice, however, there seems to have been some reluctance to pursue investor–state arbitration under Chinese bilateral investment treaties, despite their large number and the broadening of China's consent to arbitration. Although some authors cite cultural reasons (Wang 2011, 19), the reasons may be more pragmatic. Regarding inbound investment, foreign investors may be discouraged from risking resources where the chances of enforcing the award in China may be slim, as reflected by China's current legal landscape. Indeed, China expressly excluded enforceability of investor–state disputes when it acceded to the United Nations Convention on Enforcement of Foreign Arbitral Awards (Schreuer 2009, 930), and in any event, China's laws do not allow enforcement against state-owned property (Wang 2011, 24–25).

Quo Vadis?

China's transition towards becoming a major outward investor has led to a profound reformation of its investment treaty regime. The data demonstrate how China has evolved from a purely capital-importing country to a capital-exporting country. Yet, the size of China's outward FDI stock was merely US$ 730 billion in 2014, significantly smaller than that of the United States (plus US$ 6.3 trillion).

Juxtaposing the raw economic data with the investment treaty practice of China, one cannot help but notice the correlation between the language adopted in its international investment agreements and its movement on the investment spectrum. Although China has had an active bilateral investment treaty programme since the early 1980s, it is only in its recent international investment agreements that China adopted the hallmarks of EU or U.S. international investment agreements.

It remains to be seen, however, whether China will further embrace investment protection standards newly adopted by Western economies such as proceedings transparency or protection of domestic labour and of the environment (U.S. Model BIT 2012, Arts. 29 & Art. 13 & Art. 12). In light of global efforts towards encouraging "sustainable" FDI, spearheaded by the OECD and UNCTAD (the United Nations Conference on Trade and Development), China may follow the lead of other capital-exporting nations. If this is the future trajectory of China's international investment agreements, there is hope for a largely uniform international investment law and policy regime.

Acknowledgements

The authors would like to thank Louis Brennan, Filip De Beule, Christoph Dörrenbächer, Noah Rubins, Anthea Roberts, Stephan Schill and Wenhua Shan for their helpful peer reviews, as well as Camilla Gambarini, Schahram Ghalebegi, Thomas Jost, Nancy Lee, Andrei Panibratov and Adrian Torres, who prepared the host country analyses on which the second section of this chapter is based, and Kamel Aït-El-Hadj, Victor Chen, Monica DiFonzo, Ksenia Gal, Premila Nazareth Satyanand, Zhang Sheng, Yina Yang and You Zhou for their very helpful assistance in the preparation of this chapter. Special thanks go to Camilla Gambarini for helping to finalise this manuscript, which is based on a chapter by the authors on the same topic contained in *Regulating the Visible Hand? The Institutional Implications of Chinese State Capitalism*, edited by B. L. Liebman and C. J. Milhaupt, 285–312, New York: Oxford University Press, and a substantially longer version in the *Journal of International Economic Law*, Nov. 2015, 1–42.

Note

1. Extensive research was conducted between early September 2013 and the end of March 2014 on countries that accounted for some two thirds of China's outward FDI stock in 2011 (as reported by MOFCOM—see MOFCOM 2012—not counting Chinese FDI in tax havens and financial centers). Primarily newspapers and official statements in the countries concerned were consulted.

References

Austen, I. 2012. "Canada Clears $15 Billion Chinese Takeover of an Energy Company." *The New York Times*, December 7. http://dealbook.nytimes.com/2012/12/07/canada-clears-15-billion-chinese-takeover-of-an-energy-company/?_php=true&_type=blogs&_r=0.

Australian Government Foreign Investment Review Board. 2010. "2008/2009 Annual Report." www.firb.gov.au/content/Publications/AnnualReports/2008-2009/_downloads/2008-09_FIRB_AR.pdf, accessed 2015, November 25.

BCTT [Business Coalition for Transatlantic Trade]. n.d. "Competition Policy." www.transatlantictrade.org/issues/competition-policy/, accessed 2014, July 25.

Blas, J. 2014. "China's Central Bank Chief Admits Difficulties with Africa." *Financial Times*, May 22. www.ft.com/intl/cms/s/0/5b212302-e1c9-11e3-b7c4-00144feabdc0.html#axzz3EolVbxrE, accessed 2015 November 25.

Chen, K. 2010. "U.S. cities seek to woo Chinese investment" *The Wall Street Journal*, http://online.wsj.com/news/articles/SB10001424052702303410404575151593460208482, accessed 2017, March 28.

China-Germany BIT [Agreement between the People's Republic of China and the Federal Republic of Germany on the Encouragement and Reciprocal Protection of Investments China-Germany Bilateral Investment Treaty]). 2003, December 1.

China-Korea BIT [Agreement between the Government of the People's Republic of China and the Government of the Republic of Korea on the Promotion and Protection of Investments]. 2007, September 7.

China-Mexico BIT [Agreement between the Government of the United Mexican States and the Government of the People's Republic of China on the Promotion and Reciprocal Protection of Investments]). 2008, July 11.

China-Mongolia BIT [Agreement between the Government of the People's Republic of China and the Government of the Mongolian People's Republic Concerning the Encouragement and Reciprocal Protection of Investments]. 1991, August 25.

China-New Zealand FTA [Free Trade Agreement between the Government of New Zealand and the Government of the People's Republic of China]. 2008, April 7.

China-Peru FTA [Free Trade Agreement between the Government of the People's Republic of China and the Government of the Republic of Peru]. 2009, April 28.

Domain-b.com. 2009. "China's CNMC to Acquire Australia's Lynas for A$505 Million." *Domain—b.com*, May 2. www.domain-b.com/industry/Mining/20090502_china_nonferrous.html, accessed 2015, November 15.

European Commission. 2015. "The Brussels G7 Summit Declaration." http://europa.eu/rapid/press-release_MEMO-14-402_en.htm, accessed 2015, November 25.

Gallagher, K. 2013. "Latin America Playing a Risky Game by Welcoming in the Chinese Dragon." *The Guardian*, May 30. www.theguardian.com/global-development/poverty-matters/2013/may/30/latin-america-risky-chinese-dragon.

Government of Canada. 2012. "News Release, Policy Statement and Revised Guidelines for Investments by State-Owned Enterprises." http://news.gc.ca/web/article-en.do?nid=711489, accessed 2015, November 25.

Inside U.S. Trade. 2012. "In Rare Move, Obama Unwinds Chinese Acquisition of U.S. Wind Farms." *Inside U.S. Trade* 12(39): 16–17.

Ireland Houses of the Oireachtas. 2012. "Immigrant Investor Programme and Start-Up Entrepreneur Scheme: Statements." *Seanad Éireann Debate* 213(6). http://debates.oireachtas.ie/seanad/2012/02/09/00006.asp, accessed 2015, November 25.

Kowalski, P., Büge, M., Sztajerowska, M., and M. Egeland. 2013. *State-Owned Enterprises: Trade Effects and Policy Implications*. OECD Trade Policy Paper 147. Paris: OECD.

Li, J. 2014. "China, US 'Pragmatic about Pact.'" *China Daily*, January 16. www.chinadailyasia.com/business/2014-01/16/content_15112679.html, accessed 2015, November 25.

MOFCOM [Ministry of Commerce of the People's Republic of China]). 2012. "2011 Statistical Bulletin of China's Outward Foreign Direct Investment." http://images.mofcom.gov.cn/hzs/201309/20130923082710756.pdf, accessed 2015, November 25.

MOFCOM [Ministry of Commerce of the People's Republic of China]. 2013. "Summary 2012 Statistical Bulletin of China's Outward Foreign Direct Investment." www.mofcom.gov.cn/article/tongjiziliao/dgzz/201309/20130900295526.shtml, accessed 2015, November 25.

NDRC [China National Development and Reform Commission]. n.d. "The Approval of Overseas Investment Projects and Record Management Procedures." www.ndrc.gov.cn/zcfb/zcfbl/201404/t20140410_606600.html, accessed 2016, December 4.

OECD. 2005. "OECD Guidelines on Corporate Governance of State-Owned Enterprises." www.oecd.org/corporate/ca/corporategovernanceofstate-ownedenterprises/34803211.pdf, accessed 2015, November 25.

Panibratov, A. 2014. "Perceptions of Chinese FDI in Neighboring Emerging Economies: Different Groups' Opinions in Russia and Kazakhstan." Dissertation. St. Petersburg State University, Russia (on file with the authors).

Pheakdey, H. 2013. "Chinese Investment and Aid in Cambodia a Controversial Affair." www.eastasiaforum.org/2013/07/16/chinese-investment-and-aid-in-cambodia-a-controversial-affair, accessed 2015, November 25.

Rocha, E. 2013. "CNOOC Closes $15.1 Billion Acquisition of Canada's Nexen." www.reuters.com/article/2013/02/25/usnexen-cnooc-idUSBRE91O1A420130225#mugGmRH4ik8KqepB.97, accessed 2015, November 25.

SASAC n.d. "State-Owned Assets Supervision and Administration Commission of the State Council." www.sasac.gov.cn/n1180/n1226/n2425/index.html, accessed 2014, July 17.

Satyanand, P. N. 2015. "What Do India's MPs Want to Know about FDI: An Analysis of Written FDI Questions in Parliament (2 July 2009–21 February 2014)." www.ncaer.org/publication_details.php?pID=242, accessed 2015, November 25.

Sauvant, K. P., and V. Z. Chen. 2013. "China's Regulatory Framework for Outward Foreign Direct Investment." *China Economic Journal* 7(1): 141–163.

Sauvant, K. P., and V. Z. Chen. 2014. "China Needs to Complement Its 'Going-Out' Policy with a 'Going-In' Strategy." *Columbia FDI Perspectives* 121. http://ccsi.columbia.edu/publications/columbia-fdi-perspectives/.

Sauvant, K. P., Economou, P., Gal, K., Lim, S., and W. P. Wilinsk. 2014. "Trends in FDI, Home Country Measures and Competitive Neutrality." In *Yearbook on International Investment Law and Policy 2012–2013*, edited by A. K. Bjorklund, 3–108. New York: Oxford University Press.

Sauvant, K. P., Sachs, L. E., and W. P. F. Schmit Jongbloed. 2012. *Sovereign Investment: Concerns and Policy Reactions*. New York: Oxford University Press.

Schlager, I. A., Beahn, J. M., Tuesley, M., Gruenspecht, J. F., and J. P. Kabealo. 2014. "Court Finds CFIUS Violated Ralls Corporation's Due Process Rights." www.skadden.com/insights/court-finds-cfius-violated-ralls-corporations-due-process-rights, accessed 2015, November 25.

Schreuer, C. 2009. *The ICSID Convention: A Commentary*. 2nd Edition. New York: Cambridge University Press.

Sydney Morning Herald. 2011. "Australia Blocked China Investment on Supply Concerns." *Sydney Morning Herald*, February 15. www.smh.com.au/business/world-business/australia-blocked-china-investment-on-supply-concerns-20110215-1au8x.html

UNCTAD. 2013. "Full List of Bilateral Investment Agreements concluded, 1 June 2013." http://unctad.org/Sections/dite_pcbb/docs/bits_china.pdf, accessed 2015, November 25.

UNCTAD. 2014. "World Investment Report 2014: Investing in the SDGs: An Action Plan." http://unctad.org/en/PublicationsLibrary/wir2014_en.pdf, accessed 2015, November 25.

UNCTAD STAT. n.d. "Report Folders." http://unctadstat.unctad.org/ReportFolders/reportFolders.aspx, accessed 2015, November 25.

U.S. Congress, House of Representatives. 2005. "H. Res. 334, 109th Cong.: Expressing the Sense of the House of Representatives That a Chinese State-Owned Energy Company Exercising Control of Critical United States Energy Infrastructure and Energy Production Capacity Could Take Action That Would Threaten to Impair the National Security of the United States." www.govtrack.us/congress/bills/109/hres344/text, accessed 2015, November 25.

U.S. Model BIT [U.S. Model Bilateral Investment Treaty]). 2012. https://ustr.gov/sites/default/files/BIT%20text%20for%20ACIEP%20Meeting.pdf, accessed 2016, December 5.

Wang, G. 2011. "Investor-State Dispute Settlement in China." *Transnational Dispute Management* 5(7), www.transnational-dispute-management.com/article.asp?key=1764, accessed 2015, May 29.

Zoljarga, M. 2013. "Contractors Bring Illegal Workers While Mongolians Remain Unemployed." *The UB Post*, December 17. http://ubpost.mongolnews.mn/?p=7031.

11 Chinese Outward FDI in Germany and the U.S.

An Assessment of National and Subnational Location Strategies

Susan M. Walcott and Ingo Liefner

Introduction

This examination compares Chinese outward foreign direct investment (COFDI) in two advanced economies: Germany—the European leading economy—and the south-eastern region of the United States, a dynamic and diverse multi-state area. We seek a pattern within the context of FDI from developing countries in regard to the location decision for outward FDI that targets developed host countries and regions within them. Previous research examined motivations for Chinese firms to expand globally, along with the nature and effect of their acquisitions, but a gap remains in the investigation of their location targeting (Cardoza et al. 2014). This research considers characteristics of sending countries and host regions at the national, state, metropolitan regional and firm-level scales, particularly because the state/*Länder* is where significant location incentives are proffered, and outreach often occurs (United States Chamber of Commerce 2012). Our hypothesis asserts that business strategies and location decisions involved with COFDI are closely interrelated as they apply to host countries.

Location decisions are of great importance to any firm because plans are difficult to reverse and have a profound impact on revenues and costs. Companies differ in their abilities to acquire and process information about locations, so less capable firms tend to follow the location decisions of successful peers (Pred 1967). This behaviour contributes to firm clustering and explains why companies avoid relocations as long as the conditions at the present location do not threaten the profitability of operations. Today's Chinese investors possess very little experience regarding functioning abroad or in a competitive market economy environment. Limited ability to understand information about locations can easily lead to costly mistakes. We thus further hypothesise that Chinese investors prefer maintaining the locations of acquired companies. In cases of greenfield investment, Western firms are expected to assess information on location alternatives and choose places that offer access to customers or to localised assets (Kuemmerle 1999). We hypothesise that the location decisions of COFDI companies are based on established business clusters or on local networks of Chinese firms.

Our focus on Chinese FDI in the U.S. and Europe concerns the actions of these foreign firms regarding investment motives, experience, network operations and public incentives on location decisions. From 2008 to 2009 annual COFDI flows to Europe increased by four to six times and, by 2011, jumped by 2.5 times (see Table 11.1). Although exact amounts differ by source, as discussed in the following methodology section, overall movements and trends exhibit a consistent shape. Starting generally from less than 1 billion annually prior to 2008, COFDI to the U.S. and Europe accelerated quickly during the recession. Contributions of this research with policy implications point to geographic features that attract investment beyond pecuniary incentives. We find overall that the national origin of COFDI shapes corporate behaviour more than the particularities of the host locations examined, thus merging theoretical frameworks on business utilisation strategy from the Uppsala School's emphasis on business networks (Johanson and Vahlne 1977, 2009) and Dunning's (1991, 2000) eclectic paradigm of key ownership–location–internalisation (OLI) factors (Si et al. 2013).

Previous examinations of COFDI generally conclude that because of the various forms of ownership involved, extensions to current theoretical models are needed to better inform policies and strategies (Alon et al. 2011). Dunning's classic OLI, or "eclectic", model, considers the propensity of firms to invest abroad as a reflection of their economic development stage (Dunning 2000). Advantages of owning a firm that functions abroad include acquisition of a known trademark, techniques of production and marketing suitable for the foreign market, employees with skills such as the relevant foreign language, market knowledge and political–business connections needed to establish a position in that market. Location factors include acquisition of materials needed for the product, a better wage–skills fit for labour, obtaining incentives for investment and avoiding tariffs and/or other trade barriers by producing in the host country.

Companies from developing countries undergoing a modernisation transition benefit from a latecomer advantage by learning from corporate predecessors, thereby reducing the challenges of globalising (Mathews 2006). In order to successfully catch-up, firms utilise strategies to expand their storehouse of knowledge and absorptive capacity to embed and utilise the lessons learned. Costs of internationalisation versus cost reduction through learning are at the centre of the Uppsala School approach focusing on learning behaviours. Benefits must be sufficiently high to offset the uncertainties of being a foreign outsider, which Dunning's Eclectic Paradigm and the Uppsala Model both see as driving construction of networks for learning from internationalisation. By asserting that a firm is essentially an information exchange organisation, the Uppsala Model extends the paradigm whereas subsequent versions of the latter incorporate the key importance of interacting networks.

Table 11.1 COFDI to the U.S. and Germany

Value in Million US $	*YR 2005*	*YR 2006*	*YR 2007*	*YR 2008*	*YR 2009*	*YR 2010*	*YR 2011*	*YR 2012*	*YR 2013*
	FDI China--> USA								
USDOC Bureau of Economic Analysis	435	785	584	1105	1624	3300	3598	6943	8073
UNCTAD	232	198	196	462	909	1308	1811	4048	3873
China Statistical Yearbook	232	198	196	462	909	1308	1811	4048	3873
Rhodium Group	2000	178	345	747	696	4600	4800	7500	14000
	FDI China--> EU27								
UNCTAD	190	129	1045	467	2967	5963	7561	6120	
China Statistical Yearbook (Europe as the whole continent inclusive Russia)	505	598	1540	876	3353	6760	8251	7035	5949
Rhodium Group	700	800	1500	1000	2400	3000	10500	12000	
	FDI China--> Germany								
UNCTAD	129	77	239	183	179	412	512	799	
China Statistical Yearbook	129	767	239	183	179	412	512	799	911
Bundesbank (Million €)	235	328	428	594	681	853	1142	1338	1195

Source: Data sources compiled by the authors from the following data sources: http://bea.gov/international/di1fdiop.htm; http://unctad.org/en/Pages/DIAE/FDI%20Statistics/FDI-Statistics-Bilateral.aspx; www.stats.gov.cn/tjsj/ndsj/2014/indexeh.htm; http://rhg.com/interactive/china-investment-monitor; http://rhg.com/notes/chinese-investment-europe-vs-the-united-states; www.bundesbank.de/Navigation/DE/Statistiken/Aussenwirtschaft/Direktinvestitionen/Bestandsangaben/Tabellen/tabellen.html).

Methodology

Official statistics provide details about international capital movements, but our main focus is at the level of firms and regions. As structures and developments in two regions of Germany and the U.S. are compared, data incompatibilities limit the value of official statistics (cf. Table 11.1). Information and data are therefore combined from different sources to establish an aggregate pattern of Chinese investment, types, motivations and effects. Research reports, web pages, corporate reports, media coverage and case studies on Chinese FDI are augmented by 82 interviews carried out from 2011 to 2013 with managers, firm owners, representatives of business associations, government institutions and independent experts in the field, focusing on Germany (56 interviews) and the U.S. (26 interviews). Questions covered motivation for and length of involvement in OFDI (outward foreign direct investments), reasons for locating overseas, location in China and their assessment of benefits and challenges of locating overseas. Categories included whether the firm was a merger or acquisition, single ownership or branch of a multinational, number of OFDI employees, in manufacturing or services and plans for overseas expansion. Combining this information permits an initial understanding of the emerging phenomenon of Chinese OFDI and its potential consequences at the national and the regional level, exploring incipient trends and identifying broadly distinctive patterns (see Table 11.1).

Chinese Outward FDI

Chinese OFDI reflects macroeconomic conditions including a low interest rate, favourable exchange ratio, high export flow and abundant foreign reserves, leading the government to push firms to go abroad to balance the surplus and deflect unfavourable attention by debtor nations. Chinese firms are likely to use M&A as a strategy to hide their foreignness, gain a position in the stock market and instantly become part of a wider business network (see *Karl P. S. Sauvant* and *Michael D. Nolan* in this volume).

Increasing support of current customers is another COFDI goal in recognition of a competitive disadvantage with firms producing in their market area whose developed country customers expect this level of service follow-through. Motivations for Chinese OFDI also involve domestic conditions that hamper business expansion in the national market such as strong regional protectionism, shortage of capital due to banking regulations and lack of sufficient intellectual property protection. Moreover, Chinese producers generally suffer from the bad image of products "Made in China". Chinese management continues largely in a learning mode with little attempt to influence pre-existing firm behaviour according to interview reports. Chinese investors seem to be conscious of their need for knowledge and their willingness to learn. Many of them strategically apply the system of "2-in-the-box", which means that the basic working units are teams of two, one Chinese and one non-Chinese (Sohm et al. 2013). This ensures that many challenges of intercultural collaboration are solved at this working level and do not hamper business development.

Institutionally inflected behaviours appear with regard to how managers of Chinese invested companies are selected to go abroad, usually for two- to three-year terms. This is not universally regarded as a career promotion but, rather, one fraught with potential difficulties. Concerns include the backwardness of the U.S. or German education system compared to what the student would learn at that grade level in the highly competitive, exam-driven Chinese education system; the importance of developing and maintaining critical personal networks in the native society; and personal isolation due to distance from the home headquarters compounded by a cultural isolation because of the high degree of separation between the native and host country societal practices as well as language differences (Si and Liefner 2014). This is compounded by reluctance to join local networking organisations except in U.S. or German cities with very large ethnic concentrations—a strategy at odds with the OLI-Uppsala School of network building—with the exception of families who send their children to classes emphasising Chinese language and culture. Recent immigrants, well integrated in China's education, economic and social system, feel isolated from earlier groups of Chinese immigrants who are not their peers (Si and Liefner 2014).

Regional Comparison: COFDI in Germany and the South-eastern U.S.

COFDI to both Europe and the United States accelerated since the recession beginning in 2008, as the Chinese government turned to stimulus rather than austerity and encouraged business expansion. Since 2011, Europe received almost double the previous amount of COFDI as did the U.S., reflecting a combination of national security concerns in the U.S. and the slower economic recovery in Europe. Hanemann and Rosen's (2013) calculation of the strength of Chinese investments in U.S. and European economic sectors found that relative strength attracts investment. For the U.S., this means more FDI in consumer products and services, entertainment, software and IT services. Overall, of the top 20 countries investing in the U.S. in 2012, COFDI increased the third-most rapidly from the previous year but was only the 20th in amount invested (OII 2014). Natural resources, automobiles, industrial machinery and tools and utilities are European investment attractions (Hanemann and Huotari 2015).

These areas also reflect China's needs given its stage of development, in which case a shift to advanced services in the U.S. compared to industrial applications stronger in Europe is foreseen. The general openness of both the U.S. and the EU to FDI remained unchanged even during the financial crisis (UNCTAD, OECD 2013). Restrictions apply to investors whose

Characteristic	*U.S.*	*Germany*
National strategy	Open, but security concerns	Open, encouraging
Regional strategies	Active, site-specific pitches	Compete for FDI inflows
COFDI locations	Match w/ firm needs, specialised infrastructure, specialisations	Locate in preferred place w/ distinct industry clusters
Firm M&A	Very active	Very active

Figure 11.1 Comparative characteristics of COFDI in the U.S. and Germany

Source: The authors.

investment motives or business activities lack transparency and to cases of M&A deemed a potential threat to national security interests. More important, many Chinese investors feel encouraged by the overall political support expressed by the national governments. Strong similarities lie in the competitiveness of states/*Länder* (U.S./German terms for this political unit) and cities vying for tax and employment generators, as well as the M&A inclination of Chinese firms rather than the establishment of Chinese brand companies (see Figure 11.1).

COFDI in Germany

Annual net inflows of COFDI in Germany exceeded US$1 billion since 2011. China's share of inward FDI in Germany usually hovered around 1% or slightly higher in recent years. Chinese investors had set up 445 companies and acquired 85 firms in Germany by 2013 (Franz et al. 2015, 2). Accurate figures concerning the number of firms or their aggregate employment remain difficult to acquire.

Whereas greenfield investments frequently go into advanced business services (financial services, transport and logistics) or the marketing and distribution of goods manufactured in China, brownfield investment by Chinese capital taps into automotive (20%) and mechanical engineering (50%), areas considered the comparative strength of Germany's economy (Karius 2013). A report highlighting six cases of Chinese firms investing in Germany illustrates the existence of different routes of corporate development (Sohm et al. 2013). Chinese investment in Germany is reportedly primarily motivated by the firms' aim to tap into business leaders' resources and a desire to master production of the most advanced technology. Market access is a secondary motive, with the need to invest financial resources fundamental for building investment strategies. Two of the companies investigated entered the German market by acquiring market leaders. BEIJING NO. 1 bought DÜRKOPP ADLER and WALDRICH Coburg, whilst LENOVO absorbed IBM's

German operations, recently adding Medion. Baosteel, Minmetals and Haier exemplify the gradual approach towards establishing a strong local presence, starting with representative offices and moving slowly towards production, services, administration or R&D.

Initially, many COFDI companies in Germany failed, regardless of the investment mode chosen. Most obvious causes involved a lack of market-related knowledge and experience with Western business culture and mistakes of Chinese managers. Recent research shows that Chinese investors have become much more careful regarding the implementation of Chinese managers and business practices (see *Martina Fuchs* and *Martin Schalljo*, and *Sophie Golinski* and *Sebastian Henn* in this volume). They instead tend to interfere as little as possible with the management of firms acquired and employ German managers in cases of greenfield investment. Major obstacles still remaining include red tape slowing down decision-making of affiliates (Harders 2014).

The German federal government adopted a strategy to support Chinese investors during the initial investment stage, particularly for investments in R&D-intensive industries (Manske et al. 2012). This proactive approach reflects the position of German industry in general (APA 2013). Within Germany, the largest economy in the EU and the largest recipient of Asian FDI in Europe, FDI clusters in three regions: Düsseldorf, Hamburg and Frankfurt, comprising Germany's largest airport as well as a large portion of the nation's financial and business service industries (Si and Liefner 2014). These three locations host large shares of COFDI flowing into the states of North Rhine-Westphalia (Düsseldorf), Hamburg and Hesse (Frankfurt; cf. Table 11.1). Hesse, among the most active states in this regard, set up the "Hessen Trade & Invest GmbH" to attract and support potential investors. At the regional level, many overlapping activities seek to attract COFDI. Such activities may be carried out by individual cities' administrations, by companies set up by several cities within a metropolitan region or by private service companies (Zhou 2010).

The regions most actively seeking new investment benefit from a comparatively long history of Asian OFDI and provide specific infrastructure assets such as large airports, large ports and concentrations of financial services providers specialised in dealing with Asian clients. Localisation advantages work towards strengthening the spatial concentration of certain types of investors in the most appropriate regions. With the not insignificant exception of heightened security review through CFIUS (Committee on Foreign Investment in the United States), both countries seek foreign investment. On the part of firms this means finding a location match with a region receptive to their particular sectoral type.

COFDI in the South-eastern U.S.

In 2010, China contributed only 1% of U.S. total FDI, primarily in chemical and electrical manufacturing. The highest-ranked states for FDI employment in the U.S. (by 1,000s) are respectively California (567), Texas (428.1), New York (388.5), Pennsylvania (251) and Illinois (245.9; Hanemann and Rosen 2013). COFDI located outside these states are more reflective of niche opportunities and attraction efforts applicable to other states. The south-eastern state of Georgia hosts 39 COFDI firms, North Carolina has 37 and South Carolina contains 12.

Location of COFDI firms by sector strongly reflects the economic development level and strengths at each location. COFDI firms in Georgia overwhelming locate in Atlanta, the business centre of the South-east. Attraction of foreign businesses was accelerated by the Olympics, combined with the busiest airport in the U.S. and the major port of Savannah boosting transport firms. A large number of service firms cater to Chinese businesses and residents in the metropolitan area. Manufacturing is the major component of COFDI in low-wage South Carolina, growing with a large VOLVO CAR factory investment in early 2015 (Hanemann and Gao 2015). The economically strong and relatively international Greenville–Spartanburg area is attractive because of its closeness to interstate-linked Charlotte, the business centre of neighbouring North Carolina (Walcott 2014). The Charlotte and Research Triangle Park areas draw on nearby universities and high-tech development centres to create a welcome site for Chinese research-intensive firms. Western North Carolina (wood furniture) and the Piedmont Triad's High Point area (upholstered furniture) experienced huge losses as firms relocated to China in the late 20th century, so investment by COFDI firms is welcome (Walcott 2014).

The location choice of OFDI from various countries investing abroad demonstrates several complementary and conflicting strategies. Firms either follow pre-existing clusters or locate in new regions of emerging advantages. O'hUllachain and Reid (1992) saw a large state and sectoral affinity for clustering of firms from particular countries which they called the "border effect" combination of factors forecasting likely FDI locations drawing on similar embedded advantages. Location of Chinese firms in both Germany and the south-eastern U.S. states examined bore out this observation. The specific function of a firm at a specific site reveals some location decision refinement, such as in the case of LENOVO, which maintains a large presence in central North Carolina—not for R&D but primarily as a central warehouse and distribution site along the I-85 highway corridor linking major East Coast markets.

Re-concentration of firms to more suitable and concentrated FDI locations follows acquisition of knowledge over time about the host country. The example of SANY, a large Chinese construction machine company, illustrated this following several moves to various sites that ended with its Georgia home in metro Atlanta, utilising the facilities at the port of Savannah that also attracted a HUAWEI expansion from its original home facilities in South Carolina. Aspects differentiating latecomers include the role of interventionist national governments, regulations that become more flexible to support successful initiatives, and the utilisation of foreigners familiar with market conditions and gatekeepers (Child and Rodrigues 2005). An example of these consciously constructed networks comes from HUAWEI's hiring of a former aide to Senator Kay Bailey Hutchinson of Texas to serve as a lobbyist, utilising his well-honed ties to Washington players.

Conclusion

This article's objective was to discuss empirical evidence in the light of existing theories in order to establish a more profound understanding of COFDI motivations, relevant context factors, location decision and effects on Western economies based on examining the examples of the American south-east and Germany. Continued research is needed to monitor unfolding location specific investment patterns to see if maturation of the domestic Chinese economy curves its arc of OFDI in a direction congruent with previous theoretical patterns or if its political economic structure and size of its national market makes a difference.

Areas of increasing convergence between Dunning's Eclectic Paradigm and the Uppsala School's model of business network internationalisation include (1) the importance of network construction to aid business expansion by increasing knowledge of the workings of foreign systems, which also balances the costs involved in foreign expansion, (2) an ability to absorb and apply these lessons and (3) the role of learning in motivating outward investment. China utilised OFDI to transition from a trade-to investment-oriented global economic set of policies seeking markets, but chose a more expensive labour location that inverted the life cycle model. Resource-seeking behaviour fits well with theoretical assumptions. According to our interviews, Chinese firms look for human capital, intellectual property and established brands to extend their portfolio and technological abilities in more sophisticated products, in line with the Uppsala vision of corporations as information exchange centres. Both lines of theoretical reasoning should be extended to include the foreign investors' location decisions.

As initially hypothesised, the Chinese approach to OFDI involves stepwise learning of management routines and decision making, combined with maintaining present company locations or copying other Chinese investors' location decisions. The apparent lack of capabilities to acquire and process information contributes to cautious behaviour. This chapter's findings demonstrate that COFDI tends to cluster in established industry locations either known for certain industrial traditions and infrastructures or for a history of COFDI inflow. Hence, imitative location decisions are widespread, but increasingly accompanied by more informed location decisions. As of today, these decisions reinforce agglomerative processes in existing industrial clusters. Some important differences in COFDI assessment in Germany and the south-eastern U.S. remain. The most significant for FDI attraction lies in the greater security concerns of the U.S. Placing more restrictions on Chinese FDI attempts motivates their increased investment in the EU.

Similarities include clustering in places with a pre-existing same industry cluster: Hamburg and Savannah for port facilities, Frankfurt and Atlanta for air transport, Düsseldorf and South Carolina–Charlotte, North Carolina, for manufacturing, as well as sectoral clusters such as furniture and automobile concentrations. COFDI is associated with comparatively strong and positive effects on the firms acquired and local host economy through the insertion of new capital, the opening of new markets for existing products, stabilisation of business processes and retention of the workforce.

The match of type of OFDI firm and the development level of the location fit theory prediction and empirical patterns, but need some minor modification if they are to remain useful explanatory tools: (1) effect of a host country government that encourages OFDI without getting directly involved, (2) effect of a cautious strategy that leaves business processes of acquired firms initially untouched, even at the management level and (3) effect of divergent motivations of host country governments at various levels. Overall, studies of South–North OFDI remain of continuing importance.

Acknowledgements

The authors thank our interviewees for their time spent sharing information used in this research.

References

Alon, I., Child, J., Li, S., and J. R. McIntyre. 2011. "Globalization of Chinese Firms: Theoretical Universalism or Particularism." *Management and Organization Review* 7(2): 191–200.

APA [Asien-Pazifik-Ausschuss der deutschen Wirtschaft]. 2013. "China: Position der Deutschen Wirtschaft." www.asien-pazifikausschuss.de/index.php/positionen-archiv, accessed 2015, July 15.

Cardoza, G., Fornes, G., Li, P., Xu, N., and S. Xu. 2014. "China Goes Global: Public Policies' Influence on Small-and Medium-Sized Enterprises' International Expansion." *Asia Pacific Business Review* 21(2): 182–210.

Child, J., and S. B. Rodrigues. 2005. "The Internationalization of Chinese Firms: A Case for Theoretical Extension?" *Management and Organization Review* 1(3): 381–410.

Dunning, J. 1991. "The Eclectic Paradigm of International Production: A Personal Perspective." In *The Nature of the Transnational Firm*, edited by C. Pitelis, and R. Sugden, 117–136. London: Routledge.

Dunning, J. 2000. "The Eclectic Paradigm as an Envelope for Economic and Business Theories of MNE Activity." *International Business Review* 9(2): 163–190.

Franz, M., Henn, S., and J. Weingarten. 2015. "BRICINVEST: Investoren aus den BRIC-Staaten und Arbeitnehmerinteressen in Deutschland." www.bricinvest.de, accessed 2015, July 15.

Hanemann, T., and C. Gao. 2015. "Chinese FDI in the United States: 1H 2015 Update." http://rhg.com/notes/chinese-fdi-in-the-united-states-1h-2015-update, accessed 2015, July 15.

Hanemann, T., and M. Huotari. 2015. *Chinesische Direktinvestitionen in Deutschland und Europa. Eine neue Ära chinesischen Kapitals*. Berlin: Mercator Institute for China Studies and Rhodium Group.

Hanemann, T., and D. Rosen. 2013. "China's International Investment Position: An Update." http://rhg.com/notes/chinas-international-investment-position-an-update, accessed 2015, May 5.

Harders, M. 2014. "Chinesische Mergers & Acquisitions in Deutschland: Theoretisch-Konzeptionelle Grundlagen, Internationalisierungsmuster und empirische Schlüsselfaktoren." Bachelor's thesis. JLU Gießen, Gießen.

Johanson, J., and J.-E. Vahlne. 1977. "The Internationalization Process of the Firm: A Model of Knowledge Development and Increasing Foreign Market Commitments." *Journal of International Business Studies* 8(1): 23–32.

Johanson, J., and J.-E. Vahlne. 2009. "The Uppsala Internationalization Process Model Revisited: From Liability of Foreignness to Liability of Outsidership." *Journal of International Business Studies* 40(9): 1411–1431.

Karius, A. 2013. "Chinesische Übernahmewelle rollt." www.produktion.de/veranstaltungen/kongress-der-weltmarktfuehrer/studie-chinesische-uebernahmewelle-rollt-266.html, accessed 2015, July 15.

Kuemmerle, W. 1999. "Foreign Direct Investment in Industrial Research in the Pharmaceutical and Electronics Industries: Results from a Survey of Multinational Firms." *Research Policy* 28(2–3): 179–193.

Manske, D., Artmann, S., Berchem, S. von, Petrasch, G., Liefner, I., and B. Scharrer. 2012. *Die Internationale Dimension der Deutschen Innovationspolitik am Beispiel Asien*. Berlin: Dossier and Acatech.

Mathews, J. 2006. "Dragon Multinationals: New Players in 21st Century Globalization." *Asia Pacific Journal of Management* 23(1): 5–27.

O'hUllachain, B., and N. Reid. 1992. "Source Country Differences in the Spatial Distribution of Foreign Direct Investment in the United States." *Professional Geographer* 44(3): 272–285.

OII [Organization for International Investment]. 2014. "Foreign Direct Investment in the United States 2013 Report." www.ofii.org/resources/foreign-direct-investment, accessed 2015, July 15.

Pred, A. 1967. Behavior and Location: Foundations for a Geographic and Dynamic Location Theory, Part 1. Lund Studies in Geography: Series B 27. Lund: Gleerup.

Si, Y., and I. Liefner. 2014. "Cognitive Distance and Obstacles to Subsidiary Business Success: The Experience of Chinese Companies in Germany." *Tijdschrift voor Economische en Sociale Geografie* 105(3): 285–300.

Si, Y., Liefner, I., and T. Wang. 2013. "Foreign Direct Investment with Chinese Characteristics: A Middle Path between Ownership-Location-Internalization Model and Linkage-Leverage-Learning Model." *Chinese Geographical Science* 23(5): 594–606.

Sohm, S., Linke, B.-M., and A. M. Klossek. 2013. *Chinesische Unternehmen in Deutschland: Chancen und Herausforderungen*. Gütersloh: Bertelsmann Stiftung.

UNCTAD, OECD. 2013. "Ninth Report on G20 Investment Measures." www.bea.gov/international/dif1diop.htm, accessed 2015, July 15.

United States Chamber of Commerce. 2012. "Faces of Chinese Investment in the United States." www.uschamber.com/reports/faces-chinese-investment-united-states, accessed, 2015 June 6.

Walcott, S. 2014. "Capitalist China Comes to the Southeastern United States." *Southeastern Geographer* 54(3): 291–307.

Zhou, X. 2010. "Der chinesische M&A-Vorstoß in Deutschland: Illusion und Wirklichkeit: Eine Ableitung chinesischer M&A-Strategien für Deutschland auf der Grundlage bisher erfolgter Initiativen." *M&A Review* 11: 509–514. www.econbiz.de/Record/chinesische-vorsto%C3%9F-deutschland-illusion-wirklichkeit-ableitung-chinesischer-strategien-f%C3%BCr-deutschland-grundlage-bisher-erfolgter-initiativen-zhou/10008666406

12 The Perception of Local Institutional Quality by Multinationals in a Transition Economy Context

Empirical Evidence From Three Regions in Ukraine

Daria Zvirgzde, Daniel Schiller and Javier Revilla Diez

Introduction

The transition process of former centrally planned economies into market economies has far-reaching effects on the institutional environment of the respective countries. Although a large number of studies on transition processes focuses on the national level, the regional dimension of institutional change during transition is less well understood. Because of the interrelatedness of formal and socially embedded informal institutions, it is expected that institutional change in transition economies does not necessarily result in a level playing field for all kinds of actors at all locations. Institutional change might happen faster in some regions than in others, and new formal institutions might be enforced differently based on their congruence with informal institutions.

Previous research on regional development in Central and Eastern Europe has shown that capital regions and regions close to the EU border achieve better economic performance during the transition process than other regions (see e.g. Fedorov 2002; Heidenreich 2003). This chapter argues that similar differences can be expected in Ukraine, a transition country with a post-Soviet context. Original firm survey data on the perception of local institutional quality is used to empirically test this hypothesis. By comparing the perceptions of institutional quality of multinationals and domestic firms in three regional settings this chapter contributes to a better understanding of the interplay between multinational expectations and corporate practices and regional institutional realities. Foreign subsidiaries (greenfield and brownfield) and domestic firms (privatised state-owned firms and new private firms) were surveyed in the capital region (Kyiv), in Lviv (a region that borders the EU) and Kharkiv (a region that borders Russia) in order to understand institutional distance in relation to each regional context. The significance of differences in the perception of local institutional quality by regions and ownership types is tested by means of descriptive statistics and logistic regression models. The results are then qualitatively assessed against the specific context of the three regions, taking into account their Soviet legacy and their more recent development path during the post-Soviet transition period.

This chapter is organised as follows: the second section discusses the role of institutions in regional development with special attention to the transition context from a former planned economy toward a market economy and the potential impact of multinational companies in triggering institutional change. The third section explains the methodological approach. The following section provides the results of the empirical analysis of the enterprise survey in Ukraine; the final section provides a summary.

Institutional Embeddedness of Firms

Formal and Informal Institutions within the Local Institutional Environment

Lately, the role of institutions in national and regional development has become widely acknowledged. However, there is still no one widely accepted definition of institutions. North (1991, 97) states that "institutions are humanly devised constraints that structure political, economic and social interaction". He distinguishes formal institutions, such as political and economic rules and contracts, and informal institutions, such as codes of conduct, conventions, attitudes, values and norms of behaviour. Thus, institutions represent a set of rules that articulate and organise economic, social and political interactions between individuals and social groups, which have an impact on business activity and economic development (Thornton et al. 2011). For Malmberg and Maskell (2006) the institutional set-up across different spatial scales (global, national, regional, local) is one of the most important factors influencing the competitiveness of firms. Moreover, Maskell and Malmberg (1999) emphasise the importance of local and regional institutions in facilitating and strengthening the development of local advantage. They argue that

> it is the region's distinct institutional endowment that embeds knowledge and allows for knowledge creation which—through interaction with available physical and human resources—constitutes its capabilities and enhances or abates the competitiveness of the firms in the region.
> (Maskell and Malmberg 1999, 181)

Spatial concentration of interacting firms sharing a common social and institutional context is an obvious prerequisite to interactive learning processes and further technological and organisational upgrading. The shared attitudes, values, norms, routines and expectations—the local business culture—influence the practices of firms in the region (Asheim and Gertler 2005). The process of institution building is triggered by the establishment of "communities of practice" (Wenger 1998), when agents are bound together through day-to-day interactions, based on the same expertise, a common set of technological knowledge and similar experience with a particular set of problem-solving techniques. Communities of practice thus lead to the generation of distinct routines, conventions and other institutional arrangements. Common institutions and procedural rules are established incrementally, constantly being reshaped by experience (Lawson and Lorenz 1999).

According to DiMaggio and Powell (1983) local business culture is expressed through social code of conduct, behaviours and routines, which define social acceptance of certain formal and informal institutional rules and business practices and are widely acknowledged by the individuals residing within certain localities. Proximity plays a defining role in the formation of local business culture within certain informal institutional environments. The local business culture is thus shaped by local rationalities and traditions of behaviour, tacit knowledge and face-to-face exchange, social habits, norms and routines, and the sociology of communication and interaction in local economic networks (Amin 1999). For Amin (1999) a regional economy is not solely a collection of firms, but rather a

> composition of networks and collective influences which shape individual action; a highly diversified set of activities owing to the salient influence of culture and context; and subject to path-dependent change due to the contribution of inherited socio-institutional influences.
>
> (Amin 1999, 4)

Multinational Companies and their Impact on Local Institutions

When a multinational company enters a foreign market, it faces multiple kinds of embeddedness (Meyer et al. 2011). Not only is it embedded at the level of the home country, but it also is at the level of the host economy within a specific local context. In principle, the multinational company has two options in order to operate at a new location. Either it adopts the existing institutional framework or it tries to create its own institutional environment. Liu and Dicken (2006) distinguish between obligated and active embeddedness. Obligated embeddedness occurs when state power at the host location is high and the multinational company needs to get access to critical localised assets. The situation in Ukraine, however, is rather characterised by ubiquitous assets and weak or unreliable state power. Therefore, active voluntary embeddedness or proactive shaping of institutional conditions is expected to prevail.

Willingness to become a driver of institutional change depends very much on the motives, the size of the investment, the autonomy of the subsidiary and the local context. As Jindra et al. (2009) state, foreign subsidiaries in Eastern European transition economies tend to embed into the regional economic systems through linkages with domestic small and medium-sized enterprises. Subsidiaries create their own supplier–customer networks for business operations, resulting in specific value-chain governance forms. But the multinational company is not only dealing with suppliers when embedding locally. Multinational companies are also confronted with local government structures, local employees' associations and local region-specific regulations concerning land use and resource planning. These local institutions are "the rules, conventions and regulations that define the territory (a region or locality) and its usage, which in turn depend on sometimes conflicting values and modes of thought" (Rafiqui 2009, 345). According to Martin (2008) institutional path dependency is most significantly expressed at the regional or local level. Local business culture with its pre-existing social norms and accepted behavioural routines is also constrained by the shadow of the past. Rafiqui (2009) also refers to the path dependency of specifically local institutions and their adaptation towards pre-established local business culture. Path dependency of region specific institutions, closely related to the local business culture of a region, can have both positive and negative effects. The positive role of path dependency is expressed through the obvious need of formal institutions to co-evolve together with informal institutions and local business culture to be efficient and for the necessary evolutionary change to occur. The negative outcome of path dependency is the possibility of institutional lock-in (Rafiqui 2009). Being dependent on the social rules and norms, local institutions may resist change for further economic development. For example when local business culture is based on oral agreements and the use of personal contacts, local institutions will be unwilling to introduce contract enforcement, although this may be important for the overall enforceability of legislation and regulation policies.

Institutional Path and Place Dependency in a Transitional Context

Another important dimension of local institutions is institutional place dependency. Although institutions as such may not be the only reason for geographically uneven development, they do enable, constrain and frame economic activities in spatially different manners (Martin 2008). Local institutions become more and more important in shaping local and regional economic performance. Thus, the localisation of a certain industry within a regional economic system fosters the development of specialised local institutional arrangements, which reduce transaction costs and increase local economic competitiveness. Economic geographers also identify place-dependency of institutions at subnational level, referring to "local institutional thickness". Martin (2008) defines this with the help of four elements: strong presence of institutions such as local authorities, chambers, labour unions and research centres; intensive interaction between these institutions; availability of well-defined structures aimed at minimization of inter-institutional conflict; and collective integration into regional socio-economic development. Such "local institutional thickness" leads to the formation of a specific institutional regime that influences the local business culture. This regime facilitates the emergence and development of clusters of firms; it enables closer collaboration between firms and better knowledge transfer, which, in turn, fosters higher spillover effects among local firms (Martin 2008).

Local institutional change as induced by the transformation from a planned to a market economy is still under-researched. The Soviet past of Ukraine resulted in very uneven regional development. The socialist industrialisation strategy led to an overemphasis of heavy industry that was spatially concentrated in the eastern part of the country. Government support was channelled towards the development of technological competencies and industry-specific infrastructure. In consequence, these regions received preferential treatment. The close interrelation among state-owned enterprises, local administration and the line ministries lead to a very distinct institutional set-up compared to the less strategic regions in the western part of the country. During the Soviet period the western region had always been an important agricultural zone, receiving much less support than the heavy industrial region of the east. Nevertheless, the institutional set-up there was also influenced by the Soviet period, leading to a strong dependence on central state capital transfers. Capital regions in transition economies are often the drivers of institutional change. In the Soviet period, capital regions were the command centres of the planned economy, concentrating power, capital, science and technology, among others. Today, the capital regions are at the forefront of change, serving as commercial hubs (Meliciani 2015; Smetkowski 2013). Because of the economic importance of capital regions the state authorities are interested in renewing the institutional environment (Fedorov 2002). Capital regions in transition economies outperform the rest of the country and enjoy preferential government treatment (e.g. financial support), are the targets of foreign capital and offer better opportunities due to a more developed market as a consequence of agglomeration economies (Heidenreich 2003). Such opportunities also attract better-qualified human capital, which serves as an important driver of economic progress. Santos et al. (2012) for example find a positive relationship between the economic development of a region and the availability of highly innovative entrepreneurs. Capital regions absorb entrepreneurs who create new jobs that attract more and more knowledge and human resources over time.

Data and Methods

The empirical analysis of this paper is based on an enterprise survey that was carried out among 305 domestic small and medium-sized enterprises and 153 subsidiaries of multinational companies from the food and beverages and machinery and equipment sectors in Ukraine between April and July 2012 in collaboration with Kiev National Economic University. In order to cover the different regional institutional regimes of Ukraine, three types of regions were chosen: a region that is close to the EU border (Lviv), one that is close to the Russian border (Kharkiv) and the capital region (Kyiv).

The empirical data of the enterprise survey was generated from a standardised questionnaire focusing on the perception of the quality of the local institutional environment. The enterprises were asked about enforceability of legislation and regulation policies, protection of physical and intellectual property rights, reliability of oral contracts/agreements, central government support and regional and/or local government support.

In order to control for the different ownership forms, the following distinctions were made: foreign subsidiaries (brownfield and greenfield), privatised state-owned firms and new private firms. Brownfield investments are defined as those subsidiaries of multinational companies that entered the Ukrainian market and acquired an existing production site for future business operations. Greenfield investments encompass those subsidiaries that built new production sites in Ukraine. Privatised state-owned firms are either the spin-offs of government conglomerates or firms that were privatised or still have state ownership, that is those that have a connection to the government and the planned economy of the past. New private firms are basically Ukrainian start-ups, established by the young generation and therefore with few or no links to the Soviet past.

The binary logit regression model was run for each of the six aspects of institutional environment separately and for the composite indicator of institutional quality. For the calculation of the composite indicator the six aspects were grouped into four variables. The protection of property rights and intellectual property rights were treated as one property rights protection indicator, and central and regional government support were combined into one government support indicator. Thus, the composite indicator included equal weights of enforceability of legislation, property rights protection, reliability of oral contracts and agreements and government support. Because the questions on the preceding parameters were on a Likert scale from 1 (very bad) to 5 (very good), the institutional quality composite indicator was recoded into a dummy, with the value 1 representing good and very good quality of the institutional environment (a threshold of 3.5 and above on the Likert scale), and 0 representing average, low and very low quality of the institutional environment (below 3.5 on the Likert scale).

After a multicollinearity check the following control variables were used in the model: regional dummy, ownership dummy, size of the firm in terms of logged number of employees, total sales and total exports, sector dummy, number of employees with higher education and number of employees involved in R&D together with the embeddedness indicators, such as cooperation with foreign suppliers and customers in the current region and where the survey firm is located.

Results and Discussion

As expected, the descriptive results confirm that firms rate the institutional quality in the capital region more positively than in other regions. Except for government support, 40% of the surveyed firms assess local institutional conditions as good or very good. In the border regions of Lviv and Kharkiv, on average only about 25% of firms rate the different aspects of institutional quality as good or very good. Instead, about 50% rate the institutional quality as low. Significant differences are also observed with respect to central government support, which is rated as low by 70% of firms in Lviv and 65% in Kharkiv but only by 40% of firms in Kyiv. Interestingly, 40% of firms in Kyiv assess the reliability of oral contracts as good or very good, and thus much better than in the Kharkiv region.

Moreover, multinational companies assess the institutional quality at their location more positively than the respective private firms (Figure 12.1). The majority of private firms perceive institutional quality to be rather low. Whilst greenfield investors are quite positive about the quality of the institutional setting, new private firms gave very low scores for institutional quality. On average, up to 45% of greenfield investors rate the institutional quality at their present location as good or very good, compared to only 20% of new private firms. The assessment of central and regional government support turns out to be most divergent between the different ownership groups. Thus, whereas multinational companies still score government support as good or very good, only around 10% of new private firms do. Privatised state-owned firms rate government support more highly than new private firms, but even their assessment is below that of both brownfield and

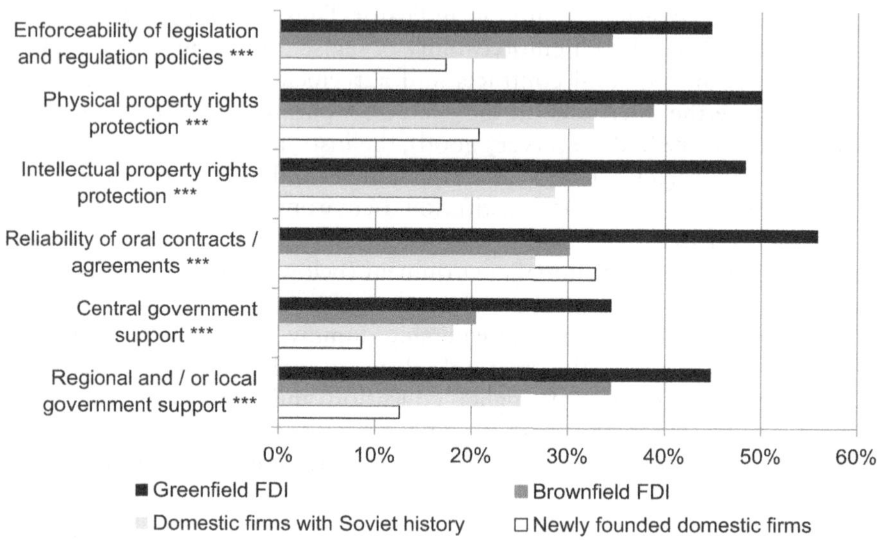

Figure 12.1 Perception of institutional quality by firm ownership

Source: The authors.

***Significant at the 0.01 level.

greenfield investors. Informal practices like oral contracts and agreements also seem more reliable to greenfield investors than private firms: more than 55% of the foreign firms regarded the oral code of conduct as highly reliable.

The outcome of the binary logit regression model in Table 12.1 is consistent with the results of the descriptive crosstab analysis. The regional and ownership dummies have a significant negative impact on the assessment of institutional quality in the cases of the Kyiv region and greenfield investments. In other words, firms in the Kyiv region and greenfield investors perceive the institutional set-up much more positively than the firms of the two border regions and the other ownership forms (especially private firms).

Cooperation with foreign suppliers in the home region turns out to have a significant positive impact on the assessment of enforceability of legislation and reliability of oral contracts and agreements. In contrast, cooperation with foreign customers in the rest of Ukraine has a significant negative impact on the institutional dimensions. This result underlines the importance of proximity for trustful arrangements and the place dependency of institutions.

The higher institutional quality of the capital Kyiv could be explained in line with regional development patterns in Central and Eastern Europe (Heidenreich 2003; Meliciani 2015; Smetkowski 2013). First, the capital region in a transition economy is a commercial hub which concentrates the best developed infrastructure, established networks of customers and suppliers, access to knowledge and technological potential. The capital thus becomes a source of opportunities, attracting business actors from other regions where the regional economic system is weaker. This leads to the emergence of the second reason why the capital region outstrips the border regions. As a high-income region, the capital attracts human capital, namely highly qualified employees and entrepreneurs who can introduce their expertise in exchange for better workplaces and more opportunities. This particularly concerns the subsidiaries of multinational companies which are based in the capital specifically to draw on these better-qualified people. In addition to highly skilled and experienced migrants coming from the peripheral regions to the capital for better opportunities, there is also a wide range of talents pulled to the capital primarily due to better educational opportunities. These are attracted by better universities and research networks in the capital. This highly skilled human capital, in turn, attracts FDI looking for experts in their fields. Against this background, the regional economic system of the capital in a transition economy becomes the driver of the national economy, which serves as an incentive for the government to further support the development and growth of the capital. This leads to the introduction of a business-friendly institutional environment which positively influences the economic and business activities of its actors. This then leads these actors to rate the given institutional quality more highly. It seems also that the more competitive environment and the economic success facilitate the breaking up of the former Soviet institutional setting.

The negative assessment of the institutional quality in the two border regions can be ascribed to institutional lock-in, as described by Fedorov

Table 12.1 Binary logit regression model on the institutional quality

	Institutional quality	*Intellectual property protection*	*Reliability of oral agreements*	*Local government support*
Regional dummies (Kyiv region as control group)				
Lviv region	–0.936***	–0.763**	0.034	–0.148
Kharkiv region	–0.867***	–0.081	–0.209	–0.332
Regional dummies (Lviv region as control group)				
Kyiv region	0.936***	0.763**	–0.034	0.148
Kharkiv region	0.069	0.682**	–0.242	–0.185
Ownership dummies (greenfield FDI as control group)				
Privatised state-owned firms	–1281***	–0.989***	–1499***	–1237***
New private firms	–1754***	–1570***	–1386***	–1867***
Brownfield investors	–0.936**	–0.911**	–1486***	–0.490
Sector dummy (food & beverages sector as control group)				
Machinery & equipment sector	–0.032	0.150	–0.095	–0.643**
Size of the firm				
Log of # of employees	0.744**	0.585**	–0.033	0.804**
Total sales	–0.019	–0.011	–0.031***	–0.005
Total exports	0.000	0.001	–0.005	–0.007
Human capital				
# of employees with higher education	–0.006	–0.005	0.009**	–0.002
# of employees involved in R&D	0.005	–0.010	0.009	0.008

Embeddedness				
Cooperation with foreign supplier in the current region	0.007	–0.011	0.030**	–0.008
Cooperation with foreign supplier in the rest of Ukraine	0.002	0.008	0.001	0.017
Cooperation with foreign customer in the current region	0.008	0.018	–0.023	0.023
Cooperation with foreign customer in the rest of Ukraine	–0.019	–0.023	–0.038*	–0.021
Model fit				
Omnibus Test of Model Coefficients (Sig.)	*0.000*	*0.000*	*0.000*	*0.000*
Correctly classified cases by the model	*0.820*	*0.760*	*0.720*	*0.790*
Nagelkerke R *Square*	*0.213*	*0.144*	*0.150*	*0.200*
N	*415*	*418*	*421*	*420*

Source: The authors.

Note: Institutional quality is the average assessment of the six dimensions analysed earlier.

*Significant at the 0.10 level; **Significant at the 0.05 level; ***Significant at the 0.01 level.

(2002) for Russia. Interestingly, firms in Kharkiv assess government support as more positive than firms in Lviv. Better support of the eastern border region appears to be a consequence of the remains of the Soviet legacy which is still in place. The lack of motivation of the political parties to transform the institutional setting of the past resulted in the government supporting the pre-existing system. This results in the neglect of potentially new sources of economic growth, for example in other parts of the country. Lviv needs government support for establishing a business-friendly environment; the socialist heritage is still observable there in the weak institutional quality. During Soviet regulation the western part of the country was an agricultural centre, making the government less interested in developing its economic and institutional infrastructure.

Multinational companies, in general, were found to rate institutional quality higher than domestic private firms. One reason may be that multinational companies tend to create their own institutional environment. The fact that greenfield investors rate the quality of the institutional environment higher than brownfield investors could possibly mean that foreign subsidiaries that enter the host economy with the intention of building their own production sites tend to introduce new customer-supplier networks and new institutional arrangements. They also receive better government treatment because they provide substantial capital and technological knowledge to the location, which all results in the emergence of a local institutional microsystem around the multinational companies. This microsystem is grounded in a certain institutional environment which is then influenced by the newcomers. This line of reasoning can be also found by Arslan and Larimo (2011), who found empirical evidence that with high informal institutional distance multinationals prefer to realise greenfield investments and thus create their own institutional environment.

Summary

The results of the enterprise survey carried out in Ukraine has shown, first, the existence of regional differences in the quality of institutions and, second, divergent perceptions of the quality of local institutional conditions by multinational companies and domestic private firms. Institutional quality is rated differently in the capital and the border regions of Ukraine, with the capital region assessed more positively than the border regions. In the latter the quality of the institutional environment is judged to be low.

Multinational companies tend to rate institutional quality better than domestic small and medium-sized enterprises. This leads to the conclusion that foreign subsidiaries may create their own institutional environments by means of deinstitutionalisation rather than opposing the institutional rules of the host economy. In addition, preferential treatment of multinational companies by national and regional governments could also play an important role. New private domestic firms seem to be the most discriminated by the local institutional environment. The negative assessment of the institutional quality by domestic private firms is a challenge to the political leaders who are not doing enough to introduce a business-friendly institutional environment for start-ups and young domestic private firms. The greater attention towards multinational companies is having a negative impact on the development of domestic firms. Especially in a transition economy, the focus should lie on providing the right institutional conditions to domestic private firms as the future backbone of economic development.

Acknowledgements

The research producing these results received funding from the European Community's Seventh Framework Program (FP7/2007–2013) under Grant Agreement Number 266834.

References

Amin, A. 1999. "An Institutionalist Perspective on Regional Economic Development." *International Journal of Urban and Regional Research* 23(2): 365–378.

Arslan, A., and J. Larimo. 2011. "Greenfield Investments or Acquisitions: Impacts of Institutional Distance on Establishment Mode Choice of Multinational Enterprises in Emerging Economies." *Journal of Global Marketing* 24(2): 345–356.

Asheim, B. T., and M. Gertler. 2005. "The Geography of Innovation: Regional Innovation Systems." In *The Oxford Handbook of Innovation*, edited by J. Fagerberg, D. C. Mowery, and R. R. Nelson, 291–317. Oxford: Oxford University Press.

DiMaggio, P. J., and W. W. Powell. 1983. "The Iron Cage Revisited: Institutional Isomorphism and Collective Rationality in Organizational Fields." *American Sociological Review* 48(2): 147–160.

Fedorov, L. 2002. "Regional Inequality and Regional Polarization in Russia 1990–1999." *World Development* 30(3): 443–456.

Heidenreich, M. 2003. "Regional Inequalities in the Enlarged Europe." *Journal of European Social Policy* 13(4): 313–333.

Jindra, B., Giroud, A., and J. Scott-Kennel. 2009. "Subsidiary Roles, Vertical Linkages and Economic Development: Lessons from Transition Economies." *Journal of World Business* 44(2): 167–179.

Lawson, C., and E. Lorenz. 1999. "Collective Learning, Tacit Knowledge and Regional Innovative Capacity." *Regional Studies* 33(4): 305–317.

Liu, W., and P. Dicken. 2006. "Transnational Corporations and 'Obligated Embeddedness': Foreign Direct Investment in China's Automobile Industry." *Environment and Planning A* 38(7): 1229–1247.

Malmberg, A., and P. Maskell. 2006. "Localized Learning Revisited." *Growth and Change* 37(1): 1–18.

Martin, R. 2008. "Institutional Approaches in Economic Geography." In *A Companion to Economic Geography*, edited by E. Sheppard, and T. J. Barnes, 77–94. Oxford: Blackwell Publishing Ltd.

Maskell, P., and A. Malmberg. 1999. "Localised Learning and Industrial Competitiveness." *Cambridge Journal of Economics* 23(2): 167–185.

Meliciani, V. 2015. Regional Disparities in the Enlarged European Union: Geography, Innovation, and Structural Change. London and New York: Routledge.

Meyer, K. E., Mudambi, R., and R. Narula. 2011. "Multinational Enterprises and Local Contexts: The Opportunities and Challenges of Multiple Embeddedness." *Journal of Management Studies* 48(2): 235–252.

North, D. C. 1991. "Institutions." *The Journal of Economic Perspectives* 5(1): 97–112.

Rafiqui, P. S. 2009. "Evolving Economic Landscapes: Why New Institutional Economics Matters for Economic Geography." *Journal of Economic Geography* 9(3): 329–353.

Santos, F. J., Romero, I., and J. Fernández-Serrano. 2012. "SMEs and Entrepreneurial Quality from a Macroeconomic Perspective." *Management Decision* 50(8): 1382–1395.

Smetkowski, M. 2013. "Regional Disparities in Central and Eastern European Countries: Trends, Drivers and Prospects." *Europe-Asia Studies* 65(8): 1529–1544.

Thornton, P. H., Ribeiro-Soriano, D., and D. Urbano. 2011. "Socio-Cultural Factors and Entrepreneurial Activity." *International Small Business Journal* 29(2): 105–118.

Wenger, E. 1998. *Communities of Practice: Learning, Meaning and Identity*. Cambridge: Cambridge University Press.

13 Realities of Responsible Business

Institutional and Structural Conditions in MNE–Local Government Bargaining

Päivi Oinas and Erja Kettunen

Introduction

How multinational enterprises (MNEs) behave in the localities they enter in different parts of the world has been keenly monitored by local agents as well as international audiences. Despite strong efforts to introduce corporate social responsibility (CSR) and the presumed widespread adoption of responsible practices in Western MNEs (Bondy et al. 2012, 281), compliance with acceptable legal and moral standards is not a given around the globe. "[C]orporations operate in a broad variety of contexts where governments are not necessarily able or willing to regulate them effectively" (Crane et al. 2014, 140). MNEs may succumb to unethical practices in such contexts, possibly regardless of explicitly subscribing to CSR and following ethical codes of conduct elsewhere. The bulk of research on CSR concerns firms originating and operating in advanced Western economies. MNEs, however, increasingly also originate in countries with inadequate government regulation. Therefore, whether MNEs with different backgrounds engage in responsible or irresponsible conduct in different contexts of operation is worthy of analysis, given that they may face starkly divergent expectations regarding corporate conduct compared to their home environments.

There is no commonly agreed definition of CSR, but in its broadest sense, it concerns "the social obligations and impacts of business in society" (Crane and Matten 2007, vi). Responsibly or ethically (we use these terms interchangeably) inclined corporations are interested in the consequences of their action and therefore are willing to acknowledge and even tackle the "systemic social and environmental problems to which they are connected" (Crane et al. 2014, 140). Much research on CSR focuses on the national scale, but our analysis concerns the *local* scale. We ask, "Under what conditions are MNEs likely to engage in ethical versus unethical conduct in the localities where they invest?" We acknowledge the central role of the interactions and negotiations between MNEs and host local governments in setting the stage for the operation of MNEs locally.

We propose what we dub here "institutional and structural conditions" as essential—though not sole (e.g. Campbell 2007, 948)—features influencing CSR on the local scale. *Institutional conditions* stem from the imprinting of features of the home versus host economy's institutional environments in the operating principles of the variously interdependent parties involved in the local scale negotiations. Imprinting is not just the long-lasting influence on organisations of the environmental conditions at the *time* of their formation (Stinchcombe 1965) but also of their geographical origin (Guthey et al. 2014). Such imprinting concerns here ethical conduct on the part of the MNEs, and good governance practices on the part of the local governments. (A firm's ethical conduct may also be based on self- or market-induced responsibility, or industry standards, but we simplify here by delimiting our discussion to "home" and "host" institutional conditions.) Corporate actors face diverse institutional settings (Meyer and Peng 2016), evidenced inter alia by the types and levels of corruption, i.e. "the abuse of entrusted power for private gain" (Transparency International 2016) around the globe. The *structural conditions* are created by MNE–locality resource interdependencies that are reflected in power relations in bargaining situations.

This chapter proposes that such conditions influence the interactions between MNEs and local governments, helping us formulate propositions as to the kinds of situations around the globe in which locally responsible versus irresponsible corporate conduct is likely. In what follows, we discuss the bargaining relations between MNEs and local governments and then introduce the two types of conditions affecting bargaining outcomes. We consider the tendencies towards ethical versus unethical conduct in the contexts influenced by those conditions and conclude by discussing implications for sustainable local development.

MNE–Host Local Government Interactions: Bargaining Relations

In the international business literature, an MNE's relation with the host state is established via negotiations, or bargaining, between the foreign firm and the host country government. The "bargaining model" (Kobrin 1987) assumes that both the MNE and the host state possess resources that are wanted by the other party. The MNEs' resources include for example technology, managerial skills, capital and export potential; the host state possesses resources such as access to the domestic market, natural resources, labour and government incentives (Kobrin 1987, 619–622). Originally, the MNE–host state relation was largely perceived as confrontational (e.g. Grosse and Behrman 1992; Vernon 1977), especially in developing countries, whereas nowadays the relation is widely considered cooperative because of perceived interdependence between firms and states under globalisation (Luo 2001; Ramamurti 2001; Wagner 2013).

Bargaining is a process, with iterative, recurrent negotiations taking place between the MNE and the host state over a range of issues (Eden et al. 2005), such as business licenses, authorisation of construction plans and inspection of implementation, safety standards and certificates of origin. Formal government policy as well as informal practices typically influence the dealings.

Although the literature on firm–state bargaining focuses on the national scale, we discuss bargaining relations at the *local scale* which is where concrete ongoing interactions take place, typically through personal contacts between MNEs and host local governments. The division of responsibilities between national and local governments varies between countries but the latter always have tasks of their own and they participate in enforcing national scale laws, rules and regulations. However, the local scale may show greater variance in their enforcement and reveal the power of informal practices (Meyer and Peng 2016, 11). MNE representatives encounter local government officials when they seek advice or approvals regarding various application procedures and the related legislation, when they inform policy-makers about their business interests in face-to-face meetings or during other encounters such as local seminars or events.

Bargaining is affected not only by economic and political factors but also by institutional factors (Eden et al. 2005, 270). Moreover, we argue here that bargaining itself also becomes a locally institutionalised relation, and the nature and outcomes of local bargaining practices bear significant consequences on corporate conduct vis-à-vis economic, social, cultural, political and environmental development of the host localities. A key issue from a locality's perspective is whether or not local governments and MNEs as parties in the bargaining relation are committed to long-term sustainable development of the locality, suggesting contributions to the advancement of activities as diverse as competent corporate management, fair wages, decent working conditions, employee training, use of natural resources, environmental protection, waste management, revitalising economic and community life, sustaining cultural heritage and supporting cultural events, among others. That, we argue, depends in part on the aforementioned institutional and structural conditions to which we turn in the following.

Institutional and Structural Conditions Affecting Local Bargaining

Institutional conditions: Agents that operate in accordance with prevailing—formal and informal (e.g. North 1990), regulatory and normative (Meyer and Rowan 1977)—institutions are considered legitimate members of their societies and communities; that is their action is perceived or assumed to be "desirable, proper, or appropriate within some socially constructed system of norms, values, beliefs, and definitions" (Suchman 1995, 574). Similar institutionalist tenets have also been adopted in the widely held institutional approach to CSR. The implication is that "firms within a given societal setting will tend to behave in a similar fashion in terms of CSR" (Young and Makhija 2014, 670). Some institutional environments create a stronger tendency towards responsible business conduct than others (Fransen 2013; Gjølberg 2009, 2010; Matten and Moon 2008). In the absence of such institutions, firms may have interests and incentives that may cause them to behave irresponsibly (Campbell 2007, 951).

Firms can be taken to act responsibly if they do "not knowingly do anything that could harm their stakeholders, notably, their investors, employees, customers, suppliers, or the local community within which they operate", and in the case that they "cause harm to their stakeholders, they must then rectify it whenever the harm is discovered and brought to their attention" (Campbell 2007, 951). However, legitimate corporate behaviour means different things in different contexts. Therefore, an MNE entering a foreign locality may perceive what is legitimate differently from its local stakeholders, facing an institutional mismatch. Formal regulation may be in place, but enforcement by local authorities may be lacking, particularly in many developing economies (Su et al. 2016). We formulate the institutional conditions as follows (F for "firm"; L for "locality"; E+ for "ethical conduct"; E– for "non-ethical conduct"):

- An MNE's home-base institutions form a strong expectation for and enforce ethical conduct (**FE+**); alternatively, they tolerate (even expect) unethical conduct (**FE–**).
- An MNE's host locality's institutions form a strong expectation for and enforce ethical conduct (**LE+**); alternatively, they tolerate (even expect) unethical conduct (**LE–**).

The possible combinations of *institutional conditions* are the following:

LE+FE+ The host local economy's and the MNE's home-base institutions enforce ethical conduct. Expectations regarding ethical conduct are shared by negotiating parties.

LE–FE+ The host local economy institutions tolerate unethical conduct, whereas the MNE's home-base institutions enforce ethical conduct, resulting in conflicting expectations in negotiations or institutional mismatch.

LE+FE– The host local economy institutions enforce ethical conduct, whereas the MNE's home-base institutions tolerate unethical conduct, resulting in conflicting expectations in negotiations or institutional mismatch.

LE–FE– Both the host local economy and the MNE's home-base institutions tolerate unethical conduct. Negotiation results likely serve the negotiating parties' private interests and shirk the local common good.

Situation LE+FE+ could involve MNEs from the world's least-corrupt countries such as Denmark, New Zealand or Finland (Transparency International 2017) investing in localities in similar countries. In contrast, situation LE–FE– would involve both MNEs and localities from the other end of the corruptness spectrum. The cases in between would be created by investments across such institutional divides.

Structural Conditions: Institutional theory posits that firms in a given institutional setting converge in their CSR strategies but does not highlight differences between firms (Young and Makhija 2014, 673). For example Gjølberg (2009) observes that the CSR literature has been unable to deal with various structural conditions, including power relations. In line with the bargaining model, the structural condition, as defined here, recognises the mutual dependencies between individual MNEs and their host localities. Dependence is taken to generate commitment and need for legitimacy.

In each locality where MNEs invest and operate, MNE–locality relations evolve that are shaped by how important the locality is to the firm in terms of significant resource provision and how important the firm is from the point of view of the development of the local economy and community. The resource interdependencies are as follows (Oinas 1995) (F for "firm"; L for "locality"; D+ for "dependent"; D– for "not dependent"):

- An MNE is locally dependent if its operation is dependent on locality-specific resources (**FD+**); otherwise, it is not locally dependent (**FD–**).
- A locality is dependent on an MNE if its development is dependent on resources controlled by the firm (**LD+**); otherwise, the locality is not dependent (**LD–**).

For simplicity of presentation, the dependence relations are dichotomised, but obviously, *de facto* dependences are matters of degree. As "one's power resides implicitly in another's dependency" (Emerson 1962, 32), these relations of dependence are manifested in the power relations between the MNE units and their host localities. They give rise to the following *structural conditions* for the local bargaining relations:

LD+FD+ Both the locality and the MNE are dependent on each other; the local government and the local MNE representatives are motivated and equal negotiators.

LD–FD+ The locality is not dependent on the MNE, but the MNE is dependent on the locality; the local government is the powerful negotiator.

LD+FD– The locality is dependent on the MNE, but the MNE is not dependent on the locality; the local MNE representative is the powerful negotiator.

LD–FD– Both the locality and the firm are not dependent on each other; the local government and the local MNE representatives are indifferent equal negotiators.

LD+ is due to the MNE being an employer, taxpayer, possibly an original innovator creating markets, connecting the region with external markets and technologies, building local networks and/or attracting other firms to the locality. The MNE's bargaining power increases when it possesses scarce and non-imitable resources helping to boost the local economy, for example sophisticated technological skills (Eden et al. 2005). Similarly, the power of the local economy increases when it has rare and location-bound resources needed by the MNE, such as central location for efficient logistics, a large market or valuable human or natural resources (see Eden et al. 2005). In situation LD+FD+, both entities desire each other's resources; for example an MNE with a new technology investing in a locality where an industrial cluster has recently laid off employees with rare competences useful in the MNE's innovative activities. In situation LD–FD–, the firm could also find its resources elsewhere, and the locality's development does not rely on a particular firm. The other situations can stem from various one-sided dependences.

Tendency Towards Corporate Social Responsibility

The institutional and structural conditions on local interactions and negotiations create tendencies towards ethical versus non-ethical conduct in MNE units as outlined in Table 13.1. The columns present the institutional (LE+/–) and structural (LD+/–) conditions from the host locality's perspective. The rows present the institutional condition of the MNE's home base, that is MNE imprinting (FE+/–) and the structural condition of the firm's dependence or non-dependence on the host locality (FD+/–). Combined, the table suggests 16 possible outcomes in terms of the tendency towards ethical conduct. Complex as it is, the table nevertheless provides just a simplified depiction of real-world circumstances. The systematic approach, however, provides an account of the diverse circumstances around the globe, where MNEs negotiate the conditions of their operations locally.

The different institutional and structural conditions brought together in Table 13.1 create tendencies towards MNE ethical or non-ethical conduct as follows:

(1) Both home and host institutional environments support a tendency towards ethical conduct (LE+FE+).

  (1a) Mutual dependence increases the likelihood of the MNE and the local government respecting each other's expectations as the stakes are high for both parties (LD+FD+). These conditions create a strong tendency towards ethical conduct.

  (1b) The MNE's dependence on the host locality strengthens the likelihood of the MNE respecting the expectations of the local government as it builds legitimacy in the non-dependent locality (LD–FD+), thus strengthening the MNE's tendency to act ethically beyond home turf.

  (1c) The locality's dependence on the non-dependent MNE (LD+FD–) makes the local government inclined to accept the MNE's requests in negotiations. They are likely not unethical but the MNE does not make long-term commitments.

  (1d) Mutually weak dependence (LD–FD–) leaves the institutional condition decisive in creating a tendency towards ethical conduct yet without long-term commitment.

Table 13.1 The institutional and structural conditions creating tendencies towards ethical versus non-ethical conduct in MNE units

LOCALITY (L): / MNE (F):		ETHICAL CONDUCT ENFORCED IN HOST LOCALITY (LE+)		UNETHICAL CONDUCT TOLERATED IN HOST LOCALITY (LE-)	
		L DEPENDENT ON F (LD+)	L NON-DEPENDENT ON F (LD-)	L DEPENDENT ON F (LD+)	L NON-DEPENDENT ON F (LD-)
ETHICAL CONDUCT ENFORCED AT HOME (FE+)	F DEP. ON HOST L (FD+)	(1a) Ethical conduct highly likely	(1b) Ethical conduct likely	(2a) Firm may yield to unethical conduct, or promote ethical conduct locally	(2b) Firm may yield to unethical conduct
	F NON-DEP. ON HOST L (FD-)	(1c) Ethical conduct likely	(1d) Ethical conduct likely	(2c) Firm may promote ethical conduct locally	(2d) Investment rare
UNETHICAL CONDUCT TOLERATED AT HOME (FE-)	F DEP. ON HOST L (FD+)	(3a) Firm likely obliged to ethical conduct	(3b) Firm may be compelled to ethical conduct	(4a) Unethical conduct highly likely	(4b) Unethical conduct highly likely
	F NON-DEP. ON HOST L (FD-)	(3c) Firm likely to push unethical solutions	(3d) Investment rare	(4c) Unethical conduct likely	(4d) Opportunistic unethical conduct likely

Source: The authors.

(2) Mixed outcomes: MNE with an ethical institutional imprinting facing institutional mismatch (LE–FE+)

(2a) Mutual dependence makes the MNE and local government equal negotiators, and the stakes are high for both parties (LD+FD+). Corporate strategy is decisive in bargaining as the MNE either adopts local practices, or alternatively, it manages to negotiate deals that promote ethical conduct locally.

(2b) The MNE's dependence on a non-dependent host locality (LD–FD+) raises its risk of yielding to corrupt local practices.

(2c) The locality's dependence on the non-dependent MNE (LD+FD–) makes the local government inclined to accept the codes of conduct the MNE insists on. The firm may showcase the changing rules of the game in the global market, and thereby contribute to the spread of CSR amongst local stakeholders and to local institutional change.

(2d) Mutual non-dependence (LD–FD–) and an institutional mismatch make investment unlikely (but if it happens, it is for other reasons that short-term deals end up ethical versus opportunistic).

(3) Mixed outcomes: MNE with an unethical institutional imprinting facing institutional mismatch (LE+FE–)

(3a) Mutual dependence makes the MNE and local government equal negotiators, and the stakes are high for both parties (LD+FD+), but the MNE may act against local rules. The local government's discretion in sanctioning unethical conduct is decisive. Tendency towards ethical outcome is strong.
(3b) MNE's dependence on non-dependent host locality (LD–FD+) increases the likelihood of negotiations leading to enforced ethical corporate conduct.
(3c) Locality's dependence on the non-dependent MNE (LD+FD–) may lead to outcomes where the local government yields to some of the MNE's unethical requests and the MNE may try to push unethical business practices amongst local stakeholders.
(3d) Mutual non-dependence (LD–FD–) and an institutional mismatch render investment unlikely (but offers an opportunity for the MNE to push unethical solutions).

(4) Tendency towards unethical conduct as both home and host institutional environments tolerate or even expect unethical conduct (LE–FE–)

(4a) Mutual dependence and the high stakes of both parties (LD+FD+) make negotiating parties tend to put effort into ascertaining each other's mutual interests. Broader local development does not weigh heavily on the agenda; institutional change is not aspired to.
(4b) The MNE's dependence on a non-dependent host locality (LD–FD+) strengthens the tendency towards unethical conduct.
(4c) The locality's dependence on the non-dependent MNE (LD+FD–) makes the local government inclined to accept the MNE's requests, strengthening tendencies towards unethical conduct.
(4d) Mutual non-dependence (LD–FD–) turns negotiations into games of opportunistic gains.

Thus, the diverging tendencies in corporate responsible action emerge as MNEs negotiate the terms of their operation locally under given circumstance. Situations 1a–d are rather clear-cut, with a strong tendency towards predominantly ethical outcomes. Also situations 4a–d suggest opportunistic solutions emerging from negotiations in a rather clear-cut fashion. Cases in the other two groups are variable—and interesting—because of the inherent institutional mismatch and unequal power relations. For example in 2b, a principally ethically operating unit of a Nordic corporation can face strong attempts at coercion to locally prevailing corrupt practices by local stakeholders in, say, the former Soviet states. In contrast, for example in 3b, an emerging economy MNE attempting to get established in a Nordic city could learn contemporary corporate transparency.

Arguably, situations 1a–d and 2a–d are the more prevalent in the world because the majority of global investments originate in and target the more advanced economies of the global North where CSR strategies are believed to be more prevalent. Situations 3a–d are less typical as investments from countries where institutions do not strongly support law enforcement and ethical practices are still less common on the world scale, although, as is well known, their numbers are increasing. We still know rather little about situations 4a–d as MNEs originating in less developed countries and targeting localities in other less-developed countries remain considerably fewer on the world scale compared to those originating in developed economies. Their numbers are growing, however, so we should get interested.

Conclusion: Negotiating Sustainable Development?

Our aim was to contribute to the systematic study of the diverse circumstances in which MNEs invest and negotiate the terms of their operations in interaction with local stakeholders, centrally local governments, and to understand the conditions in which they are likely to engage in ethical versus unethical conduct in their host localities. To this effect, we made stark delimitations which enabled us to focus on the institutional and structural conditions that we reckon are fundamental to understanding the realities of responsible business practices in localities around the world. This kept us from touching upon additional factors that are likely to influence the tendency towards corporate responsibility. These relate to corporate strategy, governance and relative independence of foreign units, corporate and locality's brand image, developments in major markets, international stakeholder relations, political systems including the role of labour unions, activities of international organisations, behaviour of other MNEs in the locality and in the MNE's global organisational field. The economic situation in host localities also plays a role: large investment hubs are distinct from smaller towns. The local government in the former has experience with potentially powerful MNEs whereas the latter might be receiving its first ever FDI.

That said, our analysis offers pointers to understanding the formation of locally institutionalised bargaining relations and their role in facilitating or hindering local development. Particularly interesting are the cases where either party is in the position to take action towards promoting ethical and transparent practices in the other party, giving rise to prospects for local institutional change. The consequence for local firms can be the opening up of opportunities to reach new markets. Initial success and the need to build legitimacy in highly competitive and institutionally robust segments in the global markets is likely to help MNEs from weak institutional backgrounds to internalise the benefits of transparency, both from the point of view of profit and from the point of view of collaborative potential arising in corporate networks and societally legitimate public–private partnerships. In localities, institutional change may facilitate the build-up of a more lucrative local institutional environment for ethical inward investment and thereby better prospects for local economic development in the long run. Most difficult are the situations where both parties are stuck with unethical practices and short-term gains. In these cases, fraudulent institutions are likely to change slowly, which tends to be reflected in local development prospects.

Acknowledgements

We thank Lucía Gómez for comments on an earlier version. Erja Kettunen is grateful for the Foundation for Economic Education for financial support.

References

Bondy, K., Moon, J., and D. Matten. 2012. "An Institution of Corporate Social Responsibility (CSR) in Multi-National Corporations (MNCs): Form and Implications." *Journal of Business Ethics* 111(2): 281–299.

Campbell, L. 2007. "Why Would Corporations Behave in Socially Responsible Ways? An Institutional Theory of Corporate Social Responsibility." *The Academy of Management Review* 32(3): 946–967.

Crane, A., and D. Matten. 2007. "Editor's Introduction: Corporate Social Responsibility as a Field of Scholarship." In *Corporate Social Responsibility*, edited by A. Crane, and D. Matten, iii-xvi. London: Sage.

Crane, A., Palazzo, G., Spence, L. J., and D. Matten. 2014. "Contesting the Value of 'Creating Shared Value'." *California Management Review* 56(2): 130–149.

Eden, L., Lenway, S., and D. A. Schuler. 2005. "From the Obsolescing Bargain to the Political Bargaining Model" In *International Business and Government Relations in the 21st Century*, edited by R. Grosse, 251–271. Cambridge: Cambridge University Press.

Emerson, R. M. 1962. "Power-Dependence Relations." *American Sociological Review* 27(1): 31–40.

Fransen, L. 2013. "The Embeddedness of Responsible Business Practice: Exploring the Interaction between National-Institutional Environments and Corporate Social Responsibility." *Journal of Business Ethics* 115(2): 213–227.

Gjølberg, M. 2009. "Measuring the Immeasurable? Constructing an Index of CSR Practices and CSR Performance in 20 Countries." *Scandinavian Journal of Management* 25(1): 10–22.

Gjølberg, M. 2010. "Varieties of Corporate Social Responsibility (CSR): CSR Meets the 'Nordic Model'." *Regulation and Governance* 4(2): 203–229.

Grosse, R., and J. N. Behrman. 1992. "Theory in International Business." *Transnational Corporations* 1(1): 93–126.

Guthey, G. T., Whiteman, G., and M. Elmes. 2014. "Place and Sense of Place: Implications for Organizational Studies of Sustainability." *Journal of Management Inquiry* 23(3): 254–265.

Kobrin, S. J. 1987. "Testing the Bargaining Hypothesis in the Manufacturing Sector in Developing Countries." *International Organization* 41(4): 609–638.

Luo, Y. 2001. "Toward a Cooperative View of MNC-Host Government Relations: Building Blocks and Performance Implications." *Journal of International Business Studies* 32(3): 401–419.

Matten, D., and J. Moon. 2008. "Implicit and Explicit CSR: A Conceptual Framework for a Comparative Understanding of Corporate Social Responsibility." *Academy of Management Review* 33(2): 404–424.

Meyer, K. E., and M. W. Peng. 2016. "Retrospective. Theoretical Foundations of Emerging Economy Business Research." *Journal of International Business Studies* 47(1): 3–22.

Meyer, J. W., and B. Rowan. 1977. "Institutionalized Organizations: Formal Structure as Myth and Ceremony." *American Journal of Sociology* 83(2): 340–363.

North, D. 1990. Institutions, Institutional Change and Economic Performance. Cambridge: Cambridge University Press.

Oinas, P. 1995. "Types of Enterprise and Local Relations." In *Human Resources and Industrial Spaces: A Perspective on Globalization and Localization*, edited by G. A. van der Knaap, and R. LeHeron, 177–195. Chichester: John Wiley and Sons.

Ramamurti, R. 2001. "The Obsolescing 'Bargaining Model'? MNC-Host Developing Country Relations Revisited." *Journal of International Business Studies* 32(1): 23–39.

Stinchcombe, A. 1965. "Social Structure and Organizations." In *Handbook of Organizations*, edited by J. March, 142–193. Chicago: Rand-McNally.

Su, W., Peng, M. W., Tan, W., and Y.-L. Cheung. 2016. "The Signaling Effect of Corporate Social Responsibility in Emerging Economies." *Journal of Business Ethics* 134(3): 479–491.

Suchman, M. C. 1995. "Managing Legitimacy: Strategic and Institutional Approaches." *The Academy of Management Review* 20(3): 571–610.

Transparency International. 2017. "Corruption Perceptions Index 2016." http://www.transparency.org/cpi2016, accessed 2017, February 6.

Vernon, R. 1977. *Storm over the Multinationals: The Real Issues*. Cambridge, MA: Harvard University Press.

Wagner, S. M. 2013. "Why Do MNEs Engage in MNE-Government Relations? Empirical Evidence from the European Union and the Automotive Industry." In *The Changing Geography of International Business*, edited by G. Cook, and J. Johns, 54–76. Basingstoke: Palgrave Macmillan.

Young, S. L., and M. V. Makhija. 2014. "Firms' Corporate Social Responsibility Behaviour: An Integration of Institutional and Profit Maximization Approaches." *Journal of International Business Studies* 45(6): 670–698.

14 Between Embeddedness and Otherness

Internationalisation of Grocery Retailers in Emerging Markets

Lech Suwala and Elmar Kulke

Introduction

Despite the unimpeded success of globalisation's benefits in general retailing, the "big picture" in grocery retailing is—with a few exceptions—somehow different. In contrast to other industries or general retailing, grocery retailing was often and still is considered a predominantly domestic economic activity in most countries. Even in the wake of general trends such as the worldwide liberalisation of retail trade, a growing middle class and higher penetration with personal vehicles or refrigerators in many developing countries, international players often operate within a limited range in (e.g. WALMART in India) or are actually absent from the key retail markets (e.g. METRO in South America). There are manifold examples showing that almost every grocery retailer that tried to expand to overseas markets has failed as often as it has succeeded (Corstjens and Lal 2012).

In the 1990s and 2000s, however, increasing internationalisation of grocery retailing resulted in a coexistence of both domestic and international structures (Dawson and Mukoyama 2014). Despite the remarkable persistence of traditional domestic retail formats like small-scale grocers, including "mom-and-pop" stores and wet markets, there is a general tendency towards "supermarketisation" and/or "hypermarketisation" of both domestic and international grocers especially in emerging markets (Reardon et al. 2004).

From our viewpoint, the coexistence of both domestic and international retail structures in emerging markets is a consequence of the considerable competitiveness and persistence of domestic retailers as well as fine-grained approaches towards internationalisation.

Against this background, the chapter takes a closer look at the latter by investigating two specific features of grocery retail internationalisation: spatial expansion patterns and foreign market strategies. Given the fact that business activities abroad generate additional costs for foreign firms in relation to their domestic counterparts, the former face certain liabilities. In order to delimit or overcome these liabilities foreign firms can choose between two opposite ends of a market development continuum: embeddedness or otherness. Although both types of market development aim to confine the competitive disadvantages arising from being a "stranger in a strange land" (Yildiz and Fey 2012) or, to put it in technical terms, the "liability of foreignness" (Zaheer 1995) or "liability of outsidership" (Johanson and Vahlne 2009), the means and approaches are fundamentally different. In our understanding, market development strategies favouring embeddedness are based on spatial and sociocultural proximity (as motived by classical Uppsala Model arguments) or mimic practices of the investors adjusting to the host country's environment, whereas market development strategies in line with otherness are characterised by flag planting in remote countries (spatial and sociocultural distance) and utilising archetypical practices or domestic capabilities abroad. We apply these market development strategies especially towards developing economies and emerging markets based on a spatial and impact analysis. Starting with an overview of theoretical approaches towards embeddedness and otherness in the context of internationalisation, we juxtapose both market development approaches with regard to (1) different types of spatial expansion patterns and (2) foreign market strategies. We show selected effects of ambivalent processes driven by these two phenomena on international grocers themselves and their competitors. The analysis is accomplished by retracing the growth history of selected retail grocers and by means of an extended literature review.

Theoretical Approaches Towards Embeddedness and Otherness in the Context of Internationalisation

Internationalisation or doing business abroad is inevitably connected with additional costs arising from spatial, sociocultural or economic distance not faced by local or domestic enterprises (Hymer 1976). At the same time, these additional costs vary with the extent of spatial, sociocultural or economic distance to foreign markets, in other words with different types of spatial expansion patterns (Johanson and Vahlne 1977). In general, inexperience of the environment was initially coined as the "liability of foreignness" (Zaheer 1995); later it was differentiated into three idiosyncratic hazard categories: unfamiliarity hazards (liability of foreignness), relational hazards (liability of outsidership) and discrimination hazards (we call it liability of racism; Eden and Miller 2001; Johanson and Vahlne 2009). By considering spatial expansion patterns alongside foreign market strategies, we also introduce the concept of spatial hazards (liability of remoteness). Because all these liabilities can result in competitive disadvantages for foreign firms, they have the choice to either assimilate/to expand in neighbouring countries (what we stylise as, approximate as and term *embeddedness* here) or to remain different/to expand in remote countries (what we stylise as, approximate as and term *otherness* here). Of course, a mixed strategy can also be thought of, which is especially relevant for grocery retailers as we will see later (e.g. TESCO is strongly embedded in remote markets).

In order to retrace firms' choices during internationalisation (spatial expansion patterns and foreign market strategies), we understand embeddedness and otherness in a twofold way. First, with regard to spatial expansion, we apprehend and portray embeddedness in the Polanyian sense (see Krippner and Alvarez 2007) as a state of being located or secured within a larger entity, context, environment, region or nation often driven by non-economic institutions (and the opposite for otherness). We link it to the internationalisation of multinational enterprise in general and their spatial expansion pattern in particular, assuming that spatial expansion patterns of grocery retailers can be illustrated by the well documented "experimental learning perspective" discussed in the so-called original Uppsala Model (Johanson and Vahlne 1977). The rationale of this approach tells us that firms undergo a learning process during their steps of international expansion. In the beginning, when international experience is still limited, expansion abroad is oriented towards countries in spatial (e.g. neighbouring countries) and sociocultural proximity (e.g. former colonies, same language, trading blocs). Spatial proximity reduces transportation costs and sociocultural proximity transaction costs. A sociocultural fit between home and host market simplifies market entry for a variety of reasons; for example it is easier for management to estimate the market volume; to offer adequate and demanded items, prices, quantities and formats; and to handle institutional conditions. Both conditions (spatial and sociocultural proximity), however, are far from being a guarantee that protects firms from market failures and divestment. In contrast, "flag planting" in remote countries in the infancy stage of internationalisation, with the purpose of diminishing risks of greater spatial and cultural–institutional distance and keeping sunk costs low, would contradict the Uppsala view. The internationalisation of grocery retailers motivated by classic Uppsala Model arguments (spatial and sociocultural proximity; Johanson and Vahlne 1977) thus aligns with the embeddedness issue, whereas flag planting in remote countries (sociocultural and organisational distance) exemplifies the otherness issue.

Second, with regard to foreign market strategies, we understand embeddedness as predominantly mimetic practices and otherness as archetypical practices of the investors—and not of the operating mode (e.g. supermarkets), a liability which could also apply to a domestic grocer—to obtain legitimacy and to pursue credibility and reliability by firms on foreign markets. These strategies have been extensively discussed by scholars from different theoretical backgrounds (institutional theory scholars, social network theorists, or supporters of the resource-based view) who favour adaptation towards the local environment either by using similar practices, thus becoming isomorphic over time (DiMaggio and Powell 1983; Rosenzweig and Nohria 1994) or by differentiating themselves from local counterparts through firm-specific managerial, organisational and technological capabilities (Buckley and Casson 1976; Dunning 1977). These findings have been reinforced by a broad range of newer studies with regard to both isomorphic practices (Eden and Miller 2001) and imported/transferred home-grown capabilities (Zaheer 1995). Although both strategies undoubtedly have their place in current debates, our arguments reach beyond this wisdom by also integrating emerging markets as host countries for multinational enterprise operations, as well as their idiosyncratic reasons for internationalising in these countries, especially with regard to otherness. Internationalisation of grocery retailers motived by isomorphic practices abroad (DiMaggio and Powell 1983) therefore supports the embeddedness issue, whereas original practices in foreign markets demonstrate the otherness issue (Zaheer 1995).

The Puzzling Spatial Expansion Patterns of International Grocery Retailers

Grocery retailing represents a low-margin business and is, therefore, forced to step into global markets to satisfy shareholders for a number of push factors (e.g. limited possibilities for market expansion, strong competition, already realised operational optimisation, and high cost pressure in saturated home markets) and pull factors such as internalisation (i.e. exploitation of economies of scale and scope), ownership (e.g. diversification of risks) or locational advantages (e.g. preventing trade or market entry barriers, new markets; Dunning 1977). Generally, internationalisation attempts and foreign ventures usually start with careful and balanced consideration of the targeted market(s). Extant literature with regard to grocery retail internationalisation in emerging markets has brought to the fore important factors and drivers from the demand side (Goldman et al. 1999; Reardon et al. 2004), supply side (Coe and Wrigley 2007; Dawson 1994, 2003) and policy side (Kulke and Suwala 2015; Wrigley and Lowe 2010). All these factors and drivers not only enable diverse global business opportunities but also represent challenges for investors when dealing with idiosyncrasies of emerging markets. The question we are addressing now is which types of spatial expansion patterns and foreign market strategies—embedded or otherness—have been pursued in grocery retail internationalisation. We begin with spatial expansion patterns.

Reviewing the list of the 250 largest retailers (food retailing and non-food retailing in 2011), we observed a total of 88 originating from Europe, 86 based in North America, and 58 located in Asia. Only eleven companies originate from South America and seven from Africa (Deloitte 2002–2014). At the same time, nine of the ten biggest global retailers (as measured by retail revenue in millions of U.S. dollars) indicated having their major business area in food retailing (see Table 14.1). The top 15 in grocery retailing were headquartered in core economies such as the U.S., Germany, the UK, France, and Japan—all of them early industrialised countries (Deloitte 2002–2014; see Table 14.1). However, none of them was able to set up a business in all key markets at the same time.

Table 14.1 Number of countries in operation and worldwide rank (in brackets) by the Top 15 Grocery Retailers (2011) among the top 250 general global retailers between 1996 and 2011

Name/Year	*1996*	*2000*	*2001*	*2003*	*2005*	*2007*	*2009*	*2011*
Walmart (U.S.)	1	1	10(1)	10(1)	11(1)	14(1)	16(1)	28(1)
Carrefour (F)	8	2	23(2)	31(2)	31(2)	33(2)	36(2)	33(2)
Tesco (UK)	18	13	12(13)	12(6)	13(5)	13(3)	13(4)	13(3)
Metro (GER)	4	5	28(6)	28(4)	30(4)	32(4)	33(3)	33(4)
Kroger (U.S.)	13	3	1(5)	1(5)	1(6)	1(6)	1(6)	1(5)
Costco (U.S.)	23	14	8(12)	8(9)	8(8)	8(9)	9(7)	9(6)
Schwarz (GER)	33	29	×	×	21(10)	24(7)	25(5)	26(7)
Aldi (GER)	×	×	12(15)	12(10)	14(11)	15(10)	18(8)	17(8)
Target (U.S.)	×	×	1(7)	1(7)	1(7)	1(8)	1(10)	1(11)
Auchan (F)	×	×	×	×	11(15)	11(14)	14(15)	12(12)
Aeon (J)	×	×	×	×	10(20)	10(21)	9(18)	9(13)
Edeka (GER)	×	×	×	×	5(17)	3(19)	1(14)	1(15)
SevenEleven (J)	×	×	×	×	4(24)	4(16)	18(16)	18(16)
Rewe (GER)	×	×	×	13(11)	14(12)	14(12)	13(12)	19(11)
Casino (F)	×	×	×	×	28(32)	11(28)	25(26)	22(26)

Source: Own calculations based on Deloitte 2002–2013.

*Due to minor interest of this study, the two biggest Australian grocery retailers have been omitted (WOOLWORTHS and WESTFARMES, 2011, rank 19th and 20th, respectively, excluded) as well as DUTCH AHOLD ranked 3rd in 2001, 26th in 2011 (balance account scandal) and ALBERTSONS ranked 8th in 2001, 239th in 2011 (M&A and split).

Abbreviations: J = Japan, GER = Germany, F = France, U.S. = United States of America, UK = United Kingdom.

Although animated by similar push and pull factors for internationalisation as general retailers, the geographic distribution of foreign ventures and spatial expansion patterns of grocery retailers are far from comprehensive. Four universal trends, however, hold true for most spatial expansion patterns.

First, next to a traditional North–North expansion that set the pace early on within grocery internationalisation (but which is not the focus here), a North–South expansion process of international retail chains has dominated internationalisation figures over the last two decades. Interestingly, this North–South expansion was accompanied by four waves of transformation that also led to a "super-/hypermarketisation" of emerging markets (Reardon et al. 2012). The first wave encompassed Latin America, Central Europe and South Africa starting in the early 1990s; the second, South-east Asia (outside transition countries like Vietnam), Central America and Mexico during mid- to late 1990s; the third, China, Vietnam, India and Russia in the late 1990s and 2000s; and, the fourth, mainly eastern/southern Africa outside of South Africa, where the supermarket revolution is just taking off. Admittedly, particular markets like China or India have idiosyncratic spatial expansion patterns not always consistent with this model. Nevertheless, these waves can be differentiated by the diverging shares of the "modern" retail market with the highest penetration in pioneering countries (Deloitte 2002–2014; Reardon et al. 2012). In particular, the second and third waves were dominated by "newborn" retail companies with aggressive "gold rush" and M&A strategies when entering emerging markets (the otherness issue; Wrigley and Lowe 2010). Motives, drivers and the sequence for this North–South internationalisation can be partly explained by the well-documented "experimental learning perspective" as discussed in the original Uppsala Model (Johanson and Vahlne 1977). This is especially relevant for modern food retailers because these stakeholders have to develop, organise and establish entire procurement systems for the continued delivery of items to the stores. In other words, when grocery retailers enter a new market, systemic market development and a far-flung network needs to be set up. Fresh food supply chains, in particular, are a logistical challenge; either efficient cross-border international delivery systems or laborious contacts to local producers or wholesalers have to be established, inevitably leading towards an intense degree of embeddedness. However, at certain stages of expansion, often more risky ventures had to be undertaken that are rather characterised by "flag planting" in remote countries, pointing more towards an otherness strategy.

Second, there is a new trend in grocery retailers originating from emerging markets with a developing middle class that clearly indicates growing South–South internationalisation (Kulke and Suwala 2016). Decades of imitation and learning associated with distinct innovations, venture capital and long-term visions of enthusiastic entrepreneurs in certain emerging countries proved sustainable in home markets and even led to entry in neighbouring countries (e.g. SPAR from South Africa; CENCOSUD from Chile). Moreover, there are delicate signs and attempts of first entries of food retailers from developing to developed economies (e.g. South African PICK N' PAY in Australia, the Mexican CHEDRAUI in the U.S.). These developments, however, neither represent a general trend nor substantial ventures that compete with national retail chains. Rather, they are experiments to exert a modest influence in niche markets (e.g. CHEDRAUI'S idea to service the Mexican community on the West Coast of the U.S.). In all cases, the embeddedness issue is predominant as spatial expansion is directed mainly towards neighbouring and often well-known customer profiles. Otherness plays only a limited role here.

Third, there are no regularities in single company expansion trajectories. Although a gradual expansion process from proximate to distant countries in the sense of spatial and cultural–institutional proximity is documented in the international expansion of several grocery-retailing enterprises (the Uppsala argument), country-based expansion itself is more reminiscent of a trial-and-error process (the otherness issue). The German METRO GROUP for example started their international expansion in the 1970s in Central and Western Europe, continued to Northern Africa in the early1990s, entered Eastern Europe and China in the mid-1990s and is now expanding in South and South-east Asia (Franz 2011). The U.S. WAL-MART GROUP was present solely in North and South America (e.g. Mexico, Argentina, Brazil, Puerto Rico) until the mid-1990s, expanded to Western Europe (Germany, UK), Central America and East Asia (Japan, South Korea) in the mid-2000s and took over numerous subsidiaries in Southern African countries in 2011 (Kulke and Suwala 2016).

Fourth, typical spatial diffusion patterns can also be observed at a national level in emerging markets (Reardon 2005). Pioneering activities of mainstream modern retailing formats (super-/hypermarkets) usually start their operation in upper-and middle-class areas of capital cities, where they expect sufficient demand due to above-average incomes and modern shopping behaviour of the residents (the otherness issue). In this instance, location-wise, super-/hypermarkets are often attached to and presented as luxury types of shopping, serving a market niche for the local elite. The auxiliary expansion process, however, diffuses hierarchically towards other parts of capital cities and later second-tier cities to intermediate towns and finally even to towns in rural areas. Finally, they enter the informal settlements of urban areas with lower incomes (e.g. in Nairobi, Kenya, or El Alto, Bolivia). This spatial expansion is driven by the ongoing competition in the higher-income market segment (other chains entering the market) and by internal cost reduction possibilities based on the development of commodity chains by the companies. Here, silent strategies are often utilised by foreign grocers where local store names or brands remain unchanged after a takeover (the embeddedness issue) in order to avoid the risk of local unrest (Kulke and Suwala 2015; Reardon 2005).

Foreign Market Strategies of Internationalisation Grocers

Our idea to reveal the embeddedness and otherness issues within foreign market strategies and the resulting business opportunities of grocery retail internationalisation in emerging markets is based on an impact analysis which focuses on the various actor groups associated with or affected by foreign retailers. Whilst our in-depth analysis (Kulke and Suwala 2015) provided exclusive consideration of the entire commodity chain behind grocery retail, starting with the agricultural product from the farm through collection and transportation to retailing and, finally, to the end consumer, here we emphasise only selective effects relevant to the embeddedness and otherness issue and restrict our analysis to aspects of market entry, business environment and competition.

Let us turn the spotlight on market entry. Setting up subunits abroad requires elaborate strategies that target the very market and retail system including domestic firms. In order to overcome the "liabilities of not being a domestic firm", foreign units often have to embed by investing a considerable amount of capital into the set-up of modern technologies. The goal is to increase operational efficiency (due to manual inventory, ordering and, in some instances, a non-existent consumer data base), and education of personnel because division of labour and task specialisation are steadily growing in the retail system of developing countries, calling for a wide range of qualifications. The same holds true, although to a lesser extent, for the establishment, organisation and maintenance of a store network, appropriate locational decision-making and operation of a smooth supply chain which necessitates highly qualified personnel, either from chain stores in advanced economies or with experience of having worked there (Dawson 2003). Here, foreign ventures have the freedom to carry out their versant practices due to the absence of "common, good or accepted" practices in emerging markets (the otherness issue). However, a segmented training approach is required. This can be delivered, sponsored or accelerated by international suppliers, government or non-governmental organisations and associations, and FDI through trade fair visits and overseas training (Hagen 2002). At the same time, internationalisation has also shown the ambiguous impact of this strategy on the profitability of foreign firms. Situational factors such as time, type and intensity of market entry, existing competitors and regulatory policies are some of the aspects that influence financial performance (the embeddedness issue). Although AHOLD's expansion in the early 2000s for example showed high returns on investment in Central America, its experience in China in the same period turned out far below expectations (Kulke and Suwala 2015).

With reference to the strategies of foreign ventures towards competitors (traditional markets, local/national chain stores, other modern international retailers), it can be said that modern international retail market entries, either as first or second movers or late-comers with major investments, have radically changed the rules of the game in developing markets (Coe and Wrigley 2007; Dawson 1994, 2003; Sunanto 2013). The underlying assumption is that significant market shares—sometimes mere market leadership—promised international grocery retailers sufficient returns on investment by means of economies of scale and scope. Although early market entry attempts in the 1990s consisted of little more than portfolio investments, "flag planting" or other short-term engagements, this infancy stage was typically accompanied by substantial follow-up investments but sometimes also by divestment and even withdrawals (Wrigley and Lowe 2010). Hence, many emerging countries witnessed a competitive "shake-out". This consolidation began when numerous international competitors initially made their entry into specific markets (e.g. Poland, Thailand), followed by selective/strategic reinvestment or even divestment, market exits and asset trade-offs among these stakeholders (Burt et al. 2003). As a result, a number of international grocery retailers concentrated their activities in certain markets to intentionally or randomly divide the pie (Kulke and Suwala 2016). For social welfare reasons, however, antitrust agencies in some countries prevented this tendency to monopolise the market (e.g. Slovakia). These facts rather point to market logics independent of the regional contexts and therefore to the otherness issue.

At best, however, this is only half the truth. Despite market leadership by international grocery retailers in some emerging markets (Corstjens and Lal 2012), both traditional and/or national retailers still show remarkable persistence and survive as strongholds in certain regions (Coe and Wrigley 2007). This persistence led to struggles of modern retailers due to customer loyalty strategies, the supply of traditional or religiously constrained products (e.g. halal foods) or just a lower critical mass for break-evens of domestic competitors in dispersed areas, to give only a few reasons (Kulke and Suwala 2015). Again, depending on the foreign market, elements of an embedded strategy are necessary in order to deal with the sheer number of street vendors, the consolidation and learning effects of local/national chains, the popularity of traditional bazaars, wet markets and street markets, the custom of bargaining and the inability of international firms to set up reliable supply networks at comparable prices and quality. Moreover, fierce defence strategies are pursued by both traditional formats and national retail chains (for Chile, see Bianchi and Ostale 2006), frequently with government support by means of low-cost capital (for China, see Reardon 2005), lobbyism and/or protective regulations.

Recent studies have observed new mixed strategies (embeddedness and otherness), such as the "supermarket-cum-wet market" (referring to supermarkets with a fresh food section as a wet market look-alike), that put further pressure on traditional retailers (e.g. for Hongkong, see Ho 2005) and have confirmed that modern retailers can outperform wet markets and street vendors in some categories (e.g. for Indonesia, see Sunanto 2013). Other mixed strategies favour cooperation agreements (e.g. joint ventures, partnerships with national grocers) as a vibrant mechanism of location adaptation with regard to consumers' needs and embeddedness (e.g. smooth and integrated sales appearances along cultural behavioural patterns or public points of view) while pursuing own practices in the background (Schlunze et al. 2013). Such strategies can be either opportunistic and short term (e.g. TESCO and their relationships with CP GROUP in Thailand, with SIME DARBY in Malaysia or with TING HSIN in China where potential rents or learning effects are only skimmed before leaving the market, Coe and Wrigley 2007) or consistent and long term (e.g. CASINO and their relationships with GDA in Brazil; with EXITO in Colombia with real lasting interest of providing markets; Deloitte 2002–2014).

Conclusion

As has been documented and analysed, doing business abroad leads to additional costs also in grocery retailing. In order to overcome these costs that can be expressed as liabilities, we have introduced a continuum of embeddedness and otherness as possible market development approaches towards spatial extension and foreign market strategies. Both the puzzling geographical patterns of the largest international grocers and the complexities of market penetration connected to different strategies during various value chain stages showed that only a balanced and fine-grained approach towards internationalisation taking both embeddedness and otherness into account can lead to successful strategies abroad. This holds true in grocery retailing more than ever, not only because of the multifaceted, highly contextual and environment-based mosaic of grocery retail internationalisation but also because of the all-embracing approach of integrating agricultural systems, procurement channels and consumers' preferences when entering a foreign market. Despite the few generalisations that are possible at this level of analysis, there are roughly two chronologically distinct spatial expansion and foreign market strategies with regard to embeddedness and otherness. We conclude that the early years of grocery internationalisation (stage 1) were predominantly characterised by expansion to spatially and/or socioculturally proximate countries (the embeddedness issue) while openly trying to assert significant structural transformation and archetypical business practices (systems, brands, workers, etc.; the otherness issue). In the current stage 2, we observe a reverse strategy: more spatially and socioculturally distant markets are targeted (the otherness issue) while preserving local store brands, parts of the network structure and certain suppliers in order to maintain legitimacy, trust and credibility among consumers (the embeddedness issue).

References

Bianchi, C., and E. Ostale. 2006. "Lessons Learned from Unsuccessful Internationalisation Attempts: Examples of Multinational Retailers in Chile." *Journal of Business Research* 59 (1): 140–147.

Buckley, P., and M. C. Casson. 1976. *The Future of the Multinational Enterprise.* London: MacMillan.

Burt, S., Dawson, J., and L. Sparks. 2003. "Failure in International Markets: Research Propositions." *International Review of Retail Distribution and Consumer Research* 13(4): 355–373.

Coe, N., and N. Wrigley. 2007. "Host Economy Impacts of Transnational Retail: The Research Agenda." *Journal of Economic Geography* 7(4): 341–371.

Corstjens, M., and R. Lal. 2012. "Retail Doesn't Cross Borders: Here's Why and What to Do about It." *Harvard Business Review* 90(4): 101–110.

Dawson, J. 1994. "Internationalisation of Retailing Operations." *Journal of Marketing Management* 10(4): 267–282.

Dawson, J. 2003. "Towards a Model of the Impacts of Retail Internationalisation." In *The Internationalisation of Retailing in Asia*, edited by J. Dawson, M. Mukoyama, C. C. Sang, and R. Larke, 189–209. London: Routledge.

Dawson, J., and M. Mukoyama. 2014. "Recent Development in Retail Internationalisation." In *Global Strategies in Retailing: Asian and European Experiences*, edited by J. Dawson, and M. Mukoyama, 5–35. London: Routledge.

Deloitte. 2002–2014. 2001–2013 Global Powers of Retailing Reports. https://www2.deloitte.com/global/en/pages/consumer-business/articles/global-powers-of-retailing.html, accessed 2016, January 8.

DiMaggio, P., and W. Powell. 1983. "The Iron Cage Revisited: Institutional Isomorphism and Collective Rationality in Organisational Fields." *American Sociological Review* 48(2): 147–160.

Dunning, J. H. 1977. "Trade, Location of Economic Activity and the MNE: A Search for an Eclectic Approach." In *The International Allocation of Economic Activity*, edited by B. Ohlin, P. O. Hesselborn, and P. M. Wijkman, 395–418. New York: Holmes and Meier.

Eden, L., and S. R. Miller. 2001. "Opening the Black Box: The Multinational Enterprise and the Cost of Doing Business Abroad." In *Best Paper Proceedings, Academy of Management Meeting*, edited by D. H. Nagao, C1—C6. Washington, DC: Academy of Management.

Franz, M. 2011. "Globalisierung im Einzelhandel: Akteure und ihre Machtbeziehungen." *Geographische Rundschau* 63(1): 4–10.

Goldman, A., Krider, R., and S. Ramaswami. 1999. "The Persistent Competitive Advantage of Traditional Food Retailers in Asia: Wet Markets' Continued Dominance in Hongkong." *Journal of Macromarketing* 19(2): 126–139.

Hagen, J. M. 2002. Causes and Consequences of Food Retailing Innovation in Developing Countries: Supermarkets in Vietnam. New York, USA: Cornell University.

Ho, S. C. 2005. "Evolution versus Tradition in Marketing Systems: The Hong Kong Food-Retailing Experience." *Journal of Public Policy and Marketing* 24(1): 90–99.

Hymer, S. H. 1976. The International Operations of National Firms: A Study of Foreign Direct Investment. Cambridge, MA: MIT Press.

Johanson, J., and J. E. Vahlne. 1977. "The Internationalisation Process of the Firm: A Model of Knowledge Development and Increasing Foreign Market Commitments." *Journal of International Business Studies* 8(1): 23–32.

Johanson, J., and J. E. Vahlne. 2009. "The Uppsala Internationalisation Process Model Revisited: From Inliability of Foreignness to Liability of Outsidership." *Journal of International Business Studies* 40(9): 1411–1431.

Krippner, G. R., and A. S. Alvarez. 2007. "Embeddedness and the Intellectual Projects of Economic Sociology." *Annual Review of Sociology* 33(1): 219–240.

Kulke, E., and L. Suwala. 2015. "Internationalisation of Grocery Retailers in Emerging Markets: General Considerations and Economic Impacts." Working Paper 5/2015, Humboldt-Universität zu Berlin. https://www.researchgate.net/publication/301694796_Internationalization_of_grocery_retailers_in_emerging_markets_-_general_considerations_and_economic_impacts, accessed 2016, January 22.

Kulke, E., and L. Suwala. 2016. "Internationalisation of Grocery Retailing in the Global South: General Conditions, Formats and Spatial Expansion Patterns of Selected MNEs." *Die Erde* 147(3): 187–200.

Reardon, T. 2005. Retail Companies as Integrators of Value Chains in Developing Countries: Diffusion, Procurement System Change, and Trade and Development Effects. Bonn: GTZ.

Reardon, T., Timmer, C. P., and J. A. Berdegué. 2004. "The Rapid Rise of Supermarkets in Developing Countries: Induced Organisational, Institutional, and Technological Change in Agrifood Systems." *Journal of Agricultural and Development Economics* 1(2): 168–183.

Reardon, T., Timmer, C. P., and B. Minten. 2012. "Supermarket Revolution in Asia and Emerging Development Strategies to Include Small Farmers." *Proceedings of the National Academy of Sciences of the United States of America* 109(31): 12332–12337.

Rosenzweig, P. M., and N. Nohria. 1994. "Influences on Human Resource Management Practices in Multinational Corporations." *Journal of International Business Studies* 25(2): 229–251.
Schlunze, R. D., Plattner, M., and W. Ji. 2013. "Co-Leadership Success by Sharing Local and Global Information Networks." In *Visuelle Netzwerkforschung*, edited by M. Schönhuth, M. Gamper, M. Kronenwett, and M. Stark, 161–178. Bielefeld: Transcript.
Sunanto, S. 2013. The Effects of Modern Food Retail Development on Consumers, Producers, Wholesalers and Traditional Retailers: The Case of West Java. Amsterdam: International Institute of Social Studies.
Wrigley, N., and M. Lowe. 2010. The Globalization of Trade in Retail Services: Report Commissioned by OECD Trade Policy Linkages and Services Division for the OECD Experts Meeting on Distribution Services. Paris: OECD Trade Policy Linkages and Services Division.
Yildiz, H. E., and C. F. Fey. 2012. "The Liability of Foreignness Reconsidered: New Insights from the Alternative Research Context of Transforming Economies." *International Business Review* 21(2): 269–280.
Zaheer, S. 1995. "Overcoming the Liability of Foreignness." *Academy of Management Journal* 38(2): 341–363.

15 Making Sense of Local Customer Relationships in Cross-border Acquisitions

Christina Öberg

Introduction

This chapter deals with sensemaking in the context of customer relationships in cross-border acquisitions. Its specific focus is on the local customer relationships of acquired parties, highlighting the differences in sensemaking that exist between local customers, local representatives of the acquired parties and strategic managers of the acquirer. Sensemaking is concerned with how individuals understand a situation (Weick 1987), which in the context of this chapter refers to both the acquisition and subsequent integration.

In the context of cross-border acquisitions, literature has focused on cultural differences between the acquirer and the acquired party but has largely been unconcerned with sensemaking. Cultural differences in M&A studies are frequently described at the organisational and national level, indicating potential complications during integration because of misalignments in how business is managed and conducted, and differing values and belief systems (Buono et al. 1985; Cartwright and Magni 2009; Weber and Drori 2008). In its focus on organisational and national cultures, literature disregards two important aspects: First, an organisation's values and belief systems may not be homogenous and how matters are understood may vary between individuals, departments, functional levels or professions. Second, the only cultures taken into account are those of the acquirer and the acquired party. Yet a cross-border acquisition is also likely to affect the customers of these parties (Öberg 2014). Because many cross-border acquisitions aim to reach customers in new geographical markets or help subsidiaries to reach international customers (Johanson and Mattsson 1988), this latter aspect is important. Hence, customer companies also need to be taken into consideration, as do the differences within and among them. These aspects are emphasised by a sensemaking focus on acquisitions.

This chapter specifically considers how strategic-level representatives of the acquirer make sense of the acquired parties' local customers, how local representatives of the acquired party understand the acquisition and how local customers (in a business-to-business setting) make sense of the acquisition. A case study illustrates differences between these parties. It points to how differences in individual understanding of the acquisition influence the continued acquisition process and lead to reactions and changes based primarily on expectations and social reinforcement. The chapter expands previous research by deepening the discussion on sensemaking related to acquisitions by taking a triadic perspective on international acquisitions (focusing on the acquirer, the acquired party and the customer) and highlighting the strategic-/operational-level chasm in such endeavours.

The chapter is organised as follows: The first section discusses sensemaking and culture in more depth. The next section places sensemaking in the specific context of cross-border acquisitions. An empirical example from the business-to-business context is then provided to illustrate the issue at hand. The case is analysed, and the chapter ends with some concluding remarks.

Sensemaking and Culture

Sensemaking reflects how individuals grasp what goes on (Weick et al. 2005) and what to do next (Taylor and Every 2000). It thus enables the construction of a rationale that guides individual activities, linking the interpretation of what is happening and what to do as a consequence. Social interaction affects sensemaking and is reflected in culture through social reinforcement (Dauber 2012). Although there are regimes within companies that attempt to guide individual values and understandings through different types of artefacts (e.g. Weick 1987), sensemaking remains based on an individual's own experience. Individuals with frequent interaction affect each other's sensemaking to larger extent than individuals with only sporadic interaction or no interaction at all (Wiley 1988). Variation among individuals may further be influenced by departments, functional levels and professions. For example the sensemaking of individuals within the same department, part of the same functional level or with the same profession may be more similar than that of disparate individuals, partly resulting from the similarity of experiences and the interactions among the individuals concerned. Interaction and organisational belonging at the level of department, at a functional level or by profession may thus lead to intra- and inter-organisational groups of individuals that have more shared understanding than others (Cooper et al. 2014). Hence, although sensemaking is an individual process, an understanding of matters is formed in interaction. Sensemaking highlights how subgroups of individuals may share understandings to a larger extent than what is expressed at the level of organisational culture. When dividing culture into subjective and objective culture (Buono et al. 1985), objective culture (management styles, etc.) can be expected to affect sensemaking in a more unilateral way; it also represents a tool of sensegiving (Maitlis and Lawrence 2007). Sensemaking, in turn, would influence yet also be influenced by subjective culture, that is the values and beliefs that are shaped in interactions. Subjective culture contributes to sensemaking beyond artefacts.

Thus, sensegiving relates to objective culture or management styles and artefacts whereas sensemaking reflects the subjective culture and is shaped by interaction among individuals. This explains how individuals belonging to different organisations while interacting may have more shared understanding of matters than individuals belonging to the same organisation.

Sensemaking in Cross-border Acquisitions

When placing sensemaking into the context of a cross-border acquisition, and specifically including the acquired party's local customers, it is evident that some subgroups interact more frequently than others, that between-group interactions occur with much less frequency and that all of these subgroups have a history. One such subgroup is the managers of the acquirer. Together with the owners, they will have a certain idea about the acquired party and its customers, including who the acquired party is, who its customers are and how they will fit into the acquirer's business (Haspeslagh and Jemison 1991; Larsson and Finkelstein 1999). Due diligence carried out before the acquisition can be expected to include a thorough analysis of the acquired party and its business, but in practice this is often limited to calculating customer contracts and the revenues of the acquired party (Koller et al. 2005). Although the idea of the acquired party's customers may be a decisive factor for the go-ahead, this view is rarely rooted in any long-term understanding of the customers or their day-to-day interaction with the acquired party. In order to promote cultural integration, managers will likely attempt to give sense to the staff of the acquired party (Lakshman 2011; Stahl et al. 2013). Provided it is reciprocal, cultural integration may well include a deepened understanding of the values and management style of the acquired party.

The acquired party's local representatives—the sales and maintenance staff that directly interact with customer representatives—can be assumed to have in-depth knowledge of the customers' day-to-day activities (their operational level). At the same time, they may not necessarily grasp the decisions taken by managers with respect to customers. This is due to the fact that some managers are part of different companies—in this case, the acquirer and the customer (Öberg 2012)—and that managers within their own organisation are at a different organisational level (Amason and Sapienza 1997; Van Der Velde and Jansen 1999). The acquired party's local representatives may potentially find it easier to understand the operational staff of the acquirer, but in the context of cross-border acquisitions may not interact with them at all. Hence, shared sensemaking may only apply at a certain functional level within one's own company and at the operational level with customers.

Local customer representatives, finally, are normally rooted in the local market of the acquired party's country. They are therefore distant to both the acquirer and its management. They will seek to comprehend what is going on from the activities of their interaction partners in the acquired party and through possible changes in the business relationship. They may share a subgroup culture with the local representatives of the acquired party (Cooper et al. 2014) or at least understand what the interaction with these parties gives them, what to expect and how to handle this accordingly.

The Example of a Finnish Software Company's Acquisition of a Swedish Firm

So what does all this mean in practice? The following example is based on previous data collected by the author, mostly based on semistructured interviews complemented by secondary data sources such as newspaper items, annual reports, and company-internal documentations (Huber and Power 1985; Welch 2000). The example was chosen specifically to illustrate dimensions of sensemaking and sensegiving related to the acquisition and integration of firms. In the description, the three perspectives outlined earlier (managers of the acquirer, local staff of the acquired party and customers' operational staff on the local market) are treated as subgroups with similar sensemaking within each, although individual differences may apply. In the analysis of data, the relevance of the three perspectives was ensured by sorting interview transcripts and notes based on within-group similarities and between-group differences.

The example describes how a Finnish software company acquired a Swedish counterpart. Prior to the acquisition, the Finnish firm had some minor representation in Sweden but aimed to increase its market there (expressed as number of customers and revenue generated from them) as part of an internationalisation scheme designed by the company's management. Prior to the acquisition the Finnish firm competed with the acquired party, so in addition to acquiring specific customer relationships, the acquisition also aimed to decrease competitive pressure. In the acquirer's calculation of benefits, the expectation was that the acquired party's customers would stay with the combined firm. Additionally, the Finnish company's management expected that the prospective customers the acquirer and the acquired party had been competing for would become customers of the combined firm.

At the same time, there was an expectation that customers would be reluctant to change. Integration of the companies was therefore put on hold for half a year following the acquisition. The integration that then happened in terms of products—where the acquired party's software was replaced by the acquirer's—was presented to customers as an upgrade rather than a different product. The financial calculations of the integration did not account for any customer losses. The acquirer's management thus had a fairly pragmatic view of the acquired party's customers. Their view was based on the companies that were presently customers of the acquired party, together with the prospective customers that the acquirer and the acquired party currently competed for. Although these customers were treated as "assets" that were expected to follow the acquired party (Anderson et al. 2001), they were still referred to as individual firms, emphasising their individual importance not only as streams of revenue but also as important reference customers and artefacts of business success vis-à-vis competitors.

The sales and maintenance staff of the acquired party understood the acquisition differently. Although the acquired party had a strong position on its domestic market, the owner had struggled with financial issues for some time, and this had come to the staff's awareness. The acquisition was therefore seen as salient by the acquired party's staff. One complicating matter was that the management of the acquirer and the local staff of the acquired party were located in different cities so that the staff of the acquired party felt somewhat alienated from the acquirer. During the time that passed between the acquisition and integration, staff tried to grasp the new situation, feeling reassured by the lack of integration that they could continue as a separate unit and continue to work with their present customers. Development projects were continued for the software and staff acted based on what they saw. When the integration was initiated, staff realised the acquirer's management intentions and responded. Development projects were closed down, and maintenance staff left the combined firm, feeling betrayed by the decision to replace the acquired party's software. Sales staff also responded by leaving the combined firm as they would have to represent the replacing product and found it difficult to sell software they had previously competed with.

Local customer representatives initially had a somewhat similar understanding of the acquisition to the sales and maintenance staff of the acquired party. They had also learned of the financial issues of the previous owner and saw the acquisition as reassurance that the software they used would continue to be maintained and developed. Local representatives based their sensemaking on what they actually heard from the acquired party's sales and maintenance staff. Because the latter communicated the idea that the acquirer and acquired party would continue as separate units, customers' operational staff also came to rely on this. In particular, the maintenance staff helped to create this shared understanding based on high levels of interaction (social reinforcement). Directly after the acquisition, but still before the integration, the maintenance staff responded to the needs and preferences of the local customer representatives by attempting to maintain business as usual. Working in close symbiosis with the maintenance staff, local customer representatives even provided ideas for further improvement of the software. Rather than being shaped through artefacts, the interaction created manifestations of sensegiving which ensured that any subsequent activities followed on from the consensus reached between these two parties.

Managers of local customers became hesitant about whether the acquired party would really continue as a separate unit, but to some degree relied on the reassurance by their local representatives. Managers looked into the general development of the acquired firm, the fit with other software, and whether the acquired party was trustworthy enough to continue its business. This last aspect caused some management concern. Managers of prospective customers started to play a waiting game to see what would happen rather than deciding on the acquirer's or the acquired party's software. This hesitation was partly rooted in previous experiences with other acquisitions (Finkelstein and Haleblian 2002) and, for some prospective customers, an option to play off two parties against one another.

When integration began, customers reacted strongly. Although presented as an upgrade, customer representatives did realise that they now were dealing with a different piece of software. For managers, its fit with other systems, the cost of changing the software and its expected future development were important aspects to consider. To a large extent, however, managers continued to rely on information from their local representatives, due in part to the particular product (software) and the need for staff experienced in its use and implementation. For local customer representatives, the change was accentuated by the fact that sales and maintenance staff left the newly combined company. This affected their continuity of interaction, causing them to react in turn. They were also receptive to comments and activities specifically of the maintenance staff, leading to a stronger sense of sharing ideas and greater commitment to that staff. As the local customer representatives turned to their managers, and based on the managers' own sensemaking of the integration, most customer companies re-evaluated their software choice rather than automatically shifting to the acquirer's software. In the end, some 60% of the customers did shift to the acquirer's software, often because other customer companies had also done so or because they were looking for continuity. Others left, also basing that decision on how other customers handled the situation or based on sensemaking in interaction with the local staff of the acquired party.

The example is of an acquisition with a time lapse between the signing of contracts and integration. The management of the acquirer had a somewhat simplified idea of the acquired party's customers: they were thought of as individual firms, and the belief was that they would follow the acquisition. Furthermore, the understanding was that they would be reluctant to change, which is why the launch of the replacement was sold as an upgrade. Although some time passed between the acquisition and integration, little effort was made to learn about the customers and their preferences, neither from the customers directly nor through the acquired party (Öberg and Tarba 2013). Influence on managers' sensemaking of local customers was therefore minor. As for the sales and maintenance staff of the acquired party and local customer representatives, frequent interaction and shared development (Thomke and Hippel 2002) had created trust and a shared understanding of matters (social reinforcement). Whilst the managers of customers found themselves questioning the continuity of the acquired party as a separate unit, local customer representatives felt reassured by the understanding they shared with the sales and maintenance staff. The managers of customers based their sensemaking on previous experience and only partly on their local representatives, whilst local representatives based their sensemaking on what they saw and heard in their day-to-day interactions. In both instances, sensemaking had little to do with what and how the acquirer's managers planned. The integration became "evidence" of the acquirer's intention as it happened. Speculations were thus replaced by reactions to actual concerns. The integration could hence be considered a first act of sensegiving (Gioia and Chittipeddi 1991), but this did not mean that sales and maintenance staff or customer representatives acted accordingly. Instead, what to do next (Taylor and Every 2000) was influenced by other customers, the influence of local customer representatives on their management and the reactions of the sales and maintenance staff.

Analysis

Sensemaking of local customer relationships in cross-border acquisitions is shown to be a process involving more parties than just the acquirer and the acquired party. In the example presented it includes managers as well as operational level staff, customers in their interaction with the companies and other customers and their ways of handling matters. Sensemaking thus occurs through interactions that may extend beyond the actual company and through transfers among individuals based on interactions (social reinforcement), leading to similar subsequent activities (Dauber 2012; Taylor and Every 2000).

The example indicates that the greater the physical distance between individuals, the greater the presence of speculation and the lesser the reliance of sensemaking on activities and shared meanings. This is exemplified by the managers of the acquired party's customers and the management of the acquirer who did not interact at all before integration and then came to negotiate contracts from quite different perspectives. In the example presented, few instances of sensegiving are found as the acquirer's intentions only became clear in the integration process itself. This implies that the management of the acquirer made no particular effort to guide the acquired party's local representation and customers, also basing decisions on speculation rather than interaction with these parties. For the managers of the acquired party's customers, grasping what went on (Weick et al. 2005) was influenced by previous activities (actual interaction), other experiences from other acquisitions, and the activities of others. Experiences from other acquisitions became important because current activities did not provide any answers; it was this that led customer managers to speculate. The consequence of speculation was that intentions became misunderstood. This not only applied to parties with no interaction but also occurred as a result of interaction. Interacting individuals strengthened each other's sensemaking through social reinforcement, but failing to interact closely with the other parties (in this case, the managers of the acquirer), their speculations had little to do with the actual intentions of these parties.

So, how can sensemaking in cross-border acquisitions be explained theoretically? Acquisitions can be interpreted as an activity that is not part of "business as usual" between companies. Individuals grasp what goes on based on their perception of the acquisition as something unusual or extraordinary. Expectations of change may take root unless evidence for continuity is the stronger force. Powers (1973) refers to the role of preconception in sensemaking processes, so previous experience may play a critical part in how the acquisition is regarded. Social interaction strengthens beliefs through social reinforcement, irrespective of whether these beliefs are correct or incorrect (Molina-Morales and Martínez-Fernández 2009). Individuals considered trustworthy are particularly important in such processes. Sensemaking is formed based on interaction, and although the interacting parties may not grasp what actually goes on, their interaction subjectively reinforces the rationale for what to do next.

Activities of others may bring clarity (sensegiving), but this does not necessarily convince individuals of what directions to take. Established values and belief systems are stronger than for instance the influence of changed management styles. Future activities are guided by interpretation of the consequences of change. In cross-border acquisitions, there is greater distance between the acquirer and the acquired party, and sensemaking is possibly influenced by value systems connected to country-specific management styles (e.g. Weber and Drori 2008). Bridging between the acquirer and the acquired party's customers thus becomes more complicated, as the local customers of the acquired party are comparably closer to the acquired party.

Conclusion

This chapter highlights that managers, local (operational) staff and customers may not give an acquisition the same meaning. The easy explanation would be that these individuals simply represent different companies. In this respect alone, the chapter contributes to the acquisition literature by including the perspective of customers. However, differences in sensemaking also result from how individuals are "located" at different organisational levels. The chapter illustrates how sensemaking is socially reinforced through interaction, and how speculations guide activities in the construction of social rationality. In the case study this is illustrated by the managers of the acquirer and how they based customer-related decisions on speculation rather than knowledge gained through direct interaction.

The practical implications of the chapter are linked to cultural integration. Literature has pointed to de-learning and the creation of something new and shared as important aspects of integration (e.g. Verbeke 2010). However, this suggests that each company has a homogeneous organisational culture rather than being constructed of subgroups with different sensemaking. Working with different types of artefacts can be helpful, but as suggested here, communication and clarification would be more important in order to avoid speculation in the practical handling of acquisitions.

References

Amason, A. C., and H. J. Sapienza. 1997. "The Effects of Top Management Team Size and Interaction Norms on Cognitive and Affective Conflict." *Journal of Management* 23(4): 495–516.

Anderson, H., Havila, V., and A. Salmi. 2001. "Can You Buy a Business Relationship? On the Importance of Customer and Supplier Relationships in Acquisitions." *Industrial Marketing Management* 30(7): 575–586.

Buono, A. F., Bowditch, J. L., and J. W. Lewis. 1985. "When Cultures Collide: The Anatomy of a Merger." *Human Relations* 38(5): 477–500.

Cartwright, C., and L. Magni. 2009. "The Value of Stories in Understanding the Past and Shaping the Future in Merged Organizations." *Advances in Mergers and Acquisitions* 8: 43–60.

Cooper, C., Öberg, C., and S. Y. Tarba. 2014. "Culture in M&As as Intra-Organizational and Inter-Organizational Value Systems." *EGOS Conference*, 2014 July 3–5, Rotterdam.

Dauber, D. 2012. "Opposing Positions in M&A Research: Culture, Integration and Performance." *Cross Cultural Management* 19(3): 375–398.

Finkelstein, S., and J. Haleblian. 2002. "Understanding Acquisition Performance: The Role of Transfer Effects." *Organization Science* 13(1): 36–47.

Gioia, D. A., and K. Chittipeddi. 1991. "Sensemaking and Sensegiving in Strategic Change Initiation." *Strategic Management Journal* 12(6): 433–448.

Haspeslagh, P. C., and D. B. Jemison. 1991. *Managing Acquisitions: Creating Value through Corporate Renewal*. New York: Free Press.

Huber, G. P., and D. J. Power. 1985. "Retrospective Reports of Strategic-Level Managers: Guidelines for Increasing Their Accuracy." *Strategic Management Journal* 6(2): 171–180.

Johanson, J., and L.-G. Mattsson. 1988. "Internationalization in Industrial Systems Internationalization: A Network Approach." In *Strategies in Global Competition*, edited by N. Hood, and J.-E. Vahlne, 287–314. Chichester and New York: John Wiley.

Koller, T., Goedhart, M., and D. Wessels. 2005. *Valuation: Measuring and Managing the Value of Companies*. Hoboken, NJ: McKinsey and Company, John Wiley and Sons, Inc.

Lakshman, C. 2011. "Postacquisition Cultural Integration in Mergers and Acquisitions: A Knowledge-Based Approach." *Human Resource Management* 50(5): 605–623.

Larsson, R., and S. Finkelstein. 1999. "Integrating Strategic, Organizational, and Human Resource Perspectives on Mergers and Acquisitions: A Case Survey of Synergy Realization." *Organizational Science* 10(1): 1–26.

Maitlis, S., and T. B. Lawrence. 2007. "Triggers and Enablers of Sensegiving in Organizations." *Academy of Management Journal* 50(1): 57–84.

Molina-Morales, F. X., and M. T. Martínez-Fernández. 2009. "Too Much Love in the Neighborhood Can Hurt: How an Excess of Intensity and Trust in Relationships May Produce Negative Effects on Firms." *Strategic Management Journal* 30(9): 1013–1023.

Öberg, C. 2012. "Using Network Pictures to Study Inter-Organisational Encounters." *Scandinavian Journal of Management* 28(2): 136–148.

Öberg, C. 2014. "Customer Relationship Challenges Following International Acquisitions." *International Marketing Review* 31(3): 259–282.

Öberg, C., and S. Y. Tarba. 2013. "What Do We Know about Post-Merger Integration Following International Acquisitions?" *Advances in International Management* 26: 469–492.

Powers, W. T. 1973. *Behavior: The Control of Perception*. Chicago: Aldine.

Stahl, G. K., Angwin, D. N., Very, P., Gomes, E., Weber, Y., Tarba, S. Y., and H. E. Yildiz. 2013. "Sociocultural Integration in Mergers and Acquisitions: Unresolved Paradoxes and Directions for Future Research." *Thunderbird International Business Review* 55(4): 333–356.

Taylor, J. R., and E. J. van Every. 2000. *The Emergent Organization: Communication as Its Site and Surface*. New Jersey: Lawrence Erlbaum.

Thomke, S., and E. von Hippel. 2002. "Customers as Innovators: A New Way to Create Value." *Harvard Business Review* 80(4): 74–81.

Van Der Velde, M. E. G., and P. G. W. Jansen. 1999. "Managerial Activities among Top and Middle Managers: Self versus Other Perceptions." *Journal of Applied Management Studies* 8(2): 161–174.

Verbeke, A. 2010. "International Acquisition Success: Social Community and Dominant Logic Dimensions." *Journal of International Business Studies* 41(1): 38–46.

Weber, Y., and I. Drori. 2008. "The Linkages between Cultural Differences, Psychological States, and Performance in International Mergers and Acquisitions." *Advances in Mergers and Acquisitions* 7: 119–142.

Weick, K. E. 1987. "Organizational Culture as a Source of High Reliability." *California Management Review* 29(2): 112–127.

Weick, K. E., Sutcliffe, K. M., and D. Obstfeld. 2005. "Organizing and the Process of Sensemaking." *Organization Science* 16(4): 409–421.

Welch, C. 2000. "The Archaeology of Business Networks: The Use of Archival Records in Case Study Research." *Journal of Strategic Marketing* 8(2): 197–208.

Wiley, N. 1988. "The Micro-Macro Problem in Social Theory." *Sociological Theory* 6: 254–261.

16 Evolving Forms of Collaborative Finance in Corporate Networks

Insights From the Automotive Industry in Germany and Brazil

Christian Baumeister and Hans-Martin Zademach

Introduction

Leading corporations today set up and operate complex production systems in different locations and countries by means of cross-border investments, particularly international M&As. These connect different socio-institutional (i.e. economic, cultural, social and legal) business environments (e.g. Markusen 2003; Zademach and Rodriguez-Pose 2009). One of the key characteristics of these global production networks (GPNs) is an intense exchange of financial means: payments for materials and intermediate products, investment in fixed assets, or debt financing and repayments precede and follow every economic transaction taking place in GPNs, or "interspaces" (see the Introduction in this volume) resulting from cross-border investments. It is evident that the organisation and configuration of these financial flows represent a key factor in these complex corporate spaces and that their management has the potential to affect the competitiveness and vulnerability of the entire production system and the places involved. Notwithstanding this relevance, both research on GPNs and M&A has only just begun to address the role of finance in the daily business of international corporate activities in general and post-merger processes in particular (Coe 2012; Coe et al. 2014; Coe and Yeung 2015; for a valuable exception see Wood et al. 2016). Yet, as the research presented in this chapter demonstrates, there is considerable value in a perspective that puts special emphasis on the exchange of financial means and varying form of (collaborative) firm finance in order to better understand the global–local dynamics related to international investments and corporate acquisitions.

Driven by the outsourcing of tasks in fragmented forms of production and a stringent working capital management by lead firms, financing requirements are increasingly shifted towards upstream suppliers (Camerinelli 2009; Hartley-Urquhart 2000; Randall and Farris 2009). Apart from the need to fund investment in fixed assets like machinery and R&D, powerful buyers demand extended payment terms that can only be partially refinanced with trade credit granted by their own suppliers. In addition, stock is reduced to a minimum by lead firms in lean forms of production and has to be held by suppliers to ensure quick response times and the demanded flexibility in supply (Hofmann and Kotzab 2010). As a result, firms that typically have greater difficulties and higher costs in raising external finance than their customers have to shoulder large parts of the financial burden and take on a financing function for their trade partners.

From an isolated, firm-centric point of view, shifting financing requirements to partners within the production network appears to be a sound strategy. However, when applying an inclusive perspective, i.e. considering the entire value chain (being more than the sum of its parts), it quickly becomes apparent that advantages achieved by lowering costs of the physical chain due to the outsourcing of tasks can be rendered void by higher overall financial costs: As competition between single firms is increasingly replaced by a competition of supply chains, eventually, lead firms themselves can be affected by higher prices (as financing costs will be incorporated in the price of goods along the value chain), higher vulnerability (because of a lower reliability of supply) and lower competitiveness (because of the lower productivity and ability to innovate due to lower funds available for investments). Put differently, in GPNs, the financial situation of the supplier firms has a distinct impact on the overall success of the lead firms, and thus their potential for further (local or cross-border) investments.

This holds true in particular for operations in developing economies with high financing costs and/or restricted access to finance due to the macroeconomic environment, the institutional and legal framework and an inefficient financial system (Beck et al. 2009). As the chapter demonstrates, the example of Brazil illustrates how financing problems of national tier 2 and 3 suppliers negatively affect the development of the automotive industry in Brazil in total. On a more general level, the contribution elucidates that the "financial" and the "productive" parts of the production network are inseparably intertwined, and that lead firms are well advised (and in some cases even do so) to be aware of and care about how their respective supply chain is financed. In other words, in order to secure their greenfield or brownfield investments, lead firms have to address the place-specific environment for corporate financing and as a consequence either adapt their sourcing strategy or develop corresponding financing instruments for their suppliers.

Conceptualising Inter-firm Financing

Despite its obvious importance, finance is still largely a blind spot in GPN research (Coe 2012, 392; Coe et al. 2014). In a similar vein, neighbouring disciplines, especially studies in supply chain management, initially paid little attention to the collaborative management of financial flows in supply chains. Slowly, however, more attention is drawn to finance in supply chain management (e.g. Pfohl et al. 2003a, b). The emerging sub-discipline of financial supply chain management gives first conceptual directions towards a better understanding of finance in production networks, and substantial progress has been made in the development of instruments of inter-firm finance (Gomm 2010; Metze 2010; Pfohl and Gomm 2009; Randall and Farris 2009). The authors argue that flows of finance, just like flows of products and information, should be analysed and managed collaboratively between supply chain partners. Financial management that blurs the boundaries of the single firm is meant to increase the competitiveness of GPNs and their capacities to cope with external shocks (Atkinson 2008; Hartley-Urquhart 2000).

Financial supply chain management itself can be divided into two closely related streams of research. The process-oriented strand of financial chain management primarily engages with the management and optimisation of financial flows. More precisely, it aims to automate and expedite flows of money and data between trading partners, logistics companies and financial intermediaries with the help of IT-systems (Pfaff et al. 2004; Skiera et al. 2004; Skiera and Pfaff 2004; Sugirin 2009). The second strand, Supply Chain Finance (SCF), focuses on the cost of financing in supply chains and is of specific interest for exploring inter-firm finance in GPNs. Because of its novelty, however, SCF is still a fuzzy concept lacking a commonly accepted definition. In general, SCF is an approach that aims to improve the way supply chains are financed, that is the financial structures and flows of capital by means of collaboration and coordination. To this end, it is necessary to evaluate who (trading partners/external investors) should finance which investments (e.g. working capital versus fixed assets) for how long, depending on the individual access to finance and capital cost rate (Gomm 2010; Hofmann and Belin 2011; Pfohl and Gomm 2009; Randall and Farris 2009).

At the heart of different SCF solutions is the idea of capitalising differences in the cost of capital and making use of exclusive information and dependencies between partners within the value chain to lower financing costs and/or problems when raising capital. Instruments comprising the integration of external investors—such as the SCF programmes described in the following—are based on information transfers from within the supply chain to external investors. Providing investors with hard information by lead firms (e.g. confirmation of receivables) renders possible interest arbitrage by enhancing the transparency and visibility of information relevant for financing decisions of external investors (Hartley-Urquhart 2000). If information concerning the risk of an investment cannot be communicated to external investors—or only at high costs—an internal financing solution within the value chain is also feasible (Pfohl and Gomm 2009). In line with contributions that explain why suppliers grant trade credit to their trading partners (e.g. Demirgüç-Kunt and Maksimović 2001; Fabbri and Klapper 2009; Petersen and Rajan 1997), Pfohl and Gomm (2009, 159) argue that actors within the supply chain have advantages in assessing and controlling risks related to the investment and in addition can realise positive external effects. Agency problems can be limited due to close interactions between capital seekers and internal investors. Problems related to hidden characteristics and information are reduced, the danger of concealed intentions is lowered, and the agent's incentives for hidden actions are narrowed inter alia because of the potential for sanctions.

In sum, the SCF literature provides strong arguments in favour of an approach that analyses and manages flows of finance, such as flows of information and materials, in a collaborative manner between supply chains partners. It points out that financial management blurring the boundaries of the single firm increases the competitiveness of GPNs and their capacities to cope with external shocks (Atkinson 2008; Hartley-Urquhart 2000). However, the related assertion that "finance is ready for inter-firm collaboration" lacks empirical proof and needs closer examination. As the following sections show, consideration of power relations, network embeddedness, the role of the institutional and sociocultural framework in which relationships between firms are embedded (e.g. the legal environment, the attitude of firms towards bank financing), as well as cultural aspects (e.g. attitudes of suppliers and buyers towards closer financial collaboration), can prove helpful to further our understanding of the use and development of collaborative forms of finance in (transnational) production systems and corporate interspaces.

Inter-firm Finance in Corporate Praxis

The results reported in this chapter have been drawn from a total of 40 interviews conducted within an exploratory study on the automotive industry in Germany and Brazil between 2011 and 2013. The interviews were conducted with experts from OEMs, suppliers, financial intermediaries as well as network partners. With one of the interview partners, a total of three interviews were conducted which proved helpful for the interpretation of preliminary findings. A qualitative research design was used as this approach provides the necessary openness to account for the novelty and limited dissemination of the topic and the lack of a commonly accepted definition of inter-firm finance in GPNs. The comparative approach addressing the two different regional contexts takes account of the theory-based assumption that the general environment for corporate finance at a certain location affects the implementation and/or design of instruments of inter-firm finance.

Brazil and Germany were selected for two reasons: First, in both countries, the automotive industry is a leading economic sector characterised by the presence of multiple OEMs and a diversified supplier industry. Second, the basic structure of their financial systems is comparable (bank based in contrast to market based) although financing conditions diverge considerably—with less favourable conditions in Brazil (average interest rates on short-term bank loans are more than six times higher than in Germany; for more details see Baumeister 2015), especially due to a different macroeconomic setting, high concentration in the banking sector and a capital-absorbing demand of the state. This allows a thorough analysis of the influence of different financial environments.

Instruments of Inter-firm Finance

During the course of the research conducted, a variety of forms of inter-firm finance was observed, most of them still in the developing phase. These forms can be summarised in three groups. The first group consists of SCF programmes in the narrow sense of the word, that is collaborative approaches that aim at reducing costs for receivables financing by interest arbitrage (focus on working capital). Key players in such programmes are OEMs—in the case of Brazil, exclusively foreign multinationals—that either set them up themselves (e.g. via captive automobile banks) or assume a leading role in programmes designed by financial intermediaries (commercial as well as development banks).

Second, we observed measures that put their focus on optimising the financing duration and/or volume, initiated either by OEMs and/or tier 1 suppliers. These measures aim to support suppliers in a specific situation, for example when supplies are exposed to certain problems for assumingly a limited period of time ("crisis-shaken" suppliers). Accordingly, we label these instruments *situative* or *reactive* forms of collaborative finance. The key mechanisms in these instruments are the adjustment of payment terms and the provision of materials. Third, collaborative approaches were observed that focus on financing investments in fixed assets such as pressing tools (*buyer-specific approach*). These forms of inter-firm finance were applied in corporate practice both with and without the involvement of financial intermediaries (for more details see also Baumeister 2015; Baumeister and Zademach 2014).

In our sample, institutionalised buyer-led SCF programmes based on (future) receivables represent the prevailing strategic approach to enhancing financing in production networks. Contrary to instruments applied on a case-by-case basis (e.g. reactive measures of support), such programmes focus on a broad range of suppliers. Although there are specific designs and disseminations, in general, SCF programmes follow the same logic and basic structure in both study contexts: receivables of suppliers from lead firms are used as collateral to provide capital in the form of early or even advanced payments. The confirmation of receivables and payment obligations vis-à-vis investors—made possible by the integration of lead firms in these programmes—enables suppliers to raise (short-term) capital based on the more favourable lead firm's rating plus a fee charged by the financial intermediary running the programme. By dint of an interest arbitrage substantial cost savings are achievable for the supplier (even if payment terms are extended) as well as for the buyer (if payment terms are extended) compared to a payment without an SCF programme. Buyers, suppliers and investors are linked to each other by an IT-based SCF platform within which payments can be requested, payment obligations confirmed and funds transferred. Funding can be provided either by banks (mostly running and offering their own SCF platforms) or via securities sold on capital markets. Patterns of such asset-based forms of supplier financing are reverse-factoring programmes offered by banks as observed in Germany and Brazil or the so-called FIDC (Fundo de Investimentos em Direitos Creditórios) specific to the Brazilian context.

FIDC is a form of asset-backed securities fund pooling short-term receivables which are refinanced through the issue of medium-term securities. Apart from access to capital via capital markets, FIDCs offer an advantage over other financing instruments, especially bank loans, in that they are exempt from tax on financial transactions (Imposto sobre Operações Financeiras). A striking example of an FIDC that links inter-firm finance to regional development is a programme by a regional Brazilian development bank. To support the productive chain of the car maker FIAT, a supplier financing programme was originated by the development bank of the state of Minas Gerais, Brazil, in which the carmaker's production site is located (BDMG 2011). Similar reverse-factoring programmes implemented by development banks are also reported from Mexico (Castañeda et al. 2011; Klapper 2006).

Although the current FIDC programmes were established by OEMs for their individual supply chains, interviewees reported considerations to implement an industry-wide supplier-financing programme also funded by an FIDC. A programme composing all, or most, of the OEMs in Brazil would offer substantial advantages compared to individual solutions such as lower overall risk, no free-rider problems and a higher impact on supplier stability. The plan to provide advanced payments for receivables up to three years in the future appears especially promising. A delivery contract serves as a guarantee and is the prerequisite for medium-term pre-shipment payments. This solution is meant to enable suppliers to make necessary investments not only in working capital (increase liquidity and reduce debt with banks) but also in machinery, among others, to achieve an increase in productivity and quality. However, up to present times (i.e. the end of our investigations in 2014 and, to our best knowledge, also beyond) the implementation of this solution has barely advanced, and interviewees come to differing judgements regarding its future prospects.

Constraints and Conducive Factors for Inter-firm Finance

The interviews conducted reveal a multitude of factors influencing the implementation, dissemination and design of instruments of inter-firm finance both on the side of the suppliers as well as of the buyers. Analytically, they can be grouped into three levels (as displayed in Figure 16.1) at which they mainly unfold—(financial) system, firm and network level—although, a clear-cut distinction cannot be made as factors on levels overlap.

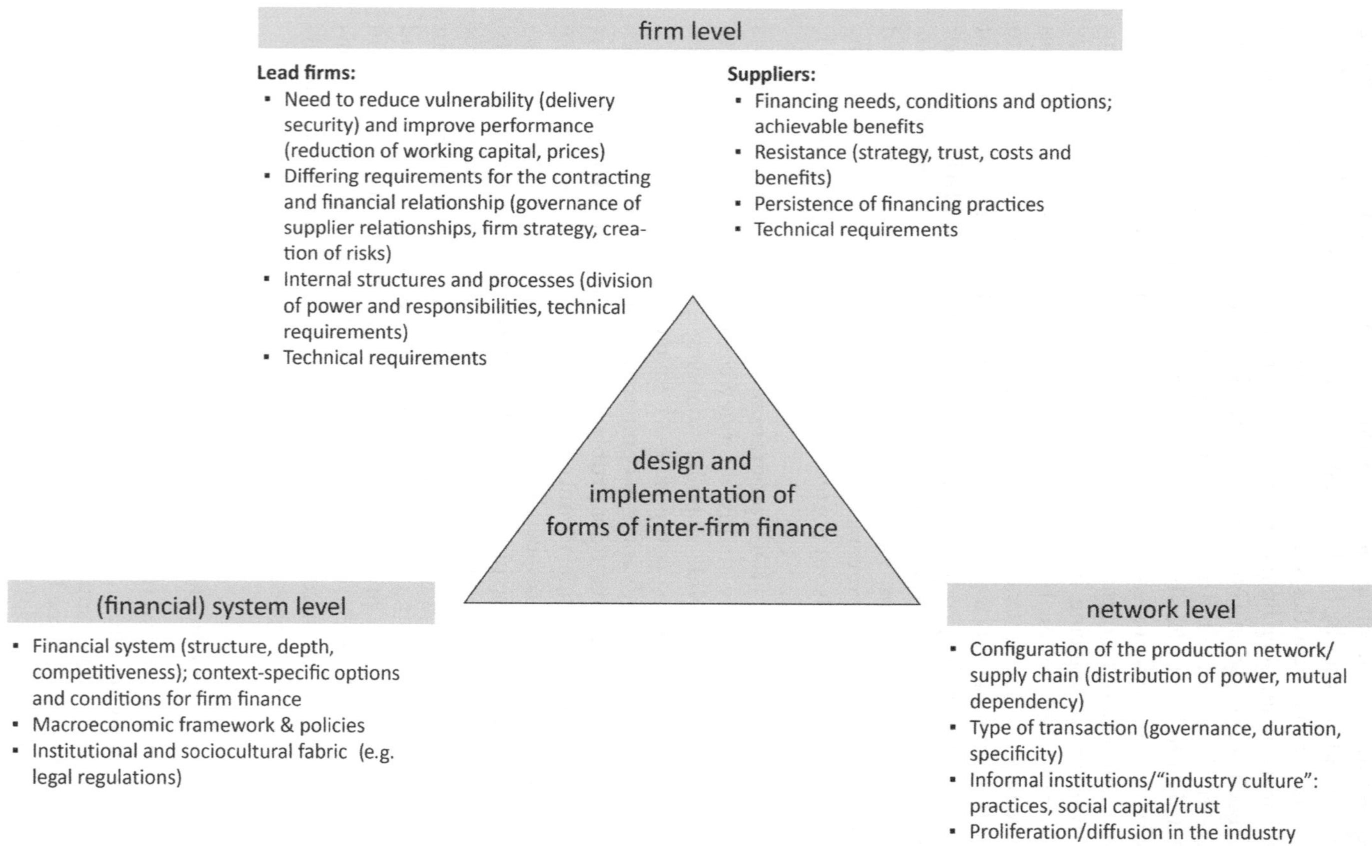

Figure 16.1 Factors influencing inter-firm finance in GPNs

Source: The authors.

The empirical data illustrates the interplay between these factors. Interviewed lead firms that became involved in the described forms of inter-firm finance typically pursue one or both of two main goals, namely the reduction of the vulnerability of the supply chain and better cost efficiency—including a reduction of their working capital by means of an extension of payment terms—leading to greater competitiveness and higher value creation. In this respect, the case of Brazil reveals how differences in the local financing conditions and institutional framework affect the use of instruments of inter-firm finance. Due to its more difficult financing environment, OEMs interviewed in Brazil perceive pronounced financing problems of suppliers, especially on tier 2 and tier 3 levels, as an obstacle for the development and competitiveness of their (sub)contractors. For example, national suppliers of small and medium-sized enterprises have difficulties accessing credit lines of the NATIONAL DEVELOPMENT BANK because of legal requirements attached to the loans provided.

SCF programmes (especially FIDCs) are developed and implemented to counter financing problems of local suppliers and thus ultimately enable local value creation. Representatives of OEMs having implemented SCF programmes emphasise that their use is closely linked to these problems and the need to adapt to the local business environment. In this context, the interviewee of an OEM in Brazil illustrates the company's motives to implement a supplier-financing programme:

> The objective of OEMs is to develop a strong national industry of auto parts with high levels of quality, productivity and reliability. Priority of the programme are tier 2 and tier 3 suppliers because only three to four tier 1 suppliers are Brazilian companies, while the rest consists of multinational firms with diverse possibilities to access capital.

The case of the FIDC illustrates how the embeddedness of financing relationships in a system of legal regulations (namely the exemption from a local tax on financial transactions) influences the configuration and spread of instruments of inter-firm finance. In a similar vein, multinational lead firms have repeatedly adapted their routines and created or implemented innovative forms of finance for their supply chain partners in order to cope with challenges of the specific local environment in which their production network touches down. Among the better-known further examples for such product and process innovations resulting from a context-specific adaptation are the development of flexfuel cars (cars that can run with different blends of bioethanol and gasoline) and the so-called consórcio modular—a factory layout of MAN/VOLKSWAGEN in Resende, in which seven key suppliers carry out the entire assembly under one roof controlled by the OEM (Sako 2009).

Yet, a number of constraints affect the design and implementation of different forms of inter-firm finance. Regarding the key limitations, interestingly, the Brazilian and German cases again exhibit striking parallels, thus substantiating the observation that particular settings co-evolve between the global company and their various regional contexts, as elaborated in more detail in the Introduction of this volume. The prime concerns relate to the interlinking of contracting and the financing relationship, as well as the creation and perception of risks (see Figure 16.1). The empirical results show little inclination on the side of lead firms to engage in additional interlinked relationships that bind them to their suppliers and thereby restrict their sanctioning potential or flexibility, for example tie them closer to their suppliers by a credit provision in the form of advance payments. Instruments are therefore favoured that create no additional risks, maintain the flexibility of lead firms and keep penalty mechanisms in place.

In the same vein, mutual dependency and form of governance have an influence on the design and enforceability of financing instruments in production networks. Both vary within the automotive industry between different types of suppliers while greater differences between the Brazilian and the German context could not be observed. Relationships characterised by high asymmetry of power between buyers and their suppliers, mostly found at tier 2 and 3 levels, permit lead firms to design instruments according to their needs and put pressure on their suppliers to participate. Relationships with tier 1 suppliers, in contrast, can be characterised by a more balanced distribution of power. The same holds true for the individual type of transaction, especially its (future) duration and the dependency of the buyer on the specific product/supplier (its replaceability), which favours or discourages the involvement of lead firms.

Persuading suppliers to participate in financing programmes initiated by lead firms is one of the greatest challenges, as lead firms and bank managers report. According to interviews with suppliers and OEMs, the attitude towards such instruments is shaped by the need and/or the associated benefits, the complementarity to existing forms of finance, the firm strategy, and the characteristics of the relationship with the lead firm.

In addition the industry culture (i.e. informal institutions, especially mutual trust) also shapes the relationships between buyers and suppliers. One reason for the resistance OEMs face when trying to implement long-run strategic financing instruments is the lack of trust and social capital. This applies to the instruments themselves as well as the lead firms and their intentions in general. In theory, social capital (e.g. Bourdieu and Wacquant 1992, 119) built and reproduced in network relationships enables the provision of informal credit and other forms of inter-firm finance (Dei Ottati 1994; McMillan and Woodruff 1999). However, as the empirical results suggest, most buyer-supplier relationships in the automotive industry in Brazil as well as Germany are characterised by low levels of trust. In consequence, suppliers regard financing instruments offered by their buyers with great suspicion. The lack of trust not only impedes acceptance by suppliers but also prevents suppliers from approaching their customers to mutually develop or offer financing programmes. Such an approach is feared to be interpreted as a signal of financial instability of a supplier, which might lead OEMs to establish alternative sourcing options. The formation of trust and social capital itself is shaped by the dominant practices in the highly competitive and hierarchical structured automotive sector.

Finally, alongside the financial system, the legal framework, i.e. the embeddedness of financial relationships at the macro-level came to the fore as a further factor of impact. This impact manifests itself especially in limitations to grant credit to contractors by non-financial firms (e.g. regulated by the German Banking Act) and risks attached to such operations (e.g. liability issues). Additionally, the possibilities and time necessary to enforce legal rights also differ according to judicial systems, affecting the willingness of trade partners to engage in inter-firm financing relationships.

Conclusion

As the present study shows, the automotive industry is currently concerned with developing and implementing instruments of inter-firm finance that are used to optimise and strengthen the financial and thus the physical/productive supply chain. Instruments of inter-firm finance appear to be of specific value, especially in an economic environment that negatively affects the overall financing situation of all suppliers independent of their specific characteristics, enabling lead firms to raise their competitiveness and improve the effectiveness and resilience of their production networks. Put differently, at least for the time being, lead firms—in the case of Brazil, first and foremost foreign multinationals—represent the key actors in the implementation and design of instruments of inter-firm finance.

With regard to the success of such programmes, our results indicate that the outcomes of establishing instruments of inter-firm finance are particularly affected by two spheres of influence. The first is the selection of suitable supply relationships, for example in terms of the characteristics of a supplier relationship (interdependence, duration and complexity of transactions, level of trust) and of realisable benefits (potential to reduce costs and/or develop suppliers). Regarding this sphere, the results presented indicate that the stronger the interdependence between buyers and suppliers (i.e. the more complex and specific the transaction and the higher the difference in financing costs), the greater the potential for an inter-firm approach to finance. The second sphere of influence relates to the specific design of the financing instrument. To be accepted and implemented among supply chain partners mutual benefits have to be created and the strong interlinkage between supply and the financing relationship has to be taken into account. Preserving flexibility for the partners involved (sanctioning mechanisms, etc.) and limiting financial, as well as legal, risks for the firms involved can be seen as key success factors.

Even though the instruments observed first and foremost mirror the motives and requirements of lead firms, collaborative finance does present an approach that in actual fact can create mutual advantages for firms in production networks, that is lead to situations in which not only the OEMs but also the suppliers benefit. This is particularly the case for suppliers in markets with high interest rate levels and/or restricted access to external finance; in turn, it reflects the potential of inter-firm finance programmes to contribute to regional development. As has been reported, such valuable routines may diffuse within GPNs to different locations, or places and contexts around the globe, to use the categories elaborated on in greater detail in the Introduction to this volume. There are good reasons thus to further intensify the investigation of global–local dynamics and the interspaces of complex production networks that result from cross-border investments, with a greater focus on financial relations in general and SCF in particular.

Acknowledgements

The authors wish to thank all executives interviewed in Brazil and Germany for the time they devoted to our research. In addition, they gratefully acknowledge the financial support of the PROFOR programme of the Catholic University Eichstätt-Ingolstadt which allowed the fieldwork to be carried out in Brazil.

References

Atkinson, W. 2008. "Supply Chain Finance: The Next Big Opportunity." *Supply Chain Management Review* 12(3): 57–60.

Baumeister, C. 2015. "Unternehmensübergreifende Finanzierung in Wertschöpfungsnetzwerken: Potenziale und Grenzen am Beispiel der Automobilindustrie in Deutschland und in Brasilien." *Wirtschaftsgeographie 56*. Dissertation. Münster: Lit-Verlag.

Baumeister, C., and H. M. Zademach. 2014. "Financing GPNs through Inter-Firm Collaboration? Insights from the Automotive Industry in Germany and Brazil." Eichstätt. MDW Working Paper 21, https://papers.ssrn.com/sol3/papers.cfm?abstract_id=2354346, accessed 2017, March 28.

BDMG [Banco de Desenvolvimento de Minas Gerais]. 2011. "BDMG estrutura fundo para apoiar cadeias produtivas em Minas." www.bdmg.mg.gov.br/Listas/Ld_Noticias/DispForm.aspx?List=929719cf-567a-4adb-bef7-fc39a5159bdf&ID=224, accessed 2013, August 14.

Beck, T., Demirgüç-Kunt, A., and M. S. Martínez Perá. 2009. "Bank Financing for SMEs: Evidence across Countries and Bank-Ownership Types." *European Banking Center Discussion Paper No. 2009–20*. http://arno.uvt.nl/show.cgi?fid=96501, accessed 2013, August 15.

Bourdieu, P., and L. J. D. Wacquant. 1992. *An Invitation to Reflexive Sociology*. Cambridge: Polity Press.

Camerinelli, E. 2009. "Supply Chain Finance." *Journal of Payments Strategy and Systems* 3(2): 114–128.

Castañeda, G., Castellanos, S., and F. Hernández. 2011. "Policies and Innovations for Improving Financial Access in Mexico." www.cgdev.org/doc/LRS_case_studies/Castaneda_et_al_Mexico.pdf, accessed 2013, August 12.

Coe, N. M. 2012. "Geographies of Production II: A Global Production Network A—Z." *Progress in Human Geography* 36(3): 389–402.

Coe, N. M., Lai, K. P. Y., and D. Wójcik. 2014. "Integrating Finance into Global Production Networks." *Regional Studies* 48(5): 761–777.

Coe, N. M., and H. C. W. Yeung. 2015. Global Production Networks: Theorizing Economic Development in an Interconnected World. Oxford: Oxford University Press.

Dei Ottati, G. 1994. "Trust, Interlinking Transactions and Credit in the Industrial District." *Cambridge Journal of Economics* 18(6): 529–546.

Demirgüç-Kunt, A., and V. Maksimović. 2001. *Firms as Financial Intermediaries: Evidence from Trade Credit Data*. World Bank Policy Research Working Papers 2696. Washington, DC: World Bank.

Fabbri, D., and L. Klapper. 2009. "Trade Credit and the Supply Chain." www1.fee.uva.nl/pp/bin/859fulltext.pdf, accessed 2011, June 13.

Gomm, M. L. 2010. "Supply Chain Finance: Applying Finance Theory to Supply Chain Management to Enhance Finance in Supply Chains." *International Journal of Logistics: Research and Applications* 13(2): 133–142.

Hartley-Urquhart, W. R. 2000. "*Supply Chain Financing System and Method*." US Patent 6167385 A. Date issued: 2000, December 26.

Hofmann, E., and H. Kotzab. 2010. "A Supply Chain-Oriented Approach of Working Capital Management." *Journal of Business Logistics* 31(2): 305–330.

Hofmann, E., and O. Belin. 2011. Supply Chain Finance Solutions: Relevance, Propositions, Market Value. Berlin: Springer.

Klapper, L. 2006. "The Role of Factoring for Financing Small and Medium Enterprises." *Journal of Banking and Finance* 30(11): 3111–3130.

McMillan, J., and C. Woodruff. 1999. "Interfirm Relationships and Informal Credit in Vietnam." *Quarterly Journal of Economics* 114(4): 1285–1320.

Markusen, A. 2003. "An Actor-Centered Approach to Regional Economic Change." *Annals of the Association of Japanese Geographers* 49(5): 395–408.

Metze, T. 2010. Supply Chain Finance: Die wertorientierte Analyse und Optimierung des Working Capital in Supply Chains. Lohmar: Josef Eul.

Petersen, M., and R. Rajan. 1997. "Trade Credit: Theories and Evidence." *The Review of Financial Studies* 10(3): 661–691.

Pfaff, D., Skiera, B., and J. Weiss. 2004. *Financial Supply Chain Management, SAP Press*. Bonn: Galileo Press.

Pfohl, H.-C., Elbert, R., and E. Hofmann. 2003a. "Management der 'finanziellen' Supply Chain: Charakterisierung, Aufgabenbereiche, Interdependenzen." In *Finanzierung: Eine neue Dimension der Logistik*, edited by G. Backfisch, 1–64. Berlin: Schmidt.

Pfohl, H.-C., and M. Gomm. 2009. "Supply Chain Finance: Optimizing Financial Flows in Supply Chains." *Logistics Research* 1(3): 149–161.

Pfohl, H.-C., Hofmann, E., and R. Elbert. 2003b. "Financial Supply Chain Management: Neue Herausforderungen für die Finanz-und Logistikwelt." *Logistik-Management* 5(4): 10–26.

Randall, W. S., and T. M. Farris. 2009. "Supply Chain Financing: Using Cash-to-Cash Variables to Strengthen the Supply Chain." *International Journal of Physical Distribution and Logistics Management* 39(8): 669–689.

Sako, M. 2009. "Outsourcing of Tasks and Outsourcing of Assets: Evidence from Automotive Supplier Parks in Brazil." In *Platforms, Markets and Innovation*, edited by A. Gawer, 251–272. Cheltenham: Edward Elgar.

Skiera, B., König, W., Gensler, S., Weitzel, T., Beimborn, D., Blumenberg, S., Franke, J., and D. Pfaff. 2004. *Financial Chain Management: Prozessanalyse, Effizienzpotenziale und Outsourcing*. Norderstedt: Books on Demand.

Skiera, B., and D. Pfaff. 2004. "Financial Supply Chain Management." *Das Wirtschaftsstudium* 33(11): 1399–1405.

Sugirin, M. 2009. "Financial Supply Chain Management." *Journal of Corporate Treasury Management* 2(3): 237–240.

Wood, S., Wrigley, N., and N. M. Coe. 2016. "Capital Discipline and Financial Market Relations in Retail Globalization: Insights from the Case of Tesco plc." *Journal of Economic Geography* 17(1): 31–57.

Zademach, H.-M., and A. Rodriguez-Pose. 2009. "Cross-Border M&As and the Chainging Economic Geography of Europe." *European Planning Studies* 17(5): 765–789.

17 Synopsis

Building a "Global" Company: Challenges of Interspace and Regional Embeddedness

Martina Fuchs, Sebastian Henn, Martin Franz and Ram Mudambi

Introduction

By combining contributions from different academic disciplines, this book presents a unique perspective on interspatial relations and the regional embeddedness that characterise cross-border investments. On one hand, a number of contributors from the field of international business studies draw upon a long-standing tradition of M&A studies that, amongst other things, are characterised by their particular focus on perceived sociocultural differences (e.g. Hofstede 1980; for an overview see Geppert et al. 2016). On the other hand, contributors from economic geography stand in a rich research tradition that aims at analysing how global firms interact over geographical distances as well as with their local environments (e.g. Amin and Thrift 1994; Taylor and Thrift 1983); their view is, in other words, "on places and flows: situating international investment" (Dicken 2000, 275).

It is not only the combination of different approaches towards cross-border investments developed in both economic geography and international business studies that make this volume unique. Rather, by paying attention to different industrial sectors, firms and countries the chapters adopt a broad focus on the subject matter while at the same time developing a high degree of coherence, as is shown in the following.

To begin with, a number of contributions to this volume adopt a clear focus on particular industries. Some for example deal with the automotive industry as a relevant sector for both creating employment opportunities and the upgrading of remote regions along global value chains (see *Claes G. Alvstam* and *Inge Ivarsson; Christoph Scheuplein; Christian Baumeister* and *Hans-Martin Zademach* in this volume), yet other chapters deal with the chemical and pharmaceutical production (see the chapter by *Luca Giustiniano* and *Luigi De Bernardis*), the software industry (see the chapter by *Christina Öberg*) and the retail sector (see the chapter by *Lech Suwala* and *Elmar Kulke*). At the same time, by considering early investors and latecomer (see the chapter by *Susan M. Walcott and Ingo Liefner*) as well as high-tech industries (see the chapter by *Claes G. Alvstam* and *Inge Ivarsson*) and low-tech industries (see the chapter of *Huter et al.*), different types of innovators and innovation processes are taken into account. Furthermore, various types of investments play a role in this volume, such as strategic investors and private equity investors (see the chapter by *Christoph Scheuplein*) as well as private and public investors, greenfield and brownfield investments. Last but not least, the different contributions cover various countries including core economics like the U.S. and Europe as well as emerging countries, such as China, India and Brazil.

Finally, this volume combines different quantitative, qualitative and triangulated methodical approaches that allow for a multifaceted understanding of interspatial relations, and of the relations between cross-border investments and their local environments. It is this broad variety of perspectives that allows this volume as a whole to develop a high degree of coherence as is reflected in five general outcomes.

Lessons Learnt

> Lesson 1: For a comprehensive understanding of cross-border investments, future research should consider a broad variety of actors involved in both the cross-border firms and the regions affected by them.

This volume suggests that it is necessary to apply an analytic lens that considers more than the single firm only, because numerous actors are involved in cross-border investments: there are, for instance, top managers who define strategic aims linked to long-term corporate goals. In the cases of takeovers, there are also managers of the acquired firms who negotiate to reach the best for their firm. Furthermore, senior staff is affected by takeovers, for example in the human resource departments or in the distribution and marketing departments. The blue- and white-collar workers are also involved in various kinds of changes at different corporate levels. If present, employee representatives like works councils and/or trade unions may appear on the scene as well. All the actors contribute to how interspace between the home and the host location is coined, that is how the actors perceive, produce and reproduce the ties and fissures within the international encounter with various processes of rapprochement and/or distancing between the parties involved.

Usually, actors involved in "building a global company" are entangled in several sociocultural environments at the same time (see *Lucas Huter et al.* in this volume). In other words, they have to deal with the challenge of "*multiple embeddedness*" at various worldwide locations (Meyer et al. 2011, 235). As such, cross-border investments can be considered as complex organisations bridging diverse institutional and national divides (Morgan 2001). For cross-border investments, the different local arenas represent complex settings composed of actors embedded in specific economic and social networks to other regional firms, such as suppliers and customers. In addition, politicians and other representatives of chambers and business development agencies, media representatives and trade unions may also play a role. In other words, managers of cross-border investments are exposed to but at the same time actively reconfigure the given economic and social relations and institutional arrangements (Henn 2012). With regard to the concept of embeddedness, the chapters of this volume illustrate how the different actors perceive, produce and reproduce the relations between the cross-border investments and their local environments; how they approach different actors or distance themselves; and how they use economic, political and other opportunities to overcome challenges.

Lesson 2: Sociocultural distance often arises from metrical distance.

In the past, managers typically used to opt for locations in neighbouring countries (Zademach and Rodríguez-Pose 2009) mostly because they had developed long-standing ties and had gained experiences with the firms located there. In today's globalising world, however, cross-border investments often do not remain restricted to neighbouring countries only but rather span large geographical distances. The growing international competition together with the increasing importance of "rational" procedures of site selection based on key performance indicators and calculative schemes have motivated firms to invest in remote locations that offer the best conditions, thereby accepting the risks associated with interspace (Fuchs and Scharmanski 2009). In particular, springboard strategies may help get access to relevant lead markets and relevant resources overseas (see *Claes G. Alvstam* and *Inge Ivarsson* in this volume). Most of the chapters of this volume relate to such far-reaching "global" cross-border investments.

Within cross-border investments, large geographical distances often go along with sociocultural gaps between the involved actors. However, sharing close cognitive, organisational or institutional proximity between the parties may help to overcome such distance (Boschma 2005; Torre and Rallet 2005; more recently, Grabher and Ibert 2014; Ibert and Müller 2015). Still, habitually managers in global cross-border investments face frictions and gaps, that is "discontinuities" in the sociocultural interspace (Beugelsdijk and Mudambi 2013, 413). The chapters of this volume illustrate that cross-border investments typically act in specific settings of perceived sociocultural proximity/distance and organisational identity/separation that go along with specific opportunities and challenges for the company, thereby causing the need to constantly find new balances between interspace and regional embeddedness (Meyer et al. 2011, 235). This, of course, leads to the question, "Which constellations of proximity/distance and organisational identity/separation actually allow cross-border investments to succeed in new environments?" The answer is provided by studies that show that the success of cross-border investments strongly correlates with two aspects, namely with (a) the strategic objectives of both the acquiring and the acquired firm to integrate socioculturally and organisation-wise and (b) to which degree such objectives can be achieved in future (Cantwell and Mudambi 2005, 2011; Pudelko and Harzing 2007; Vahlne et al. 2011). By contrast, economic success is primarily at stake when the partners originally strove for sociocultural integration but later on failed to achieve this (Rottig et al. 2013). In such cases, executives often have lost considerable time and resources for convincing, solving conflicts and for training activities to achieve integration (Pablo 2015).

Given the manifold corporate goals related to different degrees and ways of proximity and distance, the speed and forms of sociocultural integration vary considerably (Bauer 2015, 338). *Claes G. Alvstam* and *Inge Ivarsson* use the case of Volvo Car Corporation and Geely as an example of developing a "hybrid" identity of the newly merged company. *Luca Giustiniano* and *Luigi De Bernardis* in their study show that the plurality of different identities of a company can be economically successful and organisationally sustainable with regard to future success. They suggest that understanding different identities is a typical challenge for organisations and less a one-time problem to be resolved. Such insights comply with other studies suggesting that neither close integration nor distance is directly linked to corporate performance (Grabher and Ibert 2014; Ibert and Müller 2015; Stahl and Voigt 2008).

> Lesson 3: There are various strategies to build a global company with different gradations between homogenous and heterogeneous organisation.

The chapters of this volume showed a great diversity of how cross-border investments evolve and thereby more or less embed themselves within their various local, regional and national environments. Again, similar to the findings about the different effects of distance on performance within a cross-border investment (see lesson 2 in this chapter), corporate economic efficiency cannot be regarded as a direct outcome of the degree of embeddedness in the firm's environment (Hess 2004). However, if the relevant parties have striven for local embeddedness and later on failed, often problems arise.

Critical regional relations of the cross-border investments include, for instance, counterparts in the supply chain (see *Christian Baumeister* and *Hans-Martin Zademach* in this volume), as well as the domestic customers (Dalziel 2008, 179) as *Christina Öberg* shows in her study on the software industry in this volume. *Lech Suwala* and *Elmar Kulke* provide examples for private retail customers. Furthermore, regional embeddedness also relates to how cross-border investment fits within the local labour market. Employees, for example, may feel challenged by takeovers and may develop considerable countervailing power, as *Martin Franz, Kai Bollhorn* and *Reinhard Röhrig* illustrate in their chapter. Furthermore, *industry policy* may play an important role as well (see the chapter by *Susan M. Walcott* and *Ingo Liefner* for the U.S. and Germany). The chapter by *Päivi Oinas* and *Erja Kettunen* refers to this aspect and suggests a framework of conditions under which cross-border companies bargain with local governments about ethical conduct, and the chapter by *Christian Baumeister* and *Hans-Martin Zademach* stresses the relevance of governmental financial support instruments in emerging economies. Finally, the chapter by *Daria Zvirgzde, Daniel Schiller* and *Javier Revilla Diez* mentions that foreign investors can profit from their own ability to influence the institutional conditions at a given location.

Lesson 4: Othering often implies subliminal but considerable frictions.

Although the perception of sociocultural distances within cross-border investments, or between cross-border investments and their local environments, needs not necessarily cause problems for the involved actors, problems may arise in the case of othering. The notion of othering refers to an implicit and normative social pattern to demarcate identity and foreignness and is part and parcel of the definition of boundaries (Schotter et al. 2017). As *Sophie Golinski* and *Sebastian Henn* stress in their chapter, foreign firms often face strong resentments in their host countries, even though the investments cause manifold beneficial effects there. Such resentments can prevent an investment from successfully embedding itself in the host region, for example when local or regional actors do not get involved with the company. In extreme cases they may even cause resistance on the part of local or regional actors against the investment.

Given the recent wave of cross-border investments between China and the U.S. or Europe, othering can be considered to play a major role when it comes to deal with (alleged) different attitudes of the Chinese investors. The chapters by *Muriel Durand* and by *Martina Fuchs* and *Martin Schalljo* show that it can be difficult for "Western" managers to overcome their accustomed management styles and socialised professional ethics in the dissimilar contexts of Chinese cross-border investments. The chapter by *Karl P. S. Sauvant* and *Michael D. Nolan* illustrates that problems associated with embedding "Western" management styles in Chinese contexts also result from the frictions that appear if Western principles and organisation meet different forms of coordination, as Prota (2016) explains for Vietnam (see the chapter by *Lech Suwala and Elmar Kulke* in this volume).

Lesson 5: Othering is often asymmetric; this is related to fears of inferiority.

The chapter by *Lucas Huter et al.* highlights that perceived sociocultural distances differ depending on whether inbound or outbound transactions are considered, an aspect that highlights that managers' expectations vary by country.

Asymmetric effects often reflect the fear of those already established at the top of the ladder (or at least in a better-off position than other parties involved) of losing their positions. Recently, such fears have often been related to the general scepticisms towards newly emerging—and expanding—powers as becomes obvious in labels such as "Yellow Peril" in the case of China (see the chapter by *Sophie Golinski* and *Sebastian Henn* in this volume). Worries about losing the current position obviously play an important role for othering (Lupina-Wegener et al. 2015) suggesting that power and control are closely related to this process (Mudambi 2008; Mudambi 2011).

Fears and related practices of othering do not only relate to stereotypes about particular countries as described above, but also come up as a general globalisation critique. As the chapter of *Sophie Golinski* and *Sebastian Henn* highlights, discourses on foreign investments are often framed by a global (foreign)–local (national) dichotomy, according to which global investment activities are contrasted with domestic interests and local welfare. This issue can be motivated by sound reasons, that is fears of losing the job (see *Martin Franz, Kai Bollhorn* and *Reinhard Röhrig* in this volume), but must be considered as rather problematic as it can form the outset of xenophobic attitudes.

Future Outlook for Research

In the face of these lessons learnt, we now elaborate existing research gaps, and, based on those gaps, offer suggestions for future investigation in international business studies, economic geography and related disciplines.

First and generally, it has to be taken into account that researchers focusing on cross-border investments usually deal with success stories, thereby running the risk of generating biased results. It can be assumed, however, that roughly every second cross-border investment fails as is suggested by *Huter et al.* in their chapter. Such view is confirmed by the case studies of *Christina Öberg* and *Muriel Durand* in this volume that illustrate critical situations having occurred during the cross-border investment process. Studies like the ones mentioned clearly ask for a more nuanced understanding of cross-border investments that explicitly takes failed cross-border investments, divestments and critical situations into account.

Second, while this volume offers a detailed and comprehensive view of different actors in specific settings, exploring the dusky box of the firm despite various attempts to open it is still characterised by crucial research gaps. One research gap related to ongoing debates in international business studies (see Cantwell et al. 2010; Pudelko and Harzing 2007) refers to *strategies* of cross-border investments and the multiple "micro-systems" at their worldwide locations (as *Daria Zvirgzde, Daniel Schiller* and *Javier Revilla Diez* put it in their chapter). Yet another research gap is related to *industrial relations* and workers' *skills* (see *Martin Franz, Kai Bollhorn* and *Reinhard Röhrig* in this volume). Today, production in emerging economies in most cases is associated with implementing established world market standards, low failure rates and highly motivated and well-trained workers; at the same time, the local labour markets usually do not offer the skills needed. This makes apprenticeship and training activities necessary for companies to react to such local challenges (see Fuchs et al. 2016).

Third, as shown earlier, othering has the potential of causing severe economic problems and political frictions. Although social geography has long analysed issues of identity, exclusion and segregation (e.g. Jackson 1987), economic geography has widely neglected this aspect (Schotter et al. 2017). Given the underlying fears of losing supreme positions, corporate power relations have to be analysed in interdisciplinary research to better understand how global companies are built; thereby it is necessary to include the whole process of acquisition, starting with the early acquisition which is setting the direction later on (Geppert et al. 2016; Mudambi 2008; Mudambi 2011; Mudambi and Navarra 2004).

Future Outlook for Executives and Further Practitioners

The issues raised in this volume have major implications for practitioners, as managers, politicians and representatives of trade unions, of works councils, chambers, economic promotion agencies and others that shall be explored in this final part.

First, the need for a better understanding of failed cross-border investments and critical situations implies that practitioners have to discuss frankly their perception of sociocultural gaps. It is challenging but necessary to uncover perceived frictions and sociocultural gaps, all the more so as they are often hidden in communication patterns and prejudices, among others, and the fact that managers blandish critical facts (Lupina-Wegener et al. 2015, 354), even though they often repeatedly express their will to embrace change (Fuchs and Schalljo 2016; Thurlow and Helms Mills 2009). A more problem-centred view could help to better understand cross-border investments and their contribution to economically and socially sustainable developments in the respective regions.

Second, a binocular view that simultaneously pays attention to interspace and regional embeddedness is necessary. For managers, this implies that executives constantly have to stay "cognizant of changes outside the box of just their focal acquisition situation (i.e. put it in context: What's going on in the environment?)" (Pablo 2015, 384). But also the regional actors involved in cross-border investments can better understand the whole process when being occupied with the company's worldwide linkages, for example, when regional actors develop an understanding of the corporate global strategies in their regions (e.g. strategies of central versus decentral organisation, strategies of being locally engaged or inactive). By centring such human relations the development of skills comes into play. This is true for emerging economies, but also for the core economies where business-related agents often point to future shortages of skilled workers.

Third, othering prevents firms from integrating themselves in interspace and actively embedding themselves in different locations. However, when taking into account that othering often results from a lack of knowledge about others, it becomes obvious that the degree of othering can be reduced through learning, as *Martin Franz, Kai Bollhorn* and *Reinhard Röhrig* stress in their chapter. It appears that an appropriate degree of sociocultural integration can be achieved by applying a broad set of acculturation techniques, such as the implementation of transition teams, the involvement of senior management, the rotation of key personnel, intense communication across organisational boundaries, and deep-level cultural learning interventions with an ongoing dialogue between employees of the involved firms (see *Lucas Huter et al.* in this volume).

In sum, it appears that "building a global company"—as the book title suggests—remains an ongoing challenging task for various actors at different spatial scales with dissimilar perceptions and interests who engage in different sociocultural settings. They all take part in a complex process of balancing proximity and distance in both interspace and regional embeddedness.

References

Amin, A., and N. Thrift. 1994. "Living in the Global." In *Globalization, Institutions, and Regional Development in Europe*, edited by A. Amin, and N. Thrift, 1–22. Oxford: Oxford University Press.

Bauer, F. 2015. "A Literature Review and a Suggested Future Research Agenda on Speed of Integration in M&A: Taking Stock of What We Know." In *The Routledge Companion to Mergers and Acquisitions*, edited by A. Risberg, D. King, and O. Meglio, 337–353. Abingdon: Routledge.

Beugelsdijk, S., and R. Mudambi. 2013. "MNEs as Border-Crossing Multi-Location Enterprises: The Role of Discontinuities in Geographic Space." *Journal of International Business Studies* 44(5): 413–426.

Boschma, R. 2005. "Proximity and Innovation: A Critical Assessment." *Regional Studies* 39(1): 61–74.

Cantwell, J., Dunning, J. H., and S. M. Lundan. 2010. "An Evolutionary Approach to Understanding International Business Activity: The Co-Evolution of MNEs and the Institutional Environment." *Journal of International Business Studies* 41(4): 567–586.

Cantwell, J., and R. Mudambi. 2005. "MNE Competence-Creating Subsidiary Mandates." *Strategic Management Journal* 26(12): 1109–1128.

Cantwell, J., and R. Mudambi. 2011. "Physical Attraction and the Geography of Knowledge Sourcing in Multinational Enterprises." *Global Strategy Journal* 1(3–4): 206–232.

Dalziel, M. 2008. "The Seller's Perspective on Acquisition Success: Empirical Evidence from the Communications Equipment Industry." *Journal of Engineering and Technology Management* 25(3): 168–183.

Dicken, P. 2000. "Places and Flows: Situating International Investment." In *The Oxford Handbook of Economic Geography*, edited by G. Clark, M. A. Feldman, and M. Gertler, 275–291. Oxford and New York: Oxford University Press.

Fuchs, M., and M. Schalljo. 2016. "'Western' Professional Ethics Challenged by Foreign Acquisitions: German Managers' Patterns of Interpretation Surrounding Chinese and Indian Investors." *Geoforum* 75(10): 20–28.

Fuchs, M., Schamp, E. W., and J. Wiemann. 2016. "Duale Aus-und Fortbildung Goes Global? Zur Internationalisierung von Wissen in der industriellen Fertigung durch global-lokale Qualifizierungsstrategien multinationaler Unternehmen." *Geographische Zeitschrift* 104(3): 140–157.

Fuchs, M., and A. Scharmanski. 2009. "Counteracting Path Dependencies: 'Rational' Investment Decisions in the Globalising Commercial Property Market." *Environment and Planning A* 41(11): 2724–2740.

Geppert, M., Becker-Ritterspach, F., and R. Mudambi. 2016. "Politics and Power in Multinational Companies: Integrating the International Business and Organization Studies Perspectives." *Organization Studies* 37(9): 1209–1225.

Grabher, G., and O. Ibert. 2014. "Distance as Asset? Knowledge Collaboration in Hybrid Virtual Communities." *Journal of Economic Geography* 14(1): 97–123.

Henn, S. 2012. "Transnational Entrepreneurs, Global Pipelines and Shifting Production Patterns: The Example of the Palanpuris in the Diamond Sector." *Geoforum* 43(3): 497–506.

Hess, M. 2004. "'Spatial' Relationships? Towards a Reconceptualization of Embeddedness." *Progress in Human Geography* 28(2): 165–186.

Hofstede, G. 1980. Culture's Consequences: International Differences in Work Related Values. Newbury Park: Sage.

Ibert, O., and F. C. Müller. 2015. "Network Dynamics in Constellations of Cultural Differences: Relational Distance in Innovation Processes in Legal Services and Biotechnology." *Research Policy* 44(1): 181–194.

Jackson, P. 1987. *Race and Racism: Essays in Social Geography*. London: Unwin Hyman Ltd.

Lupina-Wegener, A. A., Karamustafa, G., and S. C. Schneider. 2015. "Causes and Consequences of Different Types of Identity Threat: Perceived Legitimacy of Decisions in M&As." In *The Routledge Companion to Mergers and Acquisitions*, edited by A. Risberg, D. King, and O. Meglio, 354–366. Abingdon: Routledge.

Meyer, K. E., Mudambi, R., and R. Narula. 2011. "Multinational Enterprises and Local Contexts: The Opportunities and Challenges of Multiple-Embeddedness." *Journal of Management Studies* 48(2): 235–252.

Morgan, K. 2001. "The Multinational Firm: Organizing across Institutional and National Divides." In *The Multinational Firm: Organizing across Institutional and National Divides*, edited by K. Morgan, P. H. Kristensen, and R. Whitley, 1–24. Oxford, UK: Oxford University Press.

Mudambi, R. 2008. "Location, Control and Innovation in Knowledge-Intensive Industries." *Journal of Economic Geography* 8(5): 699–725.

Mudambi, R. 2011. "Hierarchy, Coordination and Innovation in the Multinational Enterprise." *Global Strategy Journal* 1(3–4): 317–323.

Mudambi, R., and P. Navarra. 2004. "Is Knowledge Power? Knowledge Flows, Subsidiary Power and Rent-Seeking within MNCs." *Journal of International Business Studies* 35(5): 385–406.

Pablo, A. L. 2015. "Conclusion: Deconstructing M&A Research: Paradigm Progress." In *The Routledge Companion to Mergers and Acquisitions*, edited by A. Risberg, D. King, and O. Meglio, 383–390. Abingdon: Routledge.

Prota, L. 2016. "Toward a Polanyian Network Analysis: Market and Non-Market Forms of Coordination in the Rice Economy of Vietnam." *Journal of Economic Geography* 16(6): 1135–1160.

Pudelko, M., and A. W. Harzing. 2007. "Country-of-Origin, Localization, or Dominance Effect: An Empirical Investigation of HRM Practices in Foreign Subsidiaries." *Human Resources Management* 46(4): 535–559.

Rottig, D., Reus, T. H., and S. Y. Tarba. 2013. "The Impact of Culture on Mergers and Acquisitions: A Third of a Century of Research." *Advances in Mergers and Acquisitions* 12: 135–172.

Schotter, A., Mudambi, R., Doz, Y., and A. Gaur. 2017. "Boundary Spanning in Global Organizations." *Journal of Management Studies.* First online. Article not assaigned to any printed issue yet. DOI: 10.1111/joms.12256.

Stahl, G., and A. Voigt. 2008. "Do Cultural Differences Matter in Merger and Acquisitions? A Tentative Model and Examination." *Organization Science* 19(1): 160–176.

Taylor, M., and N. Thrift. 1983. "Business Organization, Segmentation and Location." *Regional Studies* 17(6): 445–465.

Thurlow, A., and J. Helms Mills. 2009. "Change, Talk and Sensemaking." *Journal of Organizational Change Management* 22(5): 459–479.

Torre, A., and A. Rallet. 2005. "Proximity and Localization." *Regional Studies* 39(1): 47–59.

Vahlne, J.-E., Ivarsson, I., and J. Johanson. 2011. "The Tortuous Road to Globalization for Volvo's Heavy Truck Business: Extending the Scope of the Uppsala Model." *International Business Review* 20(1): 1–14.

Zademach, H.-M., and A. Rodríguez-Pose. 2009. "Cross-Border M&As and the Changing Economic Geography of Europe." *European Planning Studies* 17(5): 765–789.

Index

For Product Safety Concerns and Information please contact our EU representative GPSR@taylorandfrancis.com Taylor & Francis Verlag GmbH, Kaufingerstraße 24, 80331 München, Germany